D1559340

P100

FRIEDRICH NIETZSCHE AND THE POLITICS OF THE SOUL

STUDIES IN MORAL, POLITICAL
AND LEGAL PHILOSOPHY

General Editor: Marshall Cohen

*A list of titles in the series
appears at the back of the book*

FRIEDRICH NIETZSCHE AND THE POLITICS OF THE SOUL

A Study of Heroic Individualism

Leslie Paul Thiele

PRINCETON UNIVERSITY PRESS

PRINCETON, NEW JERSEY

Copyright © 1990 by Princeton University Press
Published by Princeton University Press,
41 William Street,
Princeton, New Jersey 08540
In the United Kingdom:
Princeton University Press, Chichester, West Sussex

Library of Congress Cataloging-in-Publication Data

Thiele, Leslie Paul.
Friedrich Nietzsche and the politics of the soul : a study of
heroic individualism / Leslie Paul Thiele.
p. cm.—(Studies in moral, political, and legal philosophy)
Includes bibliographical references.
ISBN 0-691-07376-7 (alk. paper)—ISBN 0-691-02061-2
(pbk. : alk. paper)
1. Nietzsche, Friedrich Wilhelm, 1844-1900. I. Title. II. Series.
B3317.T493   1990
193—dc20   90-32668

Publication of this book has been aided
by the Whitney Darrow Fund of Princeton University Press

This book has been composed in Linotron Palatino

Princeton University Press books are printed on acid-free paper
and meet the guidelines for permanence and durability of the
Committee on Production Guidelines for Book Longevity of the
Council on Library Resources

Printed in the United States of America
10   9   8   7   6   5

Opus vigilantibus dedicatum

It's the *soul*, my good friend, that nearly everybody seems
to have misunderstood, not realizing its nature and power.
—Plato, *The Laws*

CONTENTS

PREFACE

Reading commentaries on Nietzsche is often like listening to an explanation of a good joke. Expatiation blunts wit, the aesthetic sense is trampled by dogged argument, a far inferior style shames its superior, and all mischief loses its innocence in the chains of ratiocination. Most perturbing, however, is the neutralization of what otherwise had had a visceral effect. Inevitably the joke is never really explained, simply ruined.

What is the alternative to such exposition? One may suggest that those who do not see the humor have not had the experiences necessary for them to want to, or need to, laugh. This is Nietzsche's own defense, or better said, his criticism of those who are not caught by the "fishhooks" of his writing. They simply are not the right kind of fish. Given this understanding, what should the purpose of commentary be? Should it expound Nietzsche or describe the readership he sought? The answer, I believe, is a little of both. Indeed, the tasks are complementary. One cannot be done well without the other.

There are many readers of Nietzsche who have not bitten deeply into his hooks but have been snagged and carried along by the flights of his thought. It is primarily for these victims of Nietzsche's works that I write. In part, my aim is to describe the type of reader Nietzsche tried to catch and to intimate what it means to swallow the bait.

ACKNOWLEDGMENTS

Many thanks are due to Manfred Halpern, Alan Ryan, Richard Schacht, Tracy Strong, Maurizio Viroli, and Paul Vogt for their comments, criticisms, and editorial prowess. Foremost, I wish to thank George Kateb for the benefit of his scrupulous judgment—that art of nuance which, as Nietzsche said, constitutes the best thing we gain from life.

A NOTE ON SOURCES AND CITATIONS

I have made liberal use of Nietzsche's unpublished notes, lectures, and essays, his juvenalia, and his personal correspondence. Unfortunately, adequate English translations of most of this material do not exist. These writings constitute an invaluable source of information on the development and continuity of Nietzsche's project. Nevertheless, the extensive use of material Nietzsche did not come to publish may appear in need of further justification. Certainly its importance vis-à-vis the books Nietzsche prepared for publication or published himself is moot. In this question I believe we must turn to Nietzsche's own understanding of the philosopher as one whose every scribble and handshake allows a semiotics of his soul. This does not do away with the problem of deciding the worth and context of Nietzsche's unpublished writings, but it does offer a prima facie legitimation of their use.

The Walter Kaufmann and R. J. Hollingdale translations of all of Nietzsche's major works have been used whenever possible (along with Marianne Cowan's translation of his early essay *Philosophy in the Tragic Age of the Greeks*). All citations are given within the text; titles are abbreviated and followed by page numbers. References to Nietzsche's notes, lectures, and essays (apart from those notes posthumously collected under the title *The Will to Power*) are taken from the Musarion edition of the *Gesammelte Werke*, are also given within the text, and are signified by *GW* followed by volume and page number (for example, *GW* 14:224 means volume 14, page 224 of the *Gesammelte Werke*). *Der Werdende Nietzsche*, a compilation of the young

Nietzsche's autobiographical sketches, is also referred to by abbreviation and page number. All references to Nietzsche's personal correspondence are taken from *Nietzsche Briefwechsel, Kritische Gesamtausgabe*; the abbreviated title is followed by the date the letter or draft was written (for example, *NB* 18.4.74 means Nietzsche's letter of April 18, 1874, as taken from *Nietzsche Briefwechsel*). All translations from German sources are my own. A list of abbreviations and corresponding texts follows.

A	*The Anti-Christ*
BGE	*Beyond Good and Evil*
BT	*The Birth of Tragedy*
CW	*The Case of Wagner*
D	*Daybreak*
DD	*Dithyrambs of Dionysus*
DWN	*Der Werdende Nietzsche*
EH	*Ecce Homo*
GM	*On the Genealogy of Morals*
GS	*The Gay Science*
GW	*Gesammelte Werke*
HH	*Human, All Too Human*
NB	*Nietzsche Briefwechsel*
NCW	*Nietzsche contra Wagner*
PTG	*Philosophy in the Tragic Age of the Greeks*
TI	*Twilight of the Idols*
UM	*Untimely Meditations*
WP	*The Will to Power*
Z	*Thus Spoke Zarathustra*

FRIEDRICH NIETZSCHE AND THE
POLITICS OF THE SOUL

INTRODUCTION

An explanation of the title of this work provides the best introduction. The expression *heroic individualism* is not to be found in Nietzsche's writings. Indeed, Nietzsche might have considered the term pleonastic: in his view the individual and the hero are one and the same. The primary task of life is held to be the heroic struggle of individuation. I believe that Nietzsche's thought is best represented through this terminology. It captures the dynamics of his project. His works were written expressly to mark his own battles and victories, as milestones. They constitute a diary of his intellectual and spiritual development. They illustrate not only change, but continuity in change—an active and self-conscious growth into himself. Nietzsche sought, as he was wont to put it, to become who he was. To understand this endeavor an attempt must be made to experience what underlay his struggles of individuation. Nietzsche claimed, heroically, that his works were "written with blood." Their interpretation must not be drained of this vital fluid.

While the development of the heroic individual is here submitted as Nietzsche's foremost concern, it would be inappropriate to attribute to him a *theory* of heroic individualism. This word connotes a synthetic systematization that is foreign to Nietzsche's style and antithetical to his understanding of the individual. A theory of individualism, in this sense, is oxymoronic. The individual is precisely that for which no general formulas are applicable. Politics, on the other hand, conveys most of the meanings inherent in the development of individuality: the struggle, the ambiguity and ambivalence, the will to power, the compromises and coalitions, domination and rule, plurality and rank, the search for organic unity. Nietzsche's works constitute a political biography of his soul. They challenge the reader to engage in a similar politics. His writings were not meant to be understood apart from the existential pathos that produced them. This pathos is best limned using a palette of political expressions, the colors of which fill Nietzsche's own works.

This book does not offer a tidily packaged account of Nietzsche's politics. I have not attempted to root out of his writings the mostly vague or implicit references to concerns that are explicitly addressed within the tradition of political thought. The importance of Nietzsche does not lie in what he had to say about those things generally understood to be political realities or possibilities. Nietzsche's writings engage the reader in an ongoing experiment in thought and experience. His choice of a political vocabulary to describe the soul of man, and in particular his own soul, was not arbitrary. He believed that the role of the individual in politics should be subservient to the role of politics within the individual. That is the politico-philosophical position to be explored.

Still, Nietzsche did carve out a political niche, even if it remained obscure and undefended, and he may be held accountable for it. But the political theorist must approach Nietzsche warily. The quarry is not easily captured by definition, and he is never tamed by reasoned argument. For the most part his political convictions were voiced negatively, as barbs and broadsides. He intended his political statements to provoke. One must not, however, discount his harsher judgments as insincere hyperbole. Fascination with and admiration for such a thinker should not glaze the distastefulness of many of his pronouncements and thereby make his political pill easier to swallow. To bowdlerize Nietzsche into a democrat, a pacifist, or a proponent of political engagement is to do injustice to the virtues of democracy, peace, and political activity, to obscure their vices, and to misunderstand Nietzsche. Nietzsche is Nietzsche, and his works were written as a justification of his being so. The business of commentary is to expound this testimony without indulging in nervous remarks excusing Nietzsche for his views or excusing the commentator for addressing them. Whatever one may wish to make of him, Nietzsche need not be saved from himself. At the same time, one might recall Nietzsche's own understanding of the challenge provided by great men: not to bow down before them, but to step beyond them.

What follows leaves much of Nietzsche undiscussed; this out of necessity and inclination. In order to reveal what is believed to be the kernel of his thought, much had to be disregarded. A prefatory statement Nietzsche wrote for his essay on the pre-Socratic philosophers might serve well to introduce this work: "I have selected those doctrines which sound most clearly the personality of the individual philosopher, whereas the complete enumeration of all the transmitted doctrines, as it is the custom of the ordinary handbooks to give, has but one sure result: the complete silencing of personality" (*PTG* 25). While I have not neglected to discuss the "doctrines" typically associated with Nietzsche—such as the will to power, the advent of nihilism, the eternal recurrence, the Dionysian and the Apollonian—they do not command the structure of this book, nor do they dominate its content. Instead, the reader is offered an account of the incarnations and personae that Nietzsche proposed for the heroic individual: the philosopher, the artist, the saint, the educator, and the solitary. These "higher" men are said to have actualized their underlying potential for a heroic life. Nietzsche's writings challenge one to understand their author as an individual so engaged.

Previous scholarship on Nietzsche has by and large failed to accept this challenge. It may be divided into four broad, often overlapping fields. The fruitfulness of these fields has varied over the century that has elapsed since

INTRODUCTION

Nietzsche's work ceased. All have been repeatedly cultivated. Yet none offers a sufficiently radical interpretation
of Nietzsche. For the root of Nietzsche's philosophy is
Nietzsche himself, a man who chose to reveal himself
through his work. Nietzsche has been interpreted by some
primarily as a worldly theorist. He has been posited as the
ideologue of aristocratic or racial politics and as the harbinger of world empire. Much of this scholarship rightfully
has been discredited as deceitful or simplistic; but refined,
more interesting versions continue to appear. In contrast
to this straightforward political reading, Nietzsche also
has been presented as a literary stylist. He is then approached as an unsystematic albeit profound thinker
whose trademark is the aphorism, or, more recently, as an
author whose books' literary identities and agendas constitute the subject of inquiry. A third standpoint marks
Nietzsche above all as a philosopher. His politics no less
than his literary endeavors are mostly disregarded, if not
denied, so that his philosophical importance may be em-
phasized. The fourth interpretive practice situates Nietzsche as the herald of deconstructive thought. Herein his
writings are investigated as announcements of the demise
of systematic philosophy and the destruction of the philosophical subject.

Whatever their differences, these four fields of interpretation border a common frontier. All restrict themselves
to a conceptual comprehension of Nietzsche. All divorce
Nietzsche from his work.[1] As a political theorist Nietzsche
is taken primarily to speak for and about others, not him-

[1] Alexander Nehamas's *Nietzsche: Life as Literature* (Cambridge, Mass.:
Harvard University Press, 1985) appears exempt from this charge. Nehamas does indeed offer an account of Nietzsche that succeeds in unifying the man and his work, but his thesis is antipodal to mine. Nehamas
posits Nietzsche as having paid tribute with his life to the artistic task of
creating his own literary character. I have sought to expound Nietzsche's
literary characters as the tributes he paid to the artistic task of creating
his own life. The importance of this distinction becomes apparent in the
discussion of Nietzsche's project as an artist.

self. As a literary stylist Nietzsche is understood to be concerned with producing works of written art, relishing the detachment allowed by fiction. Those concerned with Nietzsche's reputation as a philosopher have held the status of his work to be dependent on its distinction from his personal opinions and predilections. Philosophy only waxes, it is understood, as individuality wanes. Lastly, those interested in describing Nietzsche's explosion of philosophical thought are particularly prone to isolate the writer from his writings, as the passion for truth is understood to have been extinguished by skeptical distance and irony. In short, previous scholarship has not breached the frontier that separates works of politics, art, and philosophy from biography, that is, from the individual life that produced them. Yet this is the boundary Nietzsche claimed to have crossed in word and deed. He propounded a philosophy of individualism and he lived an individualistic philosophy. He claimed his work as the vestige of his life. Conceptual accounts of Nietzsche fail to penetrate this vitality.

The philosophical portrait attempted in these pages is Nietzsche's, but it is not the only one that might have been painted. Nietzsche wore many masks. I submit a description and interpretation of some of them. I attempt as well to criticize prevalent but in my view shallow interpretations of his work, which, as Nietzsche recognized, are responsible for many of the undesirable masks that are formed around a great thinker. Heroic individualism is not presented as the thematic solution to every puzzle of Nietzsche's thought but as a characteristic feature of the masks he wore, indeed, as their most enduring expression. It allows us to appreciate the development of Nietzsche's work—despite its disruptions and reversals— as a reflection of his life. That such an approach does not itself lead to false or shallow interpretations is to be determined by the reader of this book, and more decisively by the reader of Nietzsche.

In the end, it would seem, there is a choice to be made regarding how one will come to terms with Nietzsche. One may choose to fence or to wrestle with him. Fencers never get much beyond analytic parrying. Their object is to back Nietzsche into a corner. The rules of the game allow them to dismiss many of his antics as out of order. If occasionally they cut off something considered to be of value, it is employed to fortify their own convictions. When they claim a victory, it often rings hollow. For their adversary has been domesticated. No longer dangerous, the confrontation is of little merit. On the other hand, wrestlers abandon all weapons and fail to keep their distance. If they come to feel a rapport with Nietzsche it is usually evidenced in their entanglements with him. They do not resolve his dilemma, but at best manage to explore its profundity. Their opponent usually proves too slippery to pin down, but this is shown to be part of the sport. Inevitably, they are left exhausted.

Nietzsche challenged his readers to struggle with him bare-handed. To best understand Nietzsche, one must engage him on his own terms. This is not to reject critical scholarship for an obsequious empathy. Rather, it is to recognize that in order critically to assess Nietzsche's work one must first of all be able to experience its full weight.

PART I

HEROIC INDIVIDUALISM

O N E

THE HEROIC

Struggle is the perpetual food of the soul, and it knows
well enough how to exact the sweetness from it.
                                             —*Gesammelte Werke*

God had died in Nietzsche's world. Nietzsche did not
claim responsibility for the killing, but he was enthusiastic
about celebrating the wake. Yet the modern world was
also inhospitable to heroes, the half-gods and godlike men
who might redeem life through their greatness. This was
Nietzsche's concern. For nihilism, the bane of modern life,
was just such a denial of the heroic, the denial of all greatness, the depreciation of all striving. The Nietzschean
project, in short, was to instill a passion for greatness in a
world without gods.

Thus Nietzsche was concerned—indeed, one might say
obsessed—with the fate of the hero. He recounted the decline and fall of tragic heroism. He described the ascent of
the antiheroic type who crept onto the stage with Socrates
and consummated his role in Christianity. He lamented
the absence of heroism in the modern world. But he also
rejected the romantic attempt to resuscitate heroism; idols
could not be tolerated. His genealogical studies traced the
embarrassing pedigree of ruling systems of thought, un-
dermining their authority, disgracing their heritage, and
subverting their pantheons. Man's grandeur, wrote Nietzsche, could no longer be seen as the reflection of his divine
origin. For here an ape stoops, staring back blankly and

grinning. Heroes, if they were to exist, could no longer be the epigones of gods.

Nietzsche presented a new kind of hero for modern times, one who would prove capable of establishing a golden age of order and growth, if not within society at large, then within the ranks of higher man. The overman[1] is proposed as the hero of a nihilistic age. Like his forerunners, he bears his own standards of morality and reason and attempts to vanquish the hitherto reigning traditions and values. Unlike his forerunners, the overman makes no claim to divine sanction for his deeds. He refuses to be armed by the gods, as was the boon claimed by the greatest heroes of the ancient poets. The overman is the hero of an atheistic and morally destitute world; he presents the paradox of the avid pursuit of greatness when no transcendental standards exist. He must embody his own justification.

For Nietzsche struggle is the essence of the heroic. The hero is the *agonal* spirit incarnate. He finds in struggle both his means and his end. He desires his friend to be his fiercest opponent. He bears a "spiritualized enmity" toward himself, a soul "rich in contradictions" that "does not relax, does not long for peace" (*TI* 44). Strife is not merely tolerated, it is welcomed. The hero's life is the story of battles fought and obstacles overcome; his glory a measure of the dangers involved and the courage displayed. He is an individual, a mortal plagued by the limits of the self who nevertheless continually attempts to transgress them. The heroic ideal is nothing less than apotheosis. Hubris predestines him to a tragic fate. But through his hubristic drive he attains a glimpse of immortality: fame. Virgil's

---

[1] Nietzsche's word is *Uebermensch*, literally *overman*. Unlike Kaufmann, Hollingdale translates this as *superman*, just as he translates *Ueberheld* as *superhero*. Given Nietzsche's frequent references to self-*over*coming and rising *above* oneself, I have employed the literal translation. For the sake of consistency, Hollingdale's translations have been amended to coincide with my own.

Hercules is admonished by Jupiter: "For each man his day stands fixed. For all mankind the days of life are few, and not to be restored. But to prolong fame by deeds, that is valour's task."[2] Fame is that taste of the immortality denied to man which is achieved by those who combat this denial.

Yet it is the *achieving* of fame, not its *achievement*, that constitutes heroism. The hero is above all a lover of life. In comparison to the brilliance of life, the light cast by posthumous fame is lurid and pale. The great Achilles, who secured his fame through valiant deeds, sat remorseful in Hades. Even life as an uncelebrated daylaborer, Homer has it, is worth more to Achilles than his shadowy existence in the underworld, where ambition has no place. So too did Odysseus reject Calypso's offer of immortality were he to remain with her in isolation. The urge to life as struggle is too strong. Life without challenge is just as insipid to the hero as the complacency of posthumous fame. Competition and battle are not simply the means to winning glory, but constitute ends in themselves. For there is a joy found in the midst of struggle which surpasses that of the subsequent accolades. The recipe for classical heroism is found in the words of Peleus, who "exhorted his boy Achilles always to strive for the foremost place and outdo his peers."[3] The hero is he who courageously strives for preeminence. *Arete* is to be displayed; struggle is the means of its attainment. Only the love of struggle provides the stimulus for self-overcoming, the drive to reach beyond oneself so as to achieve excellence. Competition is the forum within which borders are transgressed. This classical understanding of heroism provided a model for

[2] Virgil, *Aeneid* 10.464–70.

[3] Homer, *Iliad* 11.784. Glaucon received similar instruction from his father, Hippolochus: "Let your motto be *I lead*. Strive to be best" (*Iliad* 6.207–9). Zarathustra acknowledges that this precept was the Greeks' "path to greatness" (Z 85).

Nietzsche. Its images infuse his writings and structure his thought.

Nietzsche's earliest philosophical works already mark his captivation by the concept of the heroic. *The Birth of Tragedy*, like many of the unpublished writings preceding it, is essentially an encomium and account of the origins of the ancient tragic hero of the Greek playwrights (most notably Sophocles and Aeschylus). The dismay accompanying his downfall at the hands of Euripides and Socrates is matched with hope for the resuscitation of a tragic culture in Germany through music (most notably Wagner's). In short, Nietzsche saw himself as the prophet of a new age of "dragon-slayers" who would display "a heroic penchant for the tremendous" (*BT* 112).

The *Untimely Meditations* continue the attempt to spur the development of heroic individualism. Two of Nietzsche's own mentors, Arthur Schopenhauer and Richard Wagner, the antiheroic figure of David Strauss, and the role of history are discussed with an eye to the place of the individual in the contemporary world. The underlying theme of all four essays is the desirability of creating a heroic culture to replace the modern pseudoculture. The good life is held to be one spent creating and maintaining culture, which is defined as the favorable environment for the propagation and maintenance of great men: "How can your life, the individual life, receive the highest value, the deepest significance? How can it be least squandered? Certainly only by your living for the good of the rarest and most valuable exemplars" (*UM* 162). The essays are marked by a voluble hopefulness that the creation of such an environment is possible in Europe. The means to its establishment is the emergence of a relatively small number of heroic figures: "Satiate your soul with Plutarch and when you believe in his heroes dare at the same time to believe in yourself. With a hundred such men—raised in this unmodern way, that is to say become mature and accustomed to the heroic—the whole noisy

14

sham-culture of our age could now be silenced for ever" (*UM* 95). The task of cultural renewal itself is assessed to be of heroic proportions. One must battle the tide of history, pitting forgotten and newly created individual virtues against the powers of a mass society. In this struggle to give genius its due, Nietzsche stated explicitly, not talent but "a certain heroic basic disposition" is decisive (*UM* 176). Nietzsche's rousing of his readers to participate in this project is fervent. His criticism of the forces that entrench "cultural philistinism" is scathing.

Human, All Too Human, Nietzsche's next publication, marked a distinct break in his assessment of culture. The book does not establish a positivist worldview, as is often asserted, but it does supply a rationalistic or scientific critique of all forms of romanticism, including its author's. Nietzsche voiced suspicion of his earlier enthusiasm and engaged in polemic against his mentors. A growing skepticism is pitted against his former tendency toward naive idealism and the romantic adulation of great men. Indeed, the book, as Nietzsche later characterized it, was an attempt to put the hero "on ice" (*EH* 284). Nonetheless, Nietzsche's heroic form of philosophizing had not been altered. Only the object of his accolades had changed. The hard-nosed skeptic is submitted as the new model for emulation. His strength and courage are such that he no longer needs the intoxicants and palliatives of romantic culture. Romanticism, particularly Wagner's, is now held to be antiheroic, a doctrine not of fearless struggle but of indulgence. Nietzsche's hopes for a cultural renaissance were dashed by the discovery that the romantics' penchant for heroism was not a stimulant to self-development but a means of avoiding it, a surrogate for change. Romanticism was, at best, a vicarious heroism. Nietzsche had deceived himself into believing that he had heard a clarion call when in fact it was but a sentimental dirge. Romanticism was rejected because it lacked the fundamental quality it was originally believed to incarnate—the will to struggle.

No longer actuated by hopes of the total revivification of culture, Nietzsche nonetheless retained his own heroic status. His task was to be less sensational, but nonetheless befitting his self-understanding. Toward the end of *Human, All Too Human* Nietzsche played his own minstrel: *"This, too, is worthy of a hero.—*Here is a hero who has done nothing but shake the tree as soon as the fruit was ripe. Do you think this too little? Then take a look at the tree he shook" (*HH* 393). The timely attack on all forms of romantic decadence and moral idealism, carried out with discipline and rigor, would yield a worthy harvest, even though such unglorious labor is contrary to the hero's romanticized image. A passage of *Daybreak*, Nietzsche's next book, would reassert the status of the iconoclast: "To do things of the vilest odour of which one hardly ventures even to speak but which are useful and necessary—this too is heroic. The Greeks were not ashamed to include among the great labours of Heracles the cleansing of a stable" (*D* 185). Nietzsche's future genealogical studies of morality and religion would prove to be his own Heraclean, albeit meticulous, task of antisepsis.

The remainder of Nietzsche's corpus exhibits a similar tendency. Former positions are criticized and contradicted, regarded as steps to be overcome rather than platforms to be maintained. His so-called positivistic writings are subject to his own censure, just as his romantic writings had been. This is in keeping with Nietzsche's self-image. The hero is not so much characterized by a particular set of beliefs as by the willingness to attack his own convictions and prejudices.[4] Unchallenged convictions, Nietz-

---

[4] Regarding certain beliefs, however, Nietzsche did not escape complacency. His male chauvinism is a case in point. Nietzsche portrayed his unwillingness to challenge his misogynist tendencies as an incapacity. His "truths about 'woman as such' " were acknowledged as "signposts to the problem which we *are*—more correctly, to the great stupidity

sche maintained, are prisons for those who have not the strength to bear the burden of freedom. The hero's standards of virtue must evolve along with him. "Only he who changes remains akin to me," Nietzsche would insist (*BGE* 204). The striving for excellence is tantamount to endemic change in the individual who is always in competition with former selves.

Nietzsche's later works do not so much constitute a rejection of his earlier cultural goals as a redefinition of the relation of the heroic individual to the environment. Estranged from Wagner, no longer riding on the crest of a wave of cultural renewal, and isolated in his Basel professorship, which he subsequently abandoned for an even more reclusive life, Nietzsche's understanding of the role of great men became a reflection of his own existence. A new culture was still desired, but it would no longer be that of a folk united in adoration around its greatest exemplars. At best it would be a culture strong enough to tolerate its heroes. Nietzsche modeled his ideals on himself: the true hero was an infectious force that makes a people stronger, more resilient, even as he destroys its foundations.

The projection of the hero as both an antinomian *and* a creator of new regimes is not so much a contradiction as a recognition of his archetypical vocation. The feat of founding a state, culture, or folk is subsequent to warfare, conquest, and destruction. The great man remains essentially a creative force. But before his genius may manifest itself in an enduring work, the existing structures—be they constitutive of an aesthetic, ethical, or political regime—must be demolished and the rubble cleared: "If a temple is to be erected *a temple must be destroyed*: that is the law—let any-

---

which we are, to our spiritual fate, to the *unteachable* 'right down deep.' " With regard to his scurrilous pronouncements on women, Nietzsche admitted that "it is now understood from the outset to how great an extent these are only—*my* truths" (*BGE* 144). Arguing for one's limitations, is, however, quite the opposite of perpetual self-overcoming.

one who can show me a case in which it is not fulfilled!" (*GM* 95). The temple Nietzsche set out to destroy was that of morality. The Nietzschean hero, like his classical counterpart, is a breaker of taboos and custom. Like the proud Oedipus, the hero kills his father and sleeps with his mother. He blasphemes, he violates, and he destroys. Out of the ashes emerges a new regime. Nietzsche's "transvaluation of values" had the destruction of morality as its precondition.

Only in attacking morality does the individual find the strength and freedom to transcend morality, to create values. Strife is the medium for the actualization of virtue. Traditionally the field of battle was the womb of heroic virtue. The classical hero was typically a warrior. Nietzsche buttressed this identification. "War is a training in freedom," he insisted, and "the free man is a warrior" (*TI* 92). The glorification of war is justified with the adage, "One must need strength, otherwise one will never have it" (*TI* 93).

Nietzsche, however, was no apologist for the state. Nor was he a proponent of national wars. How literally his celebration of battle should be taken is unclear. At times he speaks of the battle of ideas, at times of real battles. Statements such as "War (but without powder) between dissimilar thoughts!" may be matched with the likes of "The *most favorable inhibitions and remedies of modernity*: 1. universal military service and real wars in which the time for joking is past" (*WP* 78). In any case, the thrust is that war is laudable because it nurtures the will to struggle. Nietzsche was no pacifist, but neither had he respect for war as such, and certainly he had no desire for the booty of war or the laurels of victory. A section of *Human, All Too Human* entitled "The Means to Real Peace" exemplifies his attitude: "The doctrine of the army as a means of self-defence must be renounced just as completely as the thirst for conquest. And perhaps there will come a great day on which a nation distinguished for wars and victories and for the highest development of military discipline and thinking, and accustomed to making the heaviest sacrifices on behalf of these things, will cry of its own free will: *'we shall shatter the sword'*—and demolish its entire military machine down to its last foundations" (*HH* 380). Peace and war have no inherent value. Either may be the proper means to the desired end of producing strong, heroic individuals. Better to fight than fear; and war is better than a peace among cowards. But peace among the courageous is best of all, for it allows time and energy to be devoted to more important things, namely, the struggle within the soul. Real battle is always only an exercise for the development of courage and strength in the realm of spirit. Of primary importance is the existence of individuals who can stand on their own, capable of sacrifice, desirous of struggle, contemptuous of "shopkeepers' " happiness.

War is extolled by Nietzsche, but not the desire for conquest. The true spoils of war are enjoyed during the battle, not after it is over. The struggle for power is of great benefit for the individual and for a people. The acquisition of power already marks the arrival of decadence: "Coming to power is a costly business: power *makes stupid*" (*TI* 60). Nietzsche viewed the German Reich as the end of German philosophy. Napoleon, whose character Nietzsche celebrated, was held to have been thoroughly corrupted by power (*GW* 14:208). Indeed, the heroic individual envisaged by Nietzsche does not bear a significant resemblance to the victorious political or military leader (*HH* 385). His glory, Nietzsche affirmed, rests not on his worldly achievements but on his spiritual status: "The 'higher nature' of the great man lies in being different, in incommunicability, in distance of rank, not in an effect of any kind—even if he made the whole globe tremble" (*WP* 468). In penning this Nietzsche must have had a relatively obscure émigré philosopher in mind, one who knew that the greatest thoughts constitute the greatest events (*BGE* 195).[5]

---

[5] Owing to his spiritualization of the heroic character, Nietzsche does

Quite likely the Nietzschean hero will remain bereft of all forms of worldly achievement. Greatness may not be measured by success (*UM* 105, 113). It is not even guaranteed longevity: "For that the favorites of the gods die early, is true in all things. . . . After all, one should not demand of what is noblest of all that it should have the durable toughness of leather" (*BT* 125).[6] The hammer Nietzsche brandishes in his "grand declaration of war" is stipulated to be a delicate instrument with which he may philosophize, a tuning fork used to sound out the hollowness of idols. The hero is not so much characterized by endurance or brute strength as by sensitivity: "The higher type represents an incomparably greater complexity—a greater sum of co-ordinated elements: so its disintegration is also incomparably more likely. The 'genius' is the sublimest machine there is—consequently the most fragile" (*WP* 363). Nietzsche knew that the genius had a tendency to self-destruct, like a fine watch that is too tightly wound.

---

not figure as a proponent of the "great man" theory of history. Whether history is reducible to the biography of a few great men, as Thomas Carlyle, William James, and Ralph Waldo Emerson, among others, maintained, or whether it is solely the product of economic, technological, or sociological forces was not Nietzsche's worry. Sidney Hook's *The Hero in History: A Study in Limitation and Possibility* (New York: The John Day Company, 1943) gives a good account of this debate. His definition of the hero as an "event-making" individual who decidedly alters history would place Nietzsche on the periphery of the controversy.

[6] Nietzsche is most often misinterpreted here. Arthur C. Danto's statement that "Nietzsche often falls into the stupidest errors of the social Darwinian, identifying survival with excellence" (*Nietzsche as Philosopher* [New York: Macmillan Company, 1965], p. 161) is absolutely false. Indeed, Nietzsche explicitly states that it is the herd animal, whose expedience and cunning far surpass that of any noble spirit, that is likely to flourish and be the bane of great men. The "song of philosophic heroism" is so seldom heard and so often stifled because "the mean and petty are everywhere in control" (*PTG* 36). Nietzsche would have echoed Matthew Arnold's lament in *Empedocles on Etna* (act 2, lines 90–94): "The brave, impetuous heart yields everywhere / To the subtle, contriving head; / Great qualities are trodden down, / And littleness united / Is become invincible." The sentiment resurfaces in Albert Einstein's observation that "great spirits have always encountered violent opposition from mediocre minds."

As a member of the spiritual elite, the great man does not solicit the adulation of the many. Fame (and the desire for it) is the mark of a lower nature, of someone capable of being appreciated by the majority or the "herd." "There lives no one who is permitted to praise me," Nietzsche wrote to express his own contempt for renown (*GW* 21:100).[7] This is the mark of a *"refined heroism* which disdains to offer itself to the veneration of the great masses, as his coarser brother does, and tends to go silently through the world and out of the world" (*HH* 134). Nietzsche spiritualized the criteria for heroism, distinguishing his understanding from the classical formulation: "The heroic consists in doing a great thing (or in *not* doing a great thing in a great fashion) without feeling oneself to be in competition *with* others *before* others. The hero always bears the wilderness and the sacred, inviolable borderline within him wherever he may go" (*HH* 391–92). This self-isolation became an increasingly significant aspect of the heroic figure in Nietzsche's writing. It appears as a projection of Nietzsche's own growing solitude.

Nietzsche was most anxious to distance himself from those coarse relatives who also were concerned with the heroic. He repudiated all forms of "hero worship," specifically Carlyle's (*EH* 261). The "romantic prostration before 'genius' and the 'hero' " was recognized to be an integral part of contemporary culture and considered antithetical to his own efforts. Hero worship, or "unconditional homage to people," was considered dangerous and quite simply "ludicrous" (*D* 103). "It has always been the greatest fatality for culture when men have been worshipped," Nietzsche remarked (*HH* 259). The cult of the hero, of the great man or genius, was condemned as a throwback to theistic times, "an echo of this reverence for gods and

---

[7] Cf. *DD* 63, "This coin with which / all the world makes payment, / fame— / I grasp this coin with gloves / with loathing I trample it beneath me."

princes" (*HH* 168).[8] Nietzsche was concerned that he not
be identified with those who erected and worshipped
golden calves in the place of forgotten gods. Among the
idols he hoped to destroy were all those that bore the
stamp of divine mimicry. This was not to reject his devotion to the creation of the cultural conditions necessary for
the emergence of great men, or his belief that the goal of
culture was contained in its highest exemplars. The truly
heroic culture, however, produces great men in order to
surpass them. The heroic individual must serve as a stimulant to further growth and the production of a still higher
type: "A people is a detour of nature to get to six or seven
great men.—Yes: and then to get around them" (*BGE* 81).
Nietzsche identified the romantic worshippers of the heroic as enemies, not allies, and treated them accordingly.

In part, what distinguishes the Nietzschean hero from
his coarser brother is that he never finishes his labors. Because his victories are self-overcomings, his opposition is
never vanquished. Release from his task could be found
only in the release from consciousness. For consciousness
is always consciousness of limitations. As Homer seems to
have indicated, the hero is tragic because he is only *half* a
god. Likewise, the Nietzschean hero's deeds of self-overcoming and his words that advertise these victories serve
as much to mark his boundaries as his achievements. Herodotus's lament might come to his lips: "Of all the sor-
rows that afflict mankind, the bitterest is this, that one
should have consciousness of much, but control over

[8] Arthur C. Danto's claim that "Nietzsche was an inveterate worship-
per of heroes" (*Nietzsche as Philosopher*, p. 198) is again a very common
and very false understanding. On this same question, Eric Bentley's *A
Century of Hero-Worship: A Study of the Idea of Heroism in Carlyle and Nietzsche, with Notes on Wagner, Spengler, Stefan George and D. H. Lawrence* (2d
ed. [Boston: Beacon Press, 1957]) is a worthwhile study of Nietzsche's
cultural context, though not especially insightful as to Nietzsche's project. While laudable for his sensitivity to the ambiguity of Nietzsche's
thought, Bentley also failed to recognize Nietzsche's opposition to hero
worship in general and romantic hero worship in particular.

nothing." The classical hero fought against this fate in his struggles with *fortuna*. To transgress his limits, the hero must win the favor of the gods, or battle with them asserting his will over their divinity. But the goddess of chance is never conquered, only temporarily subdued. The heroic penchant for adventure is the tempting of *fortuna* into doing battle again and again. The classical hero struggled with *fortuna* primarily in war and on the high seas. Nietzsche's heroes are "adventurers and circumnavigators of that inner world called 'man' " (*HH* 10). The battlefield is within the self, and the corpus of knowledge supplies all the mysteries and intrigue of uncharted waters. The hope is that a higher age "will carry heroism into the search for knowledge. . . . For believe me: the secret for harvesting from existence the greatest fruitfulness and the greatest enjoyment is—to *live dangerously*! Build your cities on the slopes of Vesuvius! Send your ships into uncharted seas! Live at war with your peers and yourselves!" (*GS* 228). The "heroism of knowledge" of which Nietzsche spoke requires all the courage possessed by its classical forerunner, but it has "at length grown subtle, spiritual, intellectual" (*Z* 313). From the greatest dangers is the greatest glory won, asserts Thucydides' Pericles. The classical hero was prone to rash and reckless deeds. Nietzsche's higher man also seeks glory, albeit a self-administered kind. The greatest dangers of the modern world, however, are not to be found at the end of a spear, but with pen in hand and during solitary walks. The free spirit consequently "tends to moderation" in action, for his energies are channeled into "the promotion of spiritual objectives" (*HH* 169). The modern hero finds his nemesis in himself as he totters on the abyss of nihilism. His payment for glory is not in the coin of sweat and blood, but in isolation, anguish, spiritual torment, and perhaps ultimately in the loss of his sanity. Valor's task is to seek out this strife and walk this precipice.

The object of self-imposed struggle and sacrifice is not a

masochistic pleasure, but a heightened sense of power. The goal is to prove oneself above common fears and aversions, to become master of one's world, including its terror and pain. The point is not to bear suffering in Stoic resignation, but to seek it out; for it offers an opportunity to test and display prowess (*GW* 11:244). The path is a hard one, and it will be trod only by those whose strength and courage allow the transformation of existential pain into spiritual pleasure: "*What makes one heroic?*—Going out to meet at the same time one's highest suffering and one's highest hope" (*GS* 219). Suffering elevates man. It raises him above himself. Better said, it is the catalyst that allows man to overcome his lower nature, his desire for comfort and a painless life. The "heroic type" finds in suffering his "greatest moments," a "Saturnalia" of the soul (*GS* 253; *TI* 82).

By heroic standards everything that contributes to strength is good. And strength is developed only through struggle. A world without struggle and its attendant suffering, therefore, is to be deprecated. So too a world without destruction. For destruction and creation are inseparable within the dynamic of self-overcoming: "You do not have the courage to burn up and perish: and so you never know that which is new. What today are my wings, power, clothes, and color, shall be my ashes tomorrow" (*GW* 14:13). The imperative is to be a phoenix. "All great things bring about their own destruction through an act of self-overcoming," Nietzsche wrote, foreseeing and lauding his own destiny (*GM* 161). All great things also are to emerge from their own ashes, stronger than before. But this rebirth is no other-worldly event. The "Kingdom of Heaven" is held to be a process of growth, of "inward change" that "comes at every moment and at every moment has not yet arrived" (*WP* 98, 99). It leaves one revitalized, but also more desirous of still greater vitality.

The hero has the fate of Tantalus, whose reach is insufficient and whose efforts unending. For the fruit of his struggle is unattainable: he is a mortal who seeks immortality, a man who desires to be a god. But as he reaches for what he cannot grasp, he also grows in power, and therefore welcomes the temptation to overstep his limits. Unaware or contemptuous of the boundaries of human life, the hero is forever in a state of transgression. He is hubristic, and he both suffers and glories in his struggles to be more than he is fated to be. "In the heroic effort of the individual to attain universality, in the attempt to transcend the curse of individuation and to become the *one* world-being, he suffers in his own person the primordial contradiction that is concealed in things, which means that he commits sacrilege and suffers" (*BT* 71). That his fate is preordained, that he is doomed to perish through his own excesses, is a matter of indifference. Or rather, the opportunity to perish in pursuit of a lofty goal beyond the reach of mortal man is deemed a blessing. Nietzsche's definition follows: "Heroism—that is the predilection of a man who strives for a goal, which reckoned with he himself no longer comes into consideration. Heroism is the good will to self-destruction" (*GW* 14:52–53). Self-sacrifice is not in itself desired; it is simply the by-product of a struggle to attain a goal that is forever out of reach. One becomes indifferent to one's pain and survival in the pursuit of an ideal.[9]

[9] Here Nietzsche exposed his Homeric heritage. Bruno Snell maintained that contrary to the Platonic Socrates' understanding, Homer's Achilles did not choose to die young in order to win immortal fame. He was not motivated by such an unheroic, instrumental calculation of the use of life. Achilles simply was consumed with vengeance and the thirst for glory. With uneasy resignation he accepts his early death as an unavoidable consequence of his ineluctable desire to slay Hector. (Cf. Bruno Snell, *Scenes from Greek Drama* [Berkeley: University of California Press, 1964], pp. 1–22.) Snell's thesis would have been warmly greeted by Nietzsche, who was anxious to paint Socrates as a rationalist. However, the texts indicate otherwise. Socrates turned Achilles less into a calculating reasoner than into a lover of justice and honor (*Apology* 28d) and a victim of love (*Symposium* 179e). While the motivating forces spoken of by Socrates may not have been Homer's, they are no more instrumental and no less consuming.

The hero must justify his existence a posteriori, by setting himself a noble goal, by making of himself something that redeems life, and by risking and often losing his life as a result. Divine ends and mortal means ensure a tragic fate. But he gladly embraces such a destiny. Nietzsche's words might serve as his motto: "I know of no better aim of life than that of perishing, *animae magnae prodigus* [careless of life], in pursuit of the great and the impossible" (*UM* 112). The impossibility of a final victory does not dissuade him from the task because his defining characteristic is not so much his having a great goal as his having great vigor. He is a "monster of energy, who demands a monster of a task" in order to expend himself. His actuating force is the will to struggle, "and the wretched spiritual game of goals and intentions and motives is only a foreground—even though weak eyes may take them for the matter itself" (*WP* 518).

The price of knowledge is suffering. Nietzsche would echo the pronouncement of the chorus from Aeschylus's *Agamemnon*: "For Zeus, who caused men to know, has ordained that man should come to knowledge through suffering." Thus the quest for knowledge demands a "heroic mood," and Nietzsche characterized his own project as requiring a "heroic way of thinking" (*GW* 11:13; *NB* 13.7.82). The heroic will to struggle is not, however, the product of a primordial yearning for knowledge. Nietzsche maintained the contrary. All genuine striving for truth is the product of "the pathos of struggle" (*GW* 6:17). The heroic disposition is primary. The quest for knowledge is merely the means employed by the modern hero to exhaust his energies. Not truth but the struggle for truth claims his heart. His world is one of adventure and mystery on an anchorless ship of discovery. Truth without opposition, a "tyranny of the true," even if possible, would be rejected as "boring, powerless and tasteless" (*D* 206). Above all the pathos of struggle must be maintained and cultivated. A heroic declaration is made: "I want no more knowledge without danger" (*GW* 21:83).

The hero of knowledge must suffer for his booty, paying for his victories with the loss of his former beliefs and identity. He glories in the necessarily endless and ultimately futile quest for truth, and proclaims the world as will to power, as the pathos of struggle between competing perspectives. He anticipates his opponents' accusations of self-contradiction as he confidently asserts the impossibility of transcendent truth and replies: "Granted this too is only interpretation—and you will be eager enough to raise this objection?—well, so much the better" (*BGE* 34). His response is made in the only manner consistent with his character—as a challenge.

T W O

INDIVIDUALISM

No matter how far a man may extend himself with his knowledge, no matter how objectively he may come to view himself, in the end it can yield to him nothing but his own biography.

—*Human, All Too Human*

The road to radical individualism, which has its greatest ramifications in the realms of politics and morality, finds its origin in epistemology. The starting point is the limitations of man's mind. Nietzsche's individualism is above all the extension of his skepticism.

Epistemology for Nietzsche is the unsuccessful attempt to separate the organ of perception, the mind, from that which is perceived, the supposed thing-in-itself. Despite the most strenuous efforts, one is never assured of attaining a true representation of some fundamental reality. One knows only one's own perceptions. Likewise, however deeply the mind is explored, its substratum is never reached. One becomes conscious only of its workings, its effects. "When we try to examine the mirror in itself we discover in the end nothing but things upon it. If we want to grasp the things we finally get hold of nothing but the mirror.—This, in the most general terms, is the history of knowledge" (*D* 141). Nietzsche's point is not that the mind is a blank slate, as Locke would have it. (In fact, he explicitly repudiated Locke's theory [*GW* 16:250].) Nor is the mind considered to be an unblemished mirror that accurately reflects an external reality. The passage has a skeptical thrust. The mirror metaphors often used to represent the mind mislead us into positing a separate reality which is reflected by or in us. Nietzsche pictured man standing with his back toward a supposed reality and the mirror of his mind before him. An uninhibited view of the world is blocked by the perceiver himself: "Why does man not see things? He is himself standing in the way: he conceals things" (D 187).

The thing-in-itself is an abstraction we arrive at by imagining a world from which its perceiver is absent. Like the infinity of reflections on two opposing mirrors, the thing-in-itself would appear if the observer between the mirrors could become transparent, no longer blocking his own view. But then, with nothing for the mirrors to reflect, our invisible observer would have nothing to observe. He must step slightly aside to see the multiple reflections of his own image, reflections whose infinite regress could be seen only from a point beyond the asymptote from which he cannot escape. All he can do is imagine the infinity of images as that which would be seen from an angle less oblique than his own. The thing-in-itself is that point beyond our purest perceptions.

The world is always and only the mind conscious of its own activity. Nietzsche refused to bestow on the world a higher status, maintaining its dependence upon the structure of the mind. At the same time, man is not congratulated for his limitations. The Protagorean pronouncement that man is the measure of all things must not be accepted without qualification. Man can know the world only as he measures it, as he perceives and interprets it. But Nietzsche does not presume man to occupy a unique position in the universe. Man's inability to measure the world without using his own scales does not mean that other scales do not exist. One must withhold judgment.

How far the perspective character of existence extends or indeed whether existence has any other character than this; whether existence without interpretation, without "sense," does not become "nonsense"; whether, on the other hand, all existence is not essentially actively engaged in *interpretation*—that cannot be decided even by the most industrious and most scrupulously conscientious analysis and self-examination of the intellect; for in the course of this analysis the human intellect cannot avoid seeing itself in its own perspectives and *only* in these. We cannot look around our own corner: it is a hopeless curiosity that wants to know what other kinds of intellect and perspectives there *might* be; for example, whether some beings might be able to experience time backward, or alternately forward and backward (which would involve another direction of life and another concept of cause and effect). But I should think that today we are at least far from the ridiculous immodesty that would be involved in decreeing from our corner that perspectives are permitted only from this corner. (*GS* 336)

Skepticism is another word for such modesty in the epistemological realm. Man's limited capacity for knowledge does not determine the boundaries of reality, but the boundaries of man—a particular species on a particular planet in a particular universe. "We are figures in the dream of God who are guessing how he dreams," Nietzsche suggested (*GW* 3:319). Man may speculate about his dreamy existence, but he must acknowledge that it may not be the only dream being dreamt. The discovery of universal laws that rule his world does not preclude the existence of other laws or other worlds.

Nietzsche's individualism is the logical extension of his skeptical evaluations. The individual, like the species, cannot see around his own corner. Each is locked into a world of his own. "The habits of our senses have woven us into lies and deception of sensation: these again are the basis of all our judgments and 'knowledge'—there is absolutely no escape, no backway or bypath into the *real world*! We sit within our net, we spiders, and whatever we may catch in it, we can catch nothing at all except that which allows itself to be caught in precisely *our* net" (*D* 73). All knowledge is experience, and all experience is individual. We may compare our experiences, but not exchange them or equate them. The point is not that we subjectivize experiences that would otherwise have some objective status. An "objective experience," to use a favorite phrase of Nietzsche's, is a *contradictio in adjecto*. It is an abstraction that cannot be even clearly thought out. The individual remains the ultimate interpreter of his cultural and social inheritance, including the meanings of words (*WP* 403). That people agree to call similar experiences by the same name and, by and large, succeed in communicating according to such schemes does not retrieve the individual from his isolation. It simply demonstrates the ingenuity of the species. Perspectivism is the name Nietzsche gave to this radically individualistic epistemology.

The problem with perspectivism as a philosophical position is that it appears to be self-refuting. If all truth is individualistic, then Nietzsche's assertion of perspectivism is true only for Nietzsche, which is to say, not *the* truth. The logical paradox involved in perspectivism is insuperable, but this should not keep one from appreciating its force. The upshot is a radically individualistic philosophy in both senses of the term. Not only does Nietzsche offer a philosophical argument for radical individualism, namely, his writings, but he also provides an individualistic argument for his philosophy, namely, his life. For any true philosophy, according to Nietzsche, must first be lived, and is only subsequently transmitted. In short, one cannot separate the philosopher from his work: the personal is the philosophical, and the philosophical is the personal. Nietzsche critically applied this understanding to himself no less than to the other subjects of his studies. Any attempt to extract an objective truth from Nietzsche's

31

philosophy while siphoning off the subjective sediment is, therefore, misconstrued.[1] At the same time, psychologizing Nietzsche may be equally misleading. To highlight the psychological, that is to say personal, origins of Nietzsche's philosophy is neither to discredit it nor to explain it away. For in Nietzsche's books there is no such thing as impersonal philosophical thought.

Already in his unpublished essay *Philosophy in the Tragic Age of the Greeks* Nietzsche had outlined his understanding of individualism. "Now philosophical systems are wholly true for their founders only," he wrote in the preface; "Taken as ultimate ends, in any event, they represent an error, hence are to be repudiated" (*PTG* 23). Nonetheless, they provide a semiological study of the individuals who founded them, revealing a "slice of *personality*." One celebrates philosophical studies because they constitute in-

[1] Walter Kaufmann, for example, attempted to play down the personal side of Nietzsche's writing so as to establish him as a philosopher (i.e., someone concerned with objective truth) and not merely a literary stylist (i.e., someone concerned with individual expression). While successful in winning esteem for Nietzsche as a philosophical thinker in the English-speaking world, Kaufmann's project was at odds with a major element of Nietzsche's philosophical thought, an element far too infrequently acknowledged, namely, his contention that the personal and the philosophical are inseparable. Karl Jaspers' study *Nietzsche: An Introduction to the Understanding of His Philosophical Activity* (Tucson: University of Arizona Press, 1965) is an exception to this tendency in the secondary literature. Jaspers consistently affirmed the link between Nietzsche's self-understanding and his philosophy. Kaufmann's criticism of Jaspers for propagating the belief that "what made the philosopher so remarkable was not his philosophy. . . . it was his heroic, yet aimless self-laceration" (Walter Kaufmann, *From Shakespeare to Existentialism* [New York: Anchor Books, 1959], p. 296) is unfair to Jaspers' discussion of and esteem for Nietzsche as a philosopher. It also misses the point that what makes Nietzsche so remarkable as a philosopher is that he never separated his philosophy from his heroic (but hardly aimless) struggles as an individual. One of the few works on Nietzsche that attempts to account for the individualistic nature of his philosophy is Lou Andreas-Salomé's *Friedrich Nietzsche in seinen Werken* (Vienna: Carl Konegen, 1911). However, even Salomé made the mistake of trying to discredit some of his writing as mere literature spawned by his personal inclinations and predilections, and thus void of philosophical import. Nietzsche regarded such distinctions as spurious.

triguing and inspiring outlooks on the "human scene." However much subsequent research and events may refute elements of philosophical systems, such systems remain tributes to "what we *must ever love and honor* and what no subsequent enlightenment can take away: great individual human beings" (*PTG* 24). Philosophy for Nietzsche was not about truth, but about living without truth. What remains of import in philosophical works is the portrayal of individuals who have struggled with the contradictions of existence. Their writings never provide resolutions of these contradictions, but they may serve as testimonies to battles well fought. We discover that "the errors of great men are worthy of veneration, because they are more fruitful than the truths of small ones" (*GW* 1:393). The story of philosophy, in short, is the history of the errors and lies found necessary or useful by the titans of thinking.

Nietzsche may generalize as to the erroneousness of all philosophical systems because any attempt to speak of truth in a nonindividualistic manner must founder. Philosophy cannot exempt itself from perspectivism. "The task of painting *the* picture of life, however often poets and philosophers may pose it, is nonetheless senseless: even under the hands of the greatest of painter-thinkers all that has ever eventuated is pictures and miniatures *out of one* life, namely their own—and nothing else is even possible" (*HH* 218). Of course this applies to Nietzsche's painted thoughts as well, and he admitted as much. His oft-quoted declaration, "*This world is the will to power—and nothing besides!*" frequently interpreted as a doctrinaire assertion of a metaphysical truth is something quite different. It is a declaration of the impossibility of such truths. The will to power, Nietzsche stipulated, is only the "name" he has given to the world. And this world is shown to the reader in the only way possible for Nietzsche, namely, in his "own mirror" (*WP* 549–50). The world as will to power, and more specifically as a heightened sense of will to power, is a miniature portrait of Nietzsche's life. It is described the only way he could describe it, that is, as reflected in him.[2]

To the extent that one's experiences parallel those of others, an understanding may be approached. Still, the most that can be said about close relatives in the realm of thought is that they bring one into one's own company. They are spurs to the soul, awakening forgotten experi-

---

[2] Heidegger's account of Nietzsche sets itself the dubious task of describing the will to power as a radical metaphysical assertion while depreciating precisely that which makes it radical, namely, its individualistic, self-referential, and thus antimetaphysical status. Heidegger was so intent on establishing Nietzsche as the last metaphysician in the great Western tradition of philosophy that he consistently ignored the individualistic element of his thought. Thus Heidegger weakened his own argument, for Nietzsche's destruction of metaphysics is inseparable from the development of his perspectivist position. Heidegger's thesis reads: "When *Aristotle* says Being is ενεργεια, when the medieval theologians reinterpreted ενεργεια from creatio and say that Being is actus purus, when *Leibniz* says that Being is vis primativa activa, when *Kant* says that Being is objectivity and objecthood [*Objectivität und Gegendständlichkeit*], when *Hegel* says that Being is unconditional reality as absolute spirit—absolute idea, when *Nietzsche* says that Being is will to power, then all these thinkers are saying the same thing; the same thing in every stage of the history of its unfolding. With that we are at the same time taking Nietzsche out of his incongruous surroundings of literati and free-thinkers, life-reformers and banal atheists and are looking for him there where the 'personality' disappears: in the 'work' " (Martin Heidegger, *Gesamtausgabe*, vol. 48, *Nietzsche: Der Europäische Nihilismus* [Frankfurt: Vittorio Klostermann, 1986], p. 36). Here Heidegger is much at odds with Nietzsche's understanding of the philosophical work in general and his own work in particular. Walter Kaufmann's restrictive evaluation of Heidegger's writing on Nietzsche as being "important for those who want to understand Heidegger" is apposite (Walter Kaufmann, *Nietzsche: Philosopher, Psychologist, Antichrist*, 4th ed. [Princeton: Princeton University Press, 1974], p. 500). Heidegger's philosophical effort to look for Nietzsche where personality disappears ironically bears out Heidegger's own project more than it enlightens Nietzsche's. Of course, Nietzsche understood that this necessarily would be the case for any truly philosophical study. (Note: The benefit of reading Heidegger's writings on Nietzsche in the *Gesamtausgabe* is that they are mostly unedited. In the other German editions and their English translations, for example, Heidegger had expunged a number of remarks that appear as friendly to the National Socialist surroundings in which he found himself at the time his lectures on Nietzsche were given.)

ences or prompting new assessments of their significance. Anything more is impossible: "Ultimately, nobody can get more out of things, including books, than he already knows. For what one lacks access to from experience one will have no ear" (*EH* 261). Moreover, the higher one's spiritual rank, the more individualistic one's experiences become. What is common always belongs to "the herd."

The thoroughly self-referential world of the individual was a prominent theme throughout Nietzsche's writings. In 1874, at the start of his career, Nietzsche admitted that he had no right to claim to have penetrated into the world of even his most influential mentor, Arthur Schopenhauer: "I am far from believing that I have truly understood Schopenhauer, rather it is only that through Schopenhauer I have learned to understand myself a little better; which is why I owe him the greatest debt of thanks" (*GW* 7:140). Nietzsche's later works show the concept of radical individuality unchanged. In his last year of productivity, he wrote, "It is plain what I misunderstood in, equally plain what I read into, Wagner and Schopenhauer—myself" (*NCW* 669).[3] Nietzsche would challenge his readers to re-read his early essay "Wagner in Bayreuth" and substitute his or Zarathustra's name for Wagner's, claiming that "in all psychologically decisive places I alone am discussed" (*EH* 274). Of course, the sword cuts both ways. Nietzsche warned his own readers not to assume to have comprehended him: "Whoever thought he had understood something of me, had made up something out of me after his own image—not uncommonly an antithesis to me" (*EH* 261). In short, everyone pays and receives in his own coin.

The individual is in a permanent state of isolation. Experiences are never truly shared, only their simulacra. This is not simply because the written or spoken word is a poor reflection of thought. Thought itself is a lame trans-

---

[3] Although the majority of the excerpts from his earlier works that compose *Nietzsche contra Wagner* are unaltered, this line was written in 1888 and added by Nietzsche to an excerpt from *The Gay Science*.

mitter of experience. Consciousness is deemed an anti-in-
dividualistic development, the effect of a herd existence. It
is the ultimately futile attempt to turn the individual's mo-
nopoly of experience into common, communicable knowledge.

> My idea is, as you see, that consciousness does not
> really belong to man's individual existence but rather
> to his social or herd nature; that, as follows from this,
> it has developed subtlety only insofar as this is re-
> quired by social or herd utility. . . . Fundamentally,
> all our actions are altogether incomparably personal,
> unique, and infinitely individual; there is no doubt of
> that. But as soon as we translate them into conscious-
> ness *they no longer seem to be.*
>
> This is the essence of phenomenalism and perspec-
> tivism as *I* understand them: owing to the nature of
> *animal consciousness*, the world of which we can be-
> come conscious is only a surface-and-sign-world, a
> world that is made common and meaner; whatever
> becomes conscious *becomes* by the same token shal-
> low, low, thin, relatively stupid, general, sign, herd
> signal; all becoming conscious involves a great and
> thorough corruption, falsification, reduction to super-
> ficialities, and generalization. (*GS* 299–300)

Communication, or the making common of what is individually experienced, involves a necessary falsification.
We can communicate our experiences, but at the cost of
robbing them of their essential uniqueness. For communication marks a threefold corruption. Words never ade-
quately or unequivocally portray thought, and thought
never fully corresponds to experience. In turn, the recipient can only interpret the communication according to his
own pool of (unique) experiences.

The self-enclosure of the individual is complete. What
applies to the transmission of knowledge also applies to
the realm of feelings: "Ultimately one loves one's desires

and not that which is desired" (*BGE* 88). The objects of desire or aversion, no less than the objects of thought or perception, are as images in a mirror. Any attempt to grasp them yields only the reflecting surface. "In the final analysis," says Zarathustra, "one experiences only one-self" (Z 173). "Mankind" and "humanity" are misleading abstractions. Apart from the herd, all that exists are individuals, each enclosed in his own world, each a world unto himself.

Indeed, Nietzsche also held the individual to be an abstraction. He rejected the assumption that there was something called "the individual" which had a certain fixity, continuity, and duration. Nietzsche stepped beyond subjectivism to attack the idea of an enduring, unified subject. The individual was conceived as a multiplicity. If one may speak of the uniqueness of the individual, it is because of the unique composition of drives, the individual's particular yet pluralistic internal regime.

The revocation of the individual's membership in the community of mankind is accompanied by the constitution of the individual himself as a community. Perspectivism, then, provides a remedy for its own philosophical ills. The self-enclosure of the individual is counteracted by the multiple perspectives each individual is capable of maintaining. It is misleading, therefore, to accuse Nietzsche of subjectivism, for he gave the subject no single identity. Nietzsche's perspectivism first isolates and then dissolves the individual. Objectivity is understood to be nothing more than a multiplication of the personal: "There is *only* a perspective seeing, *only* a perspective "knowing"; and the *more* affects we allow to speak about one thing, the *more* eyes, different eyes, we can use to observe one thing, the more complete will our 'concept' of this thing, our 'objectivity,' be" (*GM* 119). Objectivity, Nietzsche always maintained, was nothing but an extension of subjectivity (*GW* 1:280). We cannot escape our own web, but we may establish numerous viewpoints within it.

37

The personalized nature of Nietzsche's writings—his frequent references to the state of his health, the climatic conditions, his geographic location, social relations, tastes, habits, and inclinations—served as implicit demonstrations of his individualistic philosophy. The suppression of the affects or the attempt to neutralize perception was held to be wholly undesirable. Knowledge, Nietzsche insisted, was not a product of depersonalized observation and thought, but of the stimulation of the senses and passions, of their multiplication and agglomeration. Even if one were capable of suspending passion, the result would not be more objectivity, but, to use Nietzsche's words, a castrated intellect.[4] There is another effect: moral man. The attempt to objectify observation and thought is the "bridge to morality" (GW 11:16). Marching over this bridge are the ranks of the deindividualized.

The individual is a law unto himself, unpredictable and unmanageable. Society, then, cannot be composed of individuals. It requires members. Man must be made "uniform" and "calculable"; for this purpose morality and the "social straitjacket" are employed. The purpose of establishing society and its fiction of mankind, Nietzsche contended, was to prevent people from becoming individuals, to make them "common" (GW 10:400). The price of social membership is the forfeiture of self-rule, this by means of establishing social norms: "Through his morality the individual *outvotes* himself" (HH 232).[5] The metaphor is well chosen, for the individual plays an active part in his own

---

[4] Nietzsche's remark was directed primarily at Schopenhauer, whose ideal of purified observation, freed of will and affect, was deemed as impossible as it was undesirable.

[5] Emerson's reflection in "Self-Reliance" comes to mind: "Society everywhere is in conspiracy against the manhood of every one of its members. Society is a joint-stock company, in which the members agree, for the better securing of his bread to each shareholder, to surrender the liberty and culture of the eater. The virtue in most request is conformity. Self-reliance is its aversion. It loves not realities and creators, but names and customs." '

socialization. Nietzsche was not party to the conspiracy theory of morality and civil society. Morality, while certainly a social imposition, also satisfies a basic need. Man is a herd animal, a tribal beast. He bears within him a drive to conformity: "Morality is the herd instinct in the individual" (*GS* 175). The domination of the herd instinct is the mark of socialization, of deindividuation. It constitutes the end of self-rule.

Nietzsche's individualistic valuations are the antitheses of those stemming from any generalizable moral system. The worth of an action, contrary to a Kantian morality (which Nietzsche recognized as the apogee of moral thought), is not determined by its capacity to reflect a universalizable maxim. The merit of any deed must be determined on a strictly individualistic basis: "The worth of an action depends upon *who* does it and whether it originates from one's depths or one's surface: that is, how deeply it is individual" (*GW* 16:245; cf. *Z* 118-20). Action performed out of a sense of duty or respect for law—the pseudonyms for custom and herd instinct—is worthless in terms of a higher morality. Indeed, it may be harmful. For one's spiritual metabolism requires a personalized diet: "The popular medical formulation of morality that goes back to Ariston of Chios, 'virtue is the health of the soul,' would have to be changed to become useful, at least to read: '*your* virtue is the health of *your* soul.' For there is no health as such" (*GS* 176). The health of the soul is placed in jeopardy through the adoption of general moral prescriptions. The rule of morality must be completely usurped by a personalized regime. For Nietzsche, virtue, no less than duty, must be an individual invention: "And so should each in his own manner do his best for himself—that is my moral:—the only one that still remains for me" (*NB* 7.82).

Nietzsche's approval of social disintegration and the decay of morality are part of his augury of the individual. Society holds the individual to be its greatest threat; morality serves as its weapon. "Lofty spiritual independence, the will to stand alone, great intelligence even, are felt to be dangerous; everything that raises the individual above the herd and makes his neighbour quail are henceforth called *evil*; the fair, the modest, obedient, self-effacing disposition, the *mean and average* in desires, acquires moral names and honours" (*BGE* 105). Social normalization and moralization reduce the autonomous individual to the status of a pariah. Nietzsche welcomed times of strife and the downfall of social relations as the harbingers of individualism (*GS* 97). The decay of morality provides the fertile soil from which the "ripest fruit" is harvested: "the *sovereign individual*, like only to himself, liberated again from morality of custom, autonomous and supramoral (for 'autonomous' and 'moral' are mutually exclusive)" (*GM* 59). In short, the social straitjacket must be rent before the higher man may emerge.

To be an individual is to be autonomous is to be supramoral. Timidity and indolence are the main obstacles to achieving this freedom of spirit (*UM* 127). It is simply easier—requiring less effort, less thought, less work and struggle and courage—to be a member of the herd. Hiding behind established custom and opinion is less dangerous and less demanding than striking out on one's own. But the same evaluation applies to personalized custom, that is, to habit. In Nietzsche's understanding, a man ruled by habit, regardless of how idiosyncratic, is no freer than a man ruled by social mores. In both cases thought and action are hindered. Enduring habits are tyrants that rob one of opportunities to explore and expand one's individuality (*GS* 237).

> Everything habitual draws around us an ever firmer net of spider webs; and soon we notice that the threads have become cords and that we ourself are sitting in the middle as the spider who has caught himself and has to live on his own blood. That is why the

free spirit hates all habituation and rules, everything enduring and definitive, that is why he sorrowfully again and again rends apart the net that surrounds him: even though he will as a consequence suffer numerous great and small wounds—for he has to rend those threads *from himself*, from his own body and soul.[6] (*HH* 158)

To be completely without habits, however, is neither possible nor desirable. Constant improvisation would rob one of the time and energy needed for the focused development of body and spirit. The duration and nature of one's habits become important questions. Whether habits are "the product of innumerable little cowardices and lazinesses or of your courage and inventive reason" will determine, in large part, one's order of rank (*GS* 246). Freedom from social norms has its counterpart in freedom from personal norms. The benefit of the disintegration of social and moral standards has its counterpart in the individual's need for revolutions of the soul. Within the social regime, as in the spiritual regime, autonomy and growth are inseparable.

Sorrow, pain, endless struggle, deprivation, and isolation are the costs of autonomy. Why should this price be paid? The answer, simply put, is that the dictates of a "higher morality" demand it. One seeks to develop virtues because they are *one's own* virtues, a sign of one's power and freedom. The "supramorality" of the higher man, his being "beyond good and evil," is not tantamount to dissipation and turpitude. It is a concentration of energy in the pursuit of an austere higher morality.

From society's point of view, supramorality appears as

[6] Nietzsche's own itinerant existence and mercurial relationships bear witness to this understanding of the threat of habit. Shortly after the publication of *Human, All Too Human* Nietzsche resigned his chair at the University of Basel, spending the remainder of his productive life as a "wanderer," generally separated from family and friends, living and working out of hotels and pensions in Switzerland, France, and Italy.

immorality. To be an individual is to be immoral. Nietzsche recognized that this identification was not new: "The individual has long been 'immoral'—it consequently hid itself, for example, the genius (like Homer) under the name of a hero" (*GW* 11:223). Past heroes, in any case, justified their actions by appealing to the gods. Political and religious founders and legislators often claimed to have had a special destiny allotted them, to have been the recipients of revelation, making them instruments of divine justice, and effectively thrusting responsibility for their doings onto a deity. Their destruction of old regimes and creation of new ones was based on the dictates of a newly discovered, higher morality. With the death of God, however, the modern hero is left with no apology for his self-assertion. His individuality must be self-supporting.

The distinction between Nietzschean and classical heroism is precisely the radical autonomy of the modern individual. Previous heroes were always, at least in part, representatives. They were incarnations of ideals or descendants of the gods. They were meant to serve as paradigms for their peers and their progeny, just as the gods served as models for the heroes.[7] Nietzsche understood the modern hero quite differently. He is not a representative of ideals any more than he is a divine tool. He speaks only for himself; he represents only himself. The paradigm being offered is that of one who has become sovereign and unique, a law unto himself, not others. As such, he cannot serve as an exemplar, for his virtue consists in his incom-

[7] In his study of classical heroism, Gregory Nagy offered a different view: "The hero, after all, is not a model for imitation but rather a figure who cannot be ignored; his special excellence is not integration but potency" (*The Best of the Achaeans: Concepts of the Hero in Archaic Greek Poetry* [Baltimore: Johns Hopkins University Press, 1979], p. ix). Nagy's point is well taken and reinforces the interpretation of Nietzsche as a self-styled classical hero. Undeniably, however, Nietzsche pushed the modern hero's individuality to a point never reached in classicism. Alasdair MacIntyre expands on this position in the chapter "The Virtues in Heroic Societies" of his *After Virtue: A Study in Moral Theory* (Notre Dame: University of Notre Dame Press, 1981).

mensurability. "Whatever kind of bizarre ideal one may follow (e.g., as 'Christian' or as 'free spirit' or as 'immoralist' or as *Reichsdeutscher*—), one should not demand that it be *the* ideal: for one therewith takes from it its privileged character. One should have it in order to distinguish oneself, not in order to level oneself. . . . true heroism consists, in *not* fighting under the banner of sacrifice, devotion, disinterestedness, but in *not fighting at all*—'This is what *I* am; this is what *I* want:—*you* can go to hell!'" (*WP* 190–91).[8] The curse is as much a damning of romantic idealism and hero worship as it is a sacrilege. The Nietzschean hero stands beyond man *and* God. When God died, the molds for the formation of man were broken. Now man's highest elevation is always the attainment of his individuality. Pluralism, for Nietzsche, is at a premium.[9]

Heroic individualism is not to be equated with what might be called democratic individualism. The latter was considered by Nietzsche at best an undeveloped, preparatory stage for the former.

> *Individualism* is a modest and still unconscious form of the "will to power"; here it seems sufficient for the

---

[8] In *The Philosophy of History* Hegel made a similar point: "World-historical men—the Heroes of an epoch . . . have formed purposes to satisfy themselves, not others." However, any agreement between them is overshadowed by Nietzsche's explicit rejection of Hegel's understanding of the hero as a historically necessary force, a concept Nietzsche found repugnant because it "transforms every moment into a naked admiration for success and leads to an idolatry of the factual" (*UM* 105).

[9] Nietzsche's depreciation of monotheism reflects his valorization of plurality and his fear of man's normalization through his emulation of nonindividualistic ideals or models. "Monotheism, on the other hand, this rigid consequence of the doctrine of the one normal type—the faith in one normal god beside whom there are only pseudo-gods—was perhaps the greatest danger that has yet confronted humanity. It threatened us with premature stagnation that, as far as we can see, most other species have long reached. . . . In polytheism the free-spiriting and many-spiriting of man attained its first preliminary form—the strength to create for ourselves our own new eyes—and ever again new eyes that are even more our own: hence man alone among all the animals has no eternal horizons and perspectives" (*GS* 192).

individual to get free from an overpowering domination by society (whether that of the state or of the
church). He does not oppose them as a person but
only as an individual, he represents all individuals
against the totality. That means: he instinctively posits himself as equal to all other individuals; what he
gains in this struggle he gains for himself not as a person but as a representative of individuals against the
totality. (*WP* 411)

Representation is foreign to Nietzsche's individualism because he assumed a fundamental inequality among men.
In this regard, democratic individualism—its political prescriptions and moral underpinnings—are antithetical to
his project.[10] Nietzsche made no attempt to construct a political theory with universal application: "My philosophy
aims at an ordering of rank: not at an individualistic morality. The ideas of the herd should rule in the herd—but
not reach out beyond it" (*WP* 162). The philosophy of individualism only applies to those who, in Nietzsche's evaluation, are capable of becoming individuals—and that excludes the majority. Ironically, then, the worthy recipients
of Nietzsche's individualistic philosophy are those who
would approach it critically. They would, at best, adapt it
to their personalized needs, refusing to accept it in toto.

Although the higher man disdains to pose as an exemplar for others, and has no particular cause to which he
devotes himself, this is not to say that his self-assertion is
without struggle. He fights, but under his own rules, for
himself, and, paradoxically, mostly against himself.
Rather than prove his courage by sacrificing himself for a
transcendent ideal or god, the modern individual's cour-

---

[10] Nietzsche actually maintained a certain ambivalence toward democracy. For democracy was held to spawn both the freedom that allows for
the cultivation of greatness *and* the disorder that characterizes the soul of
modern man (*BGE* 153–54). Democracy prepares the ground for the heroic individual just as it describes the ebb of that spiritual strength that
makes a true individualism possible.

age is evidenced in his capacity to live in its absence. His independence forbids the creation of idols before which he may kneel. In brief, bearing the isolation of his own individuality is his greatest challenge. Zarathustra declares: "And if someone goes through fire for his teaching—what does that prove? Truly, it is more when one's own teaching comes out of one's own burning!" (Z 116). The heroic individual is he who does not take refuge from his own burning in the temple of the gods, in the sanctuary of a herd existence and the comfort of custom, or behind the shield of habit. From the wounds incurred he then draws the ink used to transmit his experiences. His books are always "written with blood" (Z 67).

Nietzsche's brand of individualism is neither a political statement of democratic inclination nor an ethical statement of respect for the status of human life and liberty. The individual is not so much a reality as a goal. The heroic task, assumed only by the few, is to *become* a sovereign individual. We are all "sentenced" to individuality (*GS* 175). The aim is to turn the curse of individuation into the blessing of autonomy. Most escape this challenge by indulging their herd instincts, submitting to morality, and abandoning their potential for freedom. He who is born with a noble soul, who thinks and feels deeply, knows no such escape. He suffers from and curses his limitations, his isolation, his incapacity to see or feel beyond his own corner. Being an individual becomes an existential plight. But he knows this plight may be transformed into a celebration of the self: "no longer the humble expression, 'everything is *merely* subjective,' but 'it is also *our* work!—Let us be proud of it!' " (*WP* 545). One must turn the curse of individuation into a feast. Without exception it is to be a tragic feast, but throughout the voice of creative freedom is nonetheless heard.

A higher morality necessitates immorality by herd standards. It demands that the hero sacrifice himself for *his own* ideals: "We must free ourselves from morality *to be able to live morally. My free will,—my self-created ideal* wants this and that virtue from me, that is, to *perish in pursuit of virtue*. That is heroism" (GW 16:163). The individual becomes his own moral legislator, his own taskmaster and most ferocious enemy, and his own physician. Success is not measured by a long life, moral capital, fame, or worldly power, but by the courage needed to sacrifice these goods in the pursuit of one's autonomy.

The modern hero is destined for an alienated existence. His determination to celebrate the tragedy of individuation means that the social and political battles that rage about him are viewed as so many distractions. Human relations in general are seen as a threat to his allotted task: "The objective of all human arrangements is through distracting one's thoughts to cease *to be aware* of life. Why does [the great man] desire the opposite—to be aware precisely of life, that is to say to suffer from life—so strongly? Because he realizes that he is in danger of being cheated out of himself, and that a kind of agreement exists to kidnap him out of his own cave. Then he bestirs himself, pricks up his ears, and resolves: 'I will remain my own!' " (UM 154). Only the few are capable of such resolve. The majority remain happy in their masquerade, fulfilling their social roles and playing the part assigned to them in the "theatre of politics." Indeed, they become these roles. Their "puppet-play" "disperses the individual to the four winds" and serves as the testimony that the player "has not understood the lesson set him by existence." Heroism, wrote Nietzsche, consists in being done with this game and taking on the burden of being an individual (UM 154–55). Politics or statecraft (Nietzsche considered them synonymous) ought be left to the statesmen, of whom Nietzsche held no high opinion (UM 181): "Political and economic affairs are not worthy of being the enforced concern of society's most gifted spirits: such a wasteful use of the spirit is at bottom worse than having none at all" (D 107). Included among Nietzsche's Ten Commandments for Free

Spirits is the proscription, "You shall not practice politics" (*GW* 9:365). Indeed, Nietzsche intentionally made his published work politically obnoxious lest his public role as a writer constitute an infraction of this edict: "I write in such a way that neither the mob, nor the *populi*, nor the parties of any kind want to read me. . . . Neither usefully nor pleasantly—to the trio I have named" (*HH* 327–28).

Politics, in short, constitutes a threat to the individual. The purpose of the state, according to Nietzsche, ought to be the cultivation of individuals. But this is never the case. The modern state in particular is one of the major forces working against the goal of culture (*UM* 165; *GW* 7:383). In Zarathustra's words, the state was made for the masses: "it devours them, and chews them, and re-chews them! . . . Only there, where the state ceases, does the man who is not superfluous begin" (*Z* 76–77). It follows that political decline is a prerequisite for the emergence of individuals: "All great cultural epochs are epochs of political decline: that which is great in the cultural sense has been unpolitical, even *anti-political*" (*TI* 63). Ultimately, the strong individual is a product of the struggle with his own isolation. Political affairs are at best a distraction from this task, and at worst its greatest inhibitor. To be antipolitical, as Nietzsche considered himself, is the mark of individuality (*EH* 225). For the worthiest struggle is not waged within the public realm. True heroism, according to Nietzsche, slakes its agonal thirst within the soul.[11]

---

[11] Nietzsche's antipoliticism and antistatism is not out of line with the characteristics of classical heroism, although it is certainly more pervasive and extreme. Heroes have always been, at least for part of their lives, opposed to the powers that be. W.T.H. Jackson wrote: "The hero's objectives are thus personal, so far as his own life is concerned. He need not work for the good of society. . . . His conduct may be and often is detrimental to the society in which he moves and may be disturbing to the form of society and the power and position of its leader." Jackson concluded: "No epic could be composed unless, in some way, it embodied the confrontation between the hero and the king" (*The Hero and the King: An Epic Theme* [New York: Columbia University Press, 1982], pp. 12–13, 138). Nietzsche's writings bear out this epic theme.

That which typically identified the classical hero—his great adventures and slayings, and his subsequent founding or restoration of a political regime—has no place among the demands made by the modern hero of himself. War and oceanic odysseys are not his predilection; neither is politics. Like all heroes, he consciously writes his autobiography with his deeds. But these events are experienced mostly in silence. The Nietzschean hero, in distinction to his classical forerunners, spurns the intrigues and masquerades of the stage of worldly affairs to face a more demanding audience. He is a man driven inward. His tragic fate is to consume himself. His willingness to perish that he may proudly win his individuality is witnessed by his final words: *Ecce Homo*, behold the man.

PART II

THE POLITICS OF THE SOUL

T H R E E

THE SOUL AS A PLURALITY

Man appears as a plurality of beings, a union of many
spheres, from which one may look back on the other.
—*Gesammelte Werke*

In the spring of 1868, before the appearance of any of his
philosophical works, Nietzsche wrote: "The concept of the
whole does not lie in things, but in us. These unities that
we name organisms are but again multiplicities. There are
in reality no individuals, moreover individuals and organisms are nothing but abstractions" (*GW* 1:414). He maintained this thesis throughout his life. The human being,
the body, the soul, the subject, the individual, was proposed as a multiplicity. A note written in 1885 reads: "The
assumption of one single subject is perhaps unnecessary;
perhaps it is just as permissible to assume a multiplicity of
subjects, whose interaction and struggle is the basis of our
thought and our consciousness in general? . . . *My hypothesis*: The subject as multiplicity" (*WP* 270). Far from being
an ignorable oddity reflecting Nietzsche's penchant for
psychology, this *hypothesis* constitutes a cornerstone of
Nietzsche's politico-philosophical edifice.

The multiple soul, of course, was not Nietzsche's invention. The concept is at least as old as political philosophy.
Plato's "city in speech" of the *Republic* is the macrocosmic
description of what Socrates discerns in the souls of his
interlocutors. Indeed, the manifestly political aspect of the
Republic, that is, the theorization of the city, is ostensibly

proposed as the attempt better to discover the justice of a man's soul. Political philosophy is the means for the discussant "to see and found a city within himself" (592b). One looked to the order and strife of the sociopolitical realm to explore and represent the tensioned plurality within the individual. Nietzsche's theorizing is of the same genre. He attempted creatively to revitalize a mode of theorizing that had died with the Christian doctrine of *soul atomism*, wherein the soul became identified as "eternal, indivisible, as a monad, as an *atomon*." One should not get rid of "the soul," Nietzsche insisted, for it is "one of the oldest and most venerable of hypotheses." "But the road to new forms and refinements of the soul-hypothesis stands open" and invites "such conceptions as 'mortal soul' and 'soul as multiplicity of the subject' and 'soul as social structure of the drives and emotions' " (*BGE* 25). Here Nietzsche revealed the speculative core of his philosophical enterprise. Not unlike Plato, he would clothe his philosophy in political attire. For the language that best facilitates the description and analysis of the soul is political. The world of politics serves as a conceptual and terminological resource for the "reader of souls." Nietzsche observed that organization, cooperation, and patterns of domination—in short, politics—allow pluralities to bear the appearance of unities (*WP* 303). This is true for the human community no less than the community of the self. The politics of statecraft and soulcraft are analogous. The city is the soul writ large.

One must not be misled by Nietzsche's antipolitical pronouncements. To the extent that politics is equated with statecraft there can be no doubt as to his attitude: the state is a threat to the individual and the individual to the state.[1]

[1] Nietzsche's early unpublished writings on "The Greek State," however, portray the genius as he who utilizes the state for his own, mainly cultural, ends while all others remain mere tools of state power (cf. *GW* 3:283–85). With his estrangement from Wagner, Nietzsche came to see that genius itself was vulnerable to corruption: any attempt to place the

Yet the politics Nietzsche disparaged or ignored in a social context is celebrated in the self. Politics is not so much abandoned as internalized. The pluralism of the soul creates the space for a spiritual political practice. The rule of the self, the struggle of competing perspectives and their coalitions, forms its foundation.[2]

The microcosm of the individual becomes a resource that helps one better understand the social macrocosm. Writing of the "microcosm and macrocosm of culture," Nietzsche observed: "The finest discoveries concerning culture are made by the individual man within himself when he finds two heterogeneous powers ruling there" (*HH* 130). The obverse investigative exercise, however, was Nietzsche's primary concern. The history of politics serves as a guide to inner exploration. That freedom of spirit should not become an excuse for an anarchical soul; for example, the individual might look to eighteenth-century French politics "so as then to *continue* the work of the Enlightenment *in himself*, and to strangle the Revolution at birth, to make it not happen" (*HH* 367). More importantly, Nietzsche speculated that all moral and spiritual designa-

---

state in the service of genius inevitably leads to genius paying service to the state.

[2] One may speculate that the modern hero's inward turn is in large part the product of the changing nature of politics. As the socioeconomic realm becomes more a process of economic management and bureaucratic control and less a display of personal excellence, the individual seeks his freedom and self-affirmation elsewhere. Sheldon Wolin offered an illuminating illustration of the modern preconditions for the hero's internalization of politics: "The fate of the classical hero was that he could never overcome contingency or *fortuna*; the special irony of the modern hero is that he struggles in a world where contingency has been routed by bureaucratized procedures and nothing remains for the hero to contend against" (*Politics and Vision: Continuity and Change in Western Political Thought* [Boston and Toronto: Little, Brown and Company, 1960], p. 423).

In the same vein, Aldous Huxley gave a chilling vision of future politics to the readers of his *Brave New World*: " 'My dear young friend,' said Mustapha Mond, 'civilization has absolutely no need of nobility or heroism. These things are symptoms of political inefficiency. In a properly organized society like ours, nobody has any opportunity for being noble or heroic.' "

tions, most notably the concepts of good and evil, were the historical developments of political categories and struggles, namely, those between the aristocracy or nobility and the plebeians or commoners (*GM* 24–31ff). Metaphysical concepts, such as freedom of will, also have their origins in the "social-political domain" (*HH* 305). Indeed, the soul itself was held to be the product of a political process. Political organization could not tolerate the uncontrolled discharge of instincts. Consequently, instincts were turned inward. Man pitted his passions against each other rather than loosing them in the public realm: "Thus it was that man first developed what was later called his 'soul' " (*GM* 84). For Nietzsche, the origin of the soul is political. And its dynamics, he found, are best described in the language of politics. This is not to say, however, that political language and thought cannot and do not also obfuscate the nature of the soul. Our recognition of how political hierarchies have resolved themselves into a hierarchy of souls, Nietzsche asserted, has been retarded owing to a "democratic prejudice in the modern world" (*GM* 28).

Nietzsche called himself a "nutcracker" of souls who subsequently engaged in their vivisection (*GM* 113). The object, however, was not to create a scientifically grounded, psychological theory. The substrata of the self are acknowledged to be ambiguous and undefined. The atoms of the community-of-the-self remain essentially unknowable. The molecules they form receive various names, never used with complete consistency. The multiple soul is a conglomerate of passions, desires, affects, forces, feelings, emotions, drives, and instincts. In turn, these variously named molecules of human motivation coalesce to form dispositions or character. Still, Nietzsche did not pretend to have discovered or explained the atomic structure of the human soul. He claimed only to have observed its effects. The hypothesizing was not propounded as the forestage to a theory, for there was no expectation of subsequent proofs.

Nietzsche's suppositions were accompanied by a profound skepticism, a skepticism deemed particularly apposite when treating the soul. For the suppositions themselves, *ex hypothesi*, result from an indeterminate interaction of drives. Here observation is already the efflux of that about which one speculates. Thinking represents only the perceivable effect of an imperceivable process. Even the finest thought, Nietzsche wrote, corresponds to a network of drives: "Thoughts are signs of a play and struggle of affects: they always are connected with their hidden roots" (GW 16:60). The opaqueness of the human soul precludes anything more than speculative assertions. Thought divorced from its affective origins remains an abstraction. Consciousness itself is already the organized unity of unseen and unseeable affects: "Everything that comes into consciousness is the last link of a chain. . . . Each thought, each feeling, each will . . . is a *composite* . . . of our constituent drives" (GW 16:61). Seeing into the labyrinth of the soul is just as impossible, to retrieve another of Nietzsche's metaphors, as seeing around one's own corner. Our perception is restricted, as it were, to the surface of our souls. We are capable of penetrating neither ourselves nor others.

A general pattern, albeit one never strictly maintained, may be observed within the confusing array of terms Nietzsche employed to describe the workings of the soul. Drives, instincts, or affects constitute an irreducible substratum (which is only to say that by definition we are incapable of discerning their probable components). Feelings or emotions form the next level. They are the products, composite and complex, of conscious and unconscious drives. Thought forms the third tier. It is, by and large, derivative of emotion, the inner conversation that tries to make sense out of a medley of feelings: "Thoughts are the shadows of our feelings—always darker, emptier, and simpler" (GS 203). The simplicity of thought is not to be equated with its immediacy. Thoughts are simpler *because* they are emptier. They are one-dimensional representations of multidimensional emotions. Systems of thought, in turn, do not gain depth owing to their intricacy. This applies especially to philosophical thought. Regardless of how ostensibly rational or conceptually sophisticated one's philosophy, it remains, nonetheless, merely the schematic representation of affective relations. Music has long been recognized as "a sign-language of the emotions"; it remains, wrote Nietzsche, for philosophy to be similarly understood (*GW* 11:190; cf. *BGE* 92).

Despite Nietzsche's repeated acknowledgments of the power of reason, intellect, and thought, their status is consistently depreciated in his writings. For they never supply the impetus of human action. With Hume, Nietzsche held reason to be passion's slave. The intellect merely justifies and defends one's affective regime. In the battle between the passions, reason is employed as a tool and weapon. Nietzsche condemned the rationalistic degradation of passion "as if it were only in unseemly cases, and not necessarily and always, the motive force. . . . The misunderstanding of passion and reason, as if the latter were an independent entity and not rather a system of relations between various passions and desires; and as if every passion did not possess its quantum of reason" (*WP* 208). The Platonic opposition between reason and passion is fractured into the opposition between multiple passions, each with its own capacity for reason and will to dominate. Reason does not govern passion, as a charioteer steers his horses. Self-overcoming is not, therefore, the victory of reason over passion: "The will to overcome an emotion is ultimately only the will of another emotion or of several others" (*BGE* 79). The perception that reason tames the passions, that intellect may have its way despite one's emotional urges, mistakes the weapons for the actual contestants of battle. What arises to consciousness is only the aftershock of an unnoticed inner turbulence, the post hoc paperwork that spells out the settlement of an emotional dispute.

> Since only the last scenes of reconciliation and the final accounting at the end of this long process rise to our consciousness, we suppose that *intelligere* [understanding] must be something conciliatory, just, and good—something that stands essentially opposed to the instincts, while it is actually nothing but a *certain behavior of the instincts toward one another*. For the longest time, conscious thought was considered thought itself. Only now does the truth dawn on us that by far the greatest part of our spirit's activity remains unconscious and unfelt.[3] (*GS* 261–62)

In a typically Nietzschean paradox, the freest thinker is he who realizes that his thoughts are not free, being the efflux of his often imperceivable instincts and affects. The true slave of his passions is he who does not recognize his slavery. The man Zarathustra loves for his honesty is he who knows that "his head is only the bowels of his heart" (*Z* 45).

With reason and intellect out of contention as motive forces, the entire spectrum of human action and thought must be accounted for in terms of instincts or drives and their (political) relations. This is made possible by their essentially agonal character. Each has its will to dominate and exploit its competitors. In turn, the ruling drive(s) provides its own agenda and worldview. Nietzsche's understanding of perspectivism, often interpreted by his commentators as subjectivist at base, is actually much more

---

[3] In more ways than are often recognized, Nietzsche's observations prefigure Freud's theories of the unconscious. His account of dreams, for example, anticipates Freud's early work: "Days consciousness is closed to the lower intellect. Nights the higher intellect sleeps, the lower steps into consciousness (dream)" (*GW* 16:269). Herein what came to be called wish-fulfillment is said to occur: "The meaning and value of our *dreams* is precisely to *compensate* to some extent for the chance absence of 'nourishment' during the day" (*D* 75).

radical. The individual is not privy to a single, incommensurable perspective, but is a battleground of competing drives, each with its own perspective. The victory of a particular drive, or coalition of drives, determines the political rule of the community: "It is our needs that interpret the world; our drives and their For and Against. Every drive is a kind of lust to rule; each one has its perspective that it would like to compel all the other drives to accept as a norm" (*WP* 267). Nietzsche's perspectivism has its experiential roots not only or even primarily in what has come to be known as the relativity of values, that is, the supposed incommensurability of personal or cultural truths, but at the subindividual level of inner conflict, in the vicissitudes of the soul itself.

For Nietzsche, the multiple soul with its endless internal strife is the defining characteristic of man. Man is an animal whose instincts have multiplied and escaped a permanent ordering. The disorder of the soul is both the mark of humanity and the cause of its woes: "A single individual contains within him a vast confusion of contradictory valuations and consequently of contradictory drives. This is the expression of the diseased condition in man, in contrast to the animals in which all existing instincts answer to quite definite tasks" (*WP* 149). Man, Nietzsche said, is the sick animal. The disease of the human soul and the accompanying torments, however, were celebrated as the means to deeper knowledge, that is, knowledge garnered from multiple perspectives. The most profound thinkers are not those whose thoughts reflect lame passions and simple order, but the multiple, irregular, and chaotic origin of thought in strong, agonistic passions (*GS* 254). In effect, proper cultivation of the soul allows one to live multiple lives, thus sating the passion for knowledge. To have sat in "every nook" of "the modern soul" was Nietzsche's ambition (*WP* 532): "Oh, my greed! There is no selflessness in my soul but only an all-coveting self that would like to appropriate many individuals as so many additional pairs of eyes and hands. . . . Oh, that I might be reborn in a hundred beings!" (*GS* 215). This greed for experience could be satisfied in two ways: being reborn again and again, or living one life as many. Nietzsche assumed the latter charge: "Task: *Seeing* things *as they are!* Means: to be able to see them out of a hundred eyes, out of *many* persons" (*GW* 11:138). Carrying out this charge, asserted Nietzsche, demanded the stuff of heroism: "Unremitting *transformation*—: you must, within a short space of time, pass through and throughout many individuals. The means is *unremitting struggle*" (*GW* 13:418). The individual's alienation from community is redressed by its manifold internal relations. Heroic solitude bears its own compensation in a spiritual plurality.

Nietzsche displayed an unmistakable pride in having achieved a "cosmopolitanism of the spirit" (*HH* 262). The ability to see from multiple perspectives and wear many masks is celebrated throughout his writings. In the *Dithyrambs of Dionysus* he poeticized:

> My soul,
> its tongue insatiable,
> has licked at every good and evil thing,
> dived down into every depth[4]
>
> (*DD* 71)

---

[4] In the notes to his translation of these poems Hollingdale remarked that "it is probably not far-fetched to conclude that the 'Zarathustras' of the *Dithyrambs of Dionysus* are not so much repetitions of the grand central figure of *Thus Spoke Zarathustra* as *alternatives* to him." This is a peculiar statement coming from one who translated *Thus Spoke Zarathustra* and therefore should have realized that its protagonist is portrayed as a composite of individuals. The fluctuations of Zarathustra's spirit and concomitant changes of his mood and behavior—repeated to the point of being almost tiresome—provide ample demonstration of the plurality of his soul. "In every word he contradicts," Nietzsche acknowledged, "in him all opposites are blended into a new unity" (*EH* 305). Any "repetition" of Zarathustra could not be the reproduction of a grand, central figure, but must necessarily be that of a mercurial character who would illustrate the "chaos in one" needed to "give birth to a dancing star" (*Z* 46). Zarathustra thus portrays the medley of contradictions Nietzsche found in himself, and as Nietzsche claimed, depicts in the sharpest detail a picture of his own nature (*NB* 10.2.83).

The prelude to *The Gay Science* contains a similar self-congratulation:

> Sharp and mild, rough and fine,
> Strange and familiar, impure and clean,
> A place where fool and sage convene:
> All this am I and wish to mean,
> Dove as well as snake and swine
>
> (*GS* 45)

Nietzsche announced that he was "happy to harbour in himself, not 'an immortal soul', but *many mortal souls*" (*HH* 218).[5] The higher man, in other words, wears many masks. More important than an altered appearance, however, are the changes in perspective, in perception and thought, allowed with the donning of these masks. Nietzsche claimed to have regained that which is denied the individual—the capacity to look around his own corner (*EH* 223). As the dramatist he can, as it were, scrutinize Hecuba, and as Hecuba he may look back upon the dramatist. The multiple perspectives gained, however, are ultimately incommensurable. They can be compared only from the position of yet another perspective, a perspective itself no more "objective" than those it evaluates, its competitors.[6]

To be many people, to have many masks, is the precondition for knowledge and growth, the sign of a profound spirit. The contradictions of Nietzsche's thought which are the bane of his commentators must be understood in light

---

[5] Nietzsche's cultivation of his multiple soul was acknowledged by his close friends. Regarding his sharp and mild, loving and critical personalities Malwida von Meysenberg wrote: "Never have I seen in one person so resolved the separateness of 'two souls in one breast' as with him" (Sander L. Gilman, ed. [with Ingeborg Reichenbach], *Begegnungen mit Nietzsche* [Bonn: Bouvier Verlag, 1981], p. 334). Nietzsche held that such judgments "fall short of the truth by a large number of souls" (*BGE* 155). A most insightful investigation of the dynamics of having many souls in one breast is found in Hermann Hesse's *Steppenwolf*, a book that might well be called a psychological biography of Nietzsche.

[6] As Emerson deftly put it in his essay "Circles": "Our moods do not believe in each other."

of his glorification of the multiple soul. Consistency is not considered a virtue, especially for a philosopher whose primary concern should be his spiritual development and not the continuity of his intellectual endeavors. In this regard Nietzsche placed himself with Plato, Spinoza, Pascal, Rousseau, and Goethe, who displayed a "passionate history of a soul," and thus were considered philosophically superior to Kant and Schopenhauer (their intellectual excellence notwithstanding). Kant and Schopenhauer gave biographies "of a *head*" rather than biographies "of a soul" (*D* 198). Their lack of spiritual experience and development—in short, their consistency—was to their demerit.[7]

He who is concerned with growth overcomes himself, becomes different. The vicissitudes of the philosopher's soul, however, are particularly troublesome for those who wish to nail down his identity. That his own protean character would cause much misunderstanding was foreseen by Nietzsche. "We are misidentified," he wrote in *The Gay Science*, "because we ourselves keep growing, keep changing, we shed our old bark, we shed our skins every spring . . . we are no longer free to do only one particular thing, to *be* only one particular thing" (*GS* 331–32). The philosopher with a passion for learning finds a change of internal regime a welcome occurrence. The new leadership of drives brings new perspectives and experiences. The ensuing increase in knowledge serves as the stimulant to further growth, growth that inevitably will leave this knowledge behind.

The irony of Nietzsche's philosophy is that its contradictions demonstrate its consistency. The assertion that the philosopher is actually a puppet of his instincts is given credibility by the contradictions within Nietzsche's own work that represent the temporary hegemonies of his com-

---

[7] Again, words from Emerson's "Self-reliance" are to the point: "A foolish consistency is the hobgoblin of little minds, adored by little statesmen and philosophers and divines. With consistency a great soul has simply nothing to do."

peting instincts. In short, Nietzsche's defense against the charge of incoherence was a reaffirmation of his understanding of the soul as a plurality. "The highest man would have the greatest multiplicity of drives," Nietzsche claimed; and "the wisest man would be the one richest in contradictions" (WP 507, 150). Only thus does one become master of the greatest assortment of perspectives from which to view life. *The Gay Science*, for example, was prefaced with the admission that the book "seems to be written in the language of . . . contradiction." Further on the reader discovers the reason: the work demonstrates the changeability of Nietzsche's philosophy owing to the periodic changes of his internal government. Everything from culinary dishes to philosophical doctrines are held to be "brief habits" that are and should be frequently discarded, like "shedding a skin" (GS 32, 237, 246).[8]

It follows that the search for the authentic Nietzsche is misdirected. His identity can be discovered only through an examination of his masks and their recurring features. His books do not speak with the same voice, nor does any one book speak in a single voice. This is not to abandon the attempt to characterize Nietzsche's thought, but merely to emphasize that any such characterization must be receptive to his various personae and their interaction. His writing must be approached as one would a musical composition of many voices in counterpoint. One observes dissonance and its resolution, with much oblique and contrary motion between the melodic parts. Such works do not preclude interpretation, they invite it. But the discovery of a harmonic theme, or themes, is predicated on an appreciation of polyphony. To remain faithful

---

[8] Here, then, is a response to Jacques Derrida's artful demonstration that Nietzsche finds himself "a little lost in the web of his text, lost much as a spider who finds he is unequal to the web he has spun" (*Spurs: Nietzsche's Styles* [Chicago: University of Chicago Press, 1978], p. 101). In this respect, Nietzsche's prose bears out Walt Whitman's declaration in *Song of Myself*: "Do I contradict myself? / Very well then I contradict myself, / (I am large, I contain multitudes.)"

to Nietzsche's self-understanding, one must come to terms with his multiple souls, even at the price of ambivalence and its susceptibility to abuse.

The individual, then, is proposed as an agonistic political community that experiences changes in regime. The analogy to social "units" also includes the desirability of strong government. Frequent regime changes should not be invitations to anarchy. Struggle begets strength; but anarchy, in the soul and society, signifies powerlessness, a regression to barbarism. A tensioned order is the goal, and to this end leadership is found indispensable. In the soul, no less than in art, in ethics, and in politics, *laisser aller* is a mark of decadence and a recipe for dissipation (cf. *BGE* 92–94 and *TI* 95–96). The individual is a plurality that seeks unity, a chaos that must become a cosmos: "To become master of the chaos one is; to compel one's chaos to become form: to become logical, simple, unambiguous, mathematics, *law*—that is the grand ambition here" (*WP* 444). Nietzsche's writings are the self-conscious attempts to demonstrate the achievement of this ambition. Nietzsche engaged in a lifelong struggle to gain statehood for the society of his soul. His personal motto might well have been *e pluribus unum*. And like the American founding fathers, Nietzsche recognized that the strength of the union was based on the vigor achieved through ordered competition among its parts.

The creation of unity out of diversity is given the name "style." Style is the coordinated exploitation of powerful instincts. It is impossible for those whose passions are too weak or those who are incapable of harnessing strong passions. Stimulation and sublimation rather than extirpation or anaesthetization of the passions is its precondition. Grand style, as demonstrated by classicism, is the effect achieved through the harnessing of violent and varied passions, and their placement under the rule of a predominant drive. Only great passion can produce a great work.

Only a soul consumed by the quest for order can generate great passion.

Nietzsche's work may be seen as a stylized analysis of style. In other words, Nietzsche's writings, as the descriptions of his own struggles to arrange his soul, are submitted as style conscious of itself in the act of creation. To stylize something is to give it an identity, form, coherence, and strength, to lend the appearance of unity to a plurality. Nietzsche's life was one of almost constant physical misery, spiritual suffering, and social alienation. His works are as explosions of strength, energy, and gaiety. His writings were meant to describe heroic feats, to display his *arete* as it developed in struggle. With himself as the protagonist, he attempted to resurrect the substance of the ancient Greek tragedy before Euripides' banalization of the hero. "Before Euripides there were heroically stylized men whose descent from the gods and half-gods of the oldest tragedies was immediately noticed. The spectator saw in them an ideal past of Hellenism and therewith the reality of all that which in highflying moments also lived in his soul. With Euripides the spectator intruded on the stage, man in the reality of everyday life."[9] As if to undo a trend that began with Euripides and found its contemporary resurgence in the social novels of his day, Nietzsche's writings spurn the portrayal of everyday, bourgeois life. In its stead they offer stylized episodes of a life of stark individualism. The point was not to extol the glories of a heroic past, but to demonstrate the possibilities for a heroic future.[10]

[9] From "Socrates and Tragedy," found in div. 3, vol. 2, p. 26 of *Nietzsche Werke, Kritische Gesamtausgabe*, ed. Giorgio Colli and Mazzino Montinari [Berlin and New York: Walter de Gruyter, 1973]. This early essay appears only in fragmented form in the Musarion edition. Cf. also *BT* 77.

[10] Georg Lukács maintained that "the novel is the epic of a world that has been abandoned by God" (*The Theory of the Novel*, trans. Anna Bostock [Cambridge, Mass.: MIT Press, 1968], p. 88). Nietzsche's writings in general, and *Thus Spoke Zarathustra* in particular, may be seen as attempts to revitalize the classical epic for a godless world.

"I am one thing, my writings are another matter," Nietzsche began the section of his autobiography, *Ecce Homo*, entitled "Why I Write Such Good Books." It is a statement typical of someone who wished to stylize his work and understood the need for masks to achieve his purpose. To use the page as a shambles for one's cognitive or emotional dismemberment is the height of decadence in Nietzsche's eyes. It is the absence of style. Something of the heroic must always be present. Style is the exhibition of a self-overcoming: a jubilant warrior is paraded rather than a defeat bemoaned. No one remains a hero, it is said, to his *valet de chambre*. And when seen naked, Zarathustra admits, the greatest man and the smallest man are "all too similar to one another, even the greatest all too human!" (Z 236). But the point of wearing masks is not so much to deceive as to grow into them. The imposition of order upon the page limns the struggle for order within the self. In short, style is always a display of will, an exercise of power to govern a fractious soul. The mask of Nike is worn not because Eris is absent, but because order is ultimately achieved: "What happens here is what happens in every well-constructed and happy commonwealth: the ruling class identifies itself with the successes of the commonwealth. In all willing it is absolutely a question of commanding and obeying, on the basis, as I have said already, of a social structure composed of many 'souls' " (*BGE* 31). Nietzsche's glorification of the will to power, often interpreted as a eulogy of domination, is essentially a tribute to self-overcoming. The greatest struggles are not to be witnessed on the battlefield or in the sociopolitical arena, but in the rule of the self. The greatest victory is a well-ordered soul.

F O U R

THE WELL-ORDERED SOUL

The free man is a state and a society of individuals.
—*Gesammelte Werke*

To make a cosmos from the chaos of the multiple soul is
the Nietzschean task. To gain one's freedom, the internal
social relations must become a political regime, a state
must be formed from a society. Indeed, one seeks to found
a certain kind of state. The goal is not merely order, but a
specific order: the rule of the higher self or selves, an aristocracy. Nietzsche's contempt for democratic politics applied both to the world without and within the self. The
politics of the soul is laudatory, not because it gives equal
voice to every drive, but because all of one's drives are exploited in the creation of a powerful regime embodying
beauty and order.

The higher man, in short, is the man with an aristocrat-
ically ordered soul. He serves as the measure for all men.
Nietzsche was concerned with pursuing ideals, not with
establishing norms.

> Everyone has his good days where he discovers his
> higher self; and true humanity demands that every-
> one be evaluated only in the light of this condition
> and not in that of his working-day unfreedom and
> servitude. . . . Many live in awe and abasement be-
> fore their ideal and would like to deny it: they are
> afraid of their higher self because when it speaks it

speaks imperiously. It possesses, moreover, a spectral freedom to come or to stay away as it wishes; on this account it is often called a gift of the gods, whereas in reality it is everything else that is a gift of the gods (of chance): this however is man himself. (*HH* 197)

Nietzsche wished to make a rule of the exception. The higher self becomes the measuring stick against which human life is evaluated. To realize his potential, man must struggle such that his higher self may rule. One seeks, in other words, to extend the time one lives in a state of inspiration.

To be sure, the lower self is indispensable to this achievement. Its extermination is not part of the project; nor is its tyrannization. Pluralism within the soul is to be maintained. The good of the whole through the rule of the best is the aim of aristocratic politics. To this end hierarchy provides the condition for harmony *and* the stimulus for struggle. Thus the soul remains both ordered and active. The feeling of inspiration, of a heightened sense of power, is attainable only when the soul rises above itself. The will to power is always nourished by a state of hierarchy, a "pathos of distance"; and this, according to Nietzsche, as much within as without the self. Whoever demands greatness from himself is subject to unending inner struggle, "continuous work, war, victory, by day and night": thus is "distance" established from those who are happily bereft of such an unrelenting agonism (*GW* 14:240).

Nietzsche's well-known separation of men into higher and lower orders is not so much an evaluation of the different materials of their souls' composition as of the different manner in which these materials are organized and exploited. (Similarly, the ancient political typologies were grounded on the roles of a polity's constituent parts and the character of its leadership.) The various, perhaps innumerable ways the passions may be arranged and developed determines rank. And because the soul of man signifies none other than "a system of valuations and *value-affects*," its particular state of order determines moral standards: "We find among different people *the same number* of passions: these, however, differently named, evaluated and thereby differently judged. *Good* and *evil* distinguish themselves through the different order of rank among the passions and the domination of aims" (*GW* 16:281). In the soul, as in the social realm, the hegemonic powers determine the standards for the whole. The ruling passions, like a ruling class in society, exhibit a specific array of valuations and establish these valuations as universal principles under the name of morality.

With the reduction of all physical, mental, and emotional activity to a derivative of instinct or passion, Nietzsche displaced rational thought and conscience from its moral pedestal. Each drive supplies its own quantum of reason and will. A moral act, just like a physical movement or emotional outburst, is the outcome of the struggle between instincts. "Conscience," wrote Nietzsche, "is the feeling in which the *order of rank* of our drives comes into consciousness" (*GW* 14:31). That is to say, conscience is merely the awareness of one's ruling instincts.

Nietzsche did not limit himself to the assertion that all morality is fundamentally impulse. He claimed that the extent to which one attempts to act consciously constitutes the measure of one's *im*morality. Higher morality is instinctive and unconscious, free of intellectual and reflective interference. "Genius resides in instinct; goodness likewise. One acts perfectly only when one acts instinctively. Even from the viewpoint of morality, all conscious thinking is merely tentative, usually the reverse of morality. . . . It could be proved that all conscious thinking would also show a far lower standard of morality than the thinking of the same man when it is directed by his instincts" (*WP* 243).[1] Consciousness in general, and con-

---

[1] Terminological consistency never was one of Nietzsche's literary vir-

scious moral judgment in particular, is the registration of instinctual strife. Better said, it is the surfacing of unresolved strife, the display of inner hostilities which, for lack of an overpowering drive capable of commanding order and establishing a harmonious, albeit agonal, inner life, emerge as moral conundrums and tensions. To the extent that there is open conflict, there is lack of rule. Conscious moral thought betrays the rumblings of a disordered soul. Instinctive thought and action, on the other hand, being the rule of a dominating passion, are without arbitration. Their moral superiority stems from the value of the harmonious, hierarchically organized soul that produces them.

The moral superiority of instinctual activity is analogous to the physical superiority of the trained athlete. The athlete disciplines his body until his movements become second nature, that is, most efficient, easy, and free-flowing. He is said to act and react instinctively. Despite the restrictions of his training and the impositions of discipline, indeed precisely because of this, the athlete demonstrates grace. The appearance of freedom emerges from order, not anarchy. The athlete's movements are organized, being the product of a body whose parts have been trained to work in unison. Likewise, the soul displays its organic unity through the absence (or minimal presence) of conscious thought. Just as a dancer's steps are most graceful when they are most disciplined and least a product of reflection, so too do moral activities manifest freedom only when they are the efflux of a ruling drive.

Instincts, by definition, are innate. Man's drives are not as constricted as those of lower animals, but they are,

---

tues. Here *instinct* is opposed to conscious or rational thought, even though all thought was held ultimately to be derivative of instinct. The point is that conscious, rational, or intellectual activity represents an adulteration of instinct, being, as it were, a number of steps removed from its purest, primordial form. At times Nietzsche used *instinct* to denote the origin of all human activity. At times, as above, Nietzsche employed *instinct* as an approbative term, signifying pure, healthy instincts.

Nietzsche maintained, hereditary. Human potentials, the parameters of activity, are determined genetically. Already in his earliest writings Nietzsche had sketched out this position. At seventeen years of age he wrote that "the activity of man, then, does not first begin with birth, but already in the embryo and perhaps—who can here decide— already in the parents and forebears" (GW 1:68). It follows, as Nietzsche suggested in Beyond Good and Evil, that "that which his ancestors most liked to do and most constantly did cannot be erased from a man's soul" (BGE 184).

In addition to this rather loose form of genetic determinism, Nietzsche proposed a sort of physiological determinism. He reduced mental and spiritual activity to the status of physiological events, though he remained skeptical as to the possibility of determining their origins. All conscious activity was reckoned to have specific physiological roots, even though one might never know precisely "how deep and high the physis reaches" (GW 2:388). Nietzsche's analyses and critiques seldom actually limit themselves to speculations of physiological determinants. But such hypothesizing remained a force in reserve. Aesthetics and moral judgment, for example, were held to be merely the " 'subtlest nuances' of the physis" (GS 107). Nietzsche would glibly state, "My objections to the music of Wagner are physiological objections: why should I trouble to dress them up in aesthetic formulas? After all, aethestics is nothing but a kind of applied physiology. My 'fact,' my petit fait vrai, is that I no longer breathe easily when this music begins to affect me" (NCW 664). In a similar manner, Nietzsche offered an amusing explanation of pessimism: "The 'pessimists' are clever people with upset stomachs: they revenge themselves with the head for their bad digestion" (GW 9:374).[2] Behind the taunts lay an unprovable but also irrefutable suspicion that thoughts and feelings are al-

---

[2] Nietzsche himself suffered from chronic stomach problems, and this judgment serves as a self-appraisal of his early attachment to Schopenhauerian pessimism.

ways only a symptom of a physiological disturbance, rarefied effluxes of a corporeal activity.

Nietzsche had already explored this avenue as a youth. The age-old distinction between the material and the spiritual, body and soul, was denied.[3] Our senses are simply too dull to perceive gradations and hence we invent exclusive categories. The accompanying problems of free will and determinism and good and evil were dismissed as abstractions arising from a spurious positing of opposites owing to an inability to recognize the more likely continua. A section of the essay "Fate and History," written in 1862, reads:

> Fate is the endless force of resistance to free will; free will without fate is just as unthinkable as spirit without the real, good without evil. For only the opposition makes the quality. . . . Perhaps in a similar way, as the spirit is only the infinitely smallest substance, is the good only the subtlest development of evil that can come out of itself, free will nothing but the highest potency of fate. World history is then history of material, if one allows the meaning of this word to be infinitely loose. (GW 1:65–66)

Incapable of perceiving or accounting for the substance or activity called spirit, we come to believe in its independence from the forces to which the "material" world is subject. The will's freedom, then, is simply the name we give to the boundaries of our perceptual capacities. Were one omniscient, Nietzsche speculated in a manner reminiscent of Laplace, one could determine all thought and action for ages to come in the same way one could, with precise data, determine the seemingly capricious move-

---

[3] Here Nietzsche once again revealed his Homeric roots. Homer seems not to have distinguished between body and soul; indeed, he portrayed the body as a plurality of conflicting drives and members. (Cf. Bruno Snell, *The Discovery of the Mind: The Greek Origins of European Thought*, trans. T. G. Rosenmeyer [Oxford: Basil Blackwell, 1953].)

ment of a waterfall. In light of man's insurmountable cognitive limitations, however, skepticism must supplant scientific judgment.

These limitations are in fact more a boon than a curse. Unable to perceive the causal chains of our activities, we are wont to imagine our freedom. "We *are* in prison," Nietzsche announced, "we can only *dream* ourselves free, not make ourselves free" (*HH* 223). Yet the dream of freedom is necessary for life; spiritual health depends upon it. The answer to the question whether something done instinctively can truly be considered free is straightforward. Freedom is always only the appearance of freedom. To contemplate free will is (intellectually) to realize its absence and impossibility, even as we (spiritually) feel its effects. The impossibility of thought or action ex nihilo does not prevent us from believing in our freedom, for our perceptions simply are not acute enough to discern the chain of activity that culminates in our thoughts and actions. To experience one's freedom of will is a sign of spiritual health, even though intellectual integrity should prompt one to deny it. In short: "Who *feels* the will's lack of freedom is spiritually ill: who *denies* it is stupid" (*GW* 14:58). The *petit fait vrai* of Nietzsche's argument is that one feels most free when acting in accordance with a dominating passion, not when one accepts the dictates of a concluded process of ratiocination (although the *willing* to accept the dictates of reason may supply this same sense of freedom). As freedom is always only the illusion of freedom, the trick is to develop, order, and sublimate one's passions such that one is allowed the greatest draught of freedom and its accompanying sense of power. This is the case with the man of healthy instincts.

The effect must not be mistaken for the cause in these matters. Strength or weakness, virtue or vice, growth or decadence are the effects of the order or disorder of a soul. Decadence, in a people or an individual, is a symptom of the deterioration of instinct. In the political macrocosm of the social realm, as in the political microcosm of the soul, health, strength, and growth are the consequences of a harmonic order.

> The Church and morality say: "A race, a people perishes through vice and luxury." My *restored* reason says: when a people is perishing, degenerating physiologically, vice and luxury (that is to say the necessity of stronger and stronger and more and more frequent stimulants, such as every exhausted nature is acquainted with) *follow* therefrom. A young man grows prematurely pale and faded. His friends say: this and that illness is to blame. I say: *that* he became ill, *that* he failed to resist the illness, was already the consequence of an impoverished life, an hereditary exhaustion. The newspaper reader says: this party will ruin itself if it makes errors like this. My *higher* politics says: a party which makes errors like this is already finished—it is no longer secure in its instincts. Every error, of whatever kind, is a consequence of degeneration of instinct, disgregation of will: one has thereby virtually defined the *bad*. Everything *good* is instinct— and consequently easy, necessary, free. (*TI* 48)

The good, the instinctual, is necessary *and* free. That is to say, freedom and the compulsion of drives may coexist. Indeed, they are synonymous. The more dominating the instinct, the more encompassing its rule, and the more it is identified as representative of the whole, the greater the feeling of freedom and power.

With man reduced to an amalgam of instincts, the question of egoism must be reevaluated. Effectively, there is no such thing as unegoistic action; for all action is fundamentally a product of drives or their derivatives. This is not to say, however, that all deeds are of equal merit. Nietzsche was no libertine: "Libertinage, the principle of 'laisser aller,' should not be confused with the will to power (— which is the counterprinciple)" (*WP* 75). There exists a definite hierarchy of instincts, the extreme poles of which are given the names "life-affirming" and "decadent." Nietzsche wrote: "There are absolutely no 'selfless' actions. Actions in which the individual becomes untrue to his instincts and chooses them disadvantageously are signs of decadence" (GW 17:270). Being untrue to one's instincts is a misleading expression: to disregard certain instincts is to follow others. The import is that one may be untrue to one's higher, life-affirming instincts, giving way to one's decadent, lower self.

Nietzsche's ostensibly monistic portrayal of the human condition—quasi-materialistic and deterministic, with morality and action, rationality and thought, reduced to the effects of genetic and physiological factors—is, in fact, dualistic. Man may choose, to his advantage or disadvantage, which of his inherited traits to follow. The assertion that all action is unavoidably egoistic is accompanied by a distinction between life-affirming or ascending and decadent or descending forms of egoism: "The value of egoism depends on the physiological value of him who possesses it: it can be very valuable, it can be worthless and contemptible. Every individual may be regarded as representing the ascending or descending line of life. When one has decided which, one has thereby established a canon for the value of his egoism" (TI 85).[4] To represent an ascending line of life is to be ruled by strong instincts. Egoism for healthy individuals is the drive to increase the order of the soul, and thereby increase its power. Egoism among the decadent, conversely, is a recipe for dissipation. Universal egoism, Nietzsche maintained, was not a theory but a fact. The proper response to this reality is not to blind oneself

[4] As Kaufmann noted in another context, Nietzsche's understanding of egoism has its parallels to Aristotle's tenet that the good man should be a lover of self but the bad man should not, essentially owing to the worth of the object of love (cf. Nichomachean Ethics 1169a and Kaufmann's note in Ecce Homo, p. 277). Zarathustra makes the point bluntly: the higher man possesses great self-love, as he should, but among the weak and sick "even self-love stinks" (Z 211).

to the fundamental "immorality" of man: one must exploit it. Ultimately we are all cultivators of our vanity. The point is to become better gardeners.

Healthy egoism is not to be equated with a petty selfishness. The happiness of the man with strong, healthy instincts has its benefits for his neighbors. His love of self translates into an affirmation of the world. His sense of freedom and power allows a magnanimity toward others. On the other hand, the unordered soul is spiteful and dangerous, like "a knot of savage serpents that are seldom at peace among themselves—thus they go forth alone to seek prey in the world" (Z 66). Its viciousness amounts to a discontentedness with itself and a condemnation of life. For virtue, generally beneficial to one's neighbors, is that which *follows* happiness; it is a by-product of a fulfilled life.[5] Egoism or self-love should be promoted in one's neighbors, lest one later have to pay for the disquietude of an unhappy spirit: "We have cause to fear him who hates himself, for we shall be the victims of his wrath and his revenge. Let us therefore see if we cannot seduce him into loving himself" (D 207). Zarathustra's speech on love is centered in the notion of a higher egoism. "Selfless" love of others is often the fleeing of the self from its internal struggle. One turns outward because one lacks the courage to face one's solitude, or because nothing worthy of attention is found within. This love of neighbor arises from a "bad love" of the self (Z 86). An overflowing of self-love that is not an escape from struggle and self-disgust should determine one's relations with others.

Nietzsche's well-known distinction between slave morality and master morality is based on the distinction between a higher and lower egoism. The noble feels his happiness and his instinct as one. Such is the case with all representatives of ascending life. He is a self-admirerer

[5] Nietzsche attributed this thesis to Goethe, who wrote: "Joyfulness is the mother of all virtue."

who defines the good in relation to himself. His love for others is a reflection of his love of (his own) life. Everything is affirmed as an intrinsic part of his own destiny. Slave morality, in contrast, is a product of resentment. The slave defines good not as a positive extension of the self, but as a reactive denial of what lies outside, what opposes it and causes it hardship—its master in particular, life in general. "While every noble morality develops from a triumphant affirmation of itself, slave morality from the outset says No to what is 'outside,' what is 'different,' what is 'not itself'; and *this* No is its creative deed. This inversion of the value-positing eye—this *need* to direct one's view outward instead of back to oneself—is of the essence of *ressentiment*" (GM 36–37). The slave's condemnation of *his* life is extended to a condemnation of life in general. His inability to find joy in himself leads him to view all egoism as evil. Love of his neighbor, a duty-bound outward gaze, is a bad love of himself.

The concepts of master morality and slave morality are the facets of a bifurcation that runs through the corpus of Nietzsche's mature writings. All life has been placed in one of two camps: ascending or declining, growing or decadent, affirmative or resentful. Ascending, growing, affirmative life bears the name "Dionysian." Its antipode is known by various epithets: Christianity, romanticism, pessimism, and nihilism, among others. The mark of Dionysian man is his capacity for affirmation. This is not to say that his life is without suffering or strife. On the contrary, he is dubbed Dionysian precisely because he affirms in spite of suffering, and finds joy in strife. He is, in brief, heroic. Amidst all his tribulations the love of life and struggle causes him to shout, "more of the same!"

> Every art, every philosophy may be viewed as a remedy and an aid in the service of growing and struggling life; they always presuppose suffering and sufferers. But there are two kinds of sufferers: first, those

who suffer from the *over-fullness of life*—they want a Dionysian art and likewise a tragic view of life, a tragic insight—and then those who suffer from the *impoverishment of life* and seek rest, stillness, calm seas, redemption from themselves through art and knowledge, or intoxication, convulsions, anaesthesia, and madness. . . . He that is richest in the fullness of life, the Dionysian god and man, cannot only afford the sight of the terrible and questionable but even the terrible deed and any luxury of destruction, decomposition, and negation. In his case, what is evil, absurd, and ugly seems, as it were, permissible, owing to an excess of procreating, fertilizing energies that can still turn any desert into lush farmland. Conversely, those who suffer most and are poorest in life would need above all mildness, peacefulness, and goodness in thought as well as deed—if possible, also a god who would be truly a god for the sick, a healer and savior; also logic, the conceptual understandability of existence—for logic calms and gives confidence—in short, a certain warm narrowness that keeps away fear and encloses one in optimistic horizons. (*GS* 328)

The Dionysian man lives in the same world as his decadent counterpart. But he is strong enough to transform the meaninglessness of life into an occasion for celebration. Conversely, the decadent slanders existence: his gods and systems of thought are erected so as to depreciate this world, making his inability to enjoy it less irritating.

The core of Nietzsche's dualism is formed around his account of the Dionysian and the decadent man. That which does not celebrate life, including its terrifying mystery, is decadent. Passive nihilism, Nietzsche's epithet for the modern disease, exhibits this incapacity. But so too do all forms of life undistinguished by a tragic-heroic disposition. All who cannot affirm life in and for itself imagine an afterlife and redemptive gods in compensation, thus

77

betraying an inability or unwillingnes to participate in the tragic celebration of existence. Schopenhauerian pessimism, Wagnerian romanticism, Socratic rationalism, religious thought in general (with Christianity singled out for particular abuse)—all fail the test of Dionysus. *They* are nihilistic, cried Nietzsche, not *I*. For in their weakness they reject life . . . and for what? There *is* nothing else. They reject life for *nothing*! They deserve to be called nihilistic "because they all have glorified the concept contrary to life, *nothing(ness)*, as end, as highest good, as 'God' " (*GW* 14:328). Nietzsche turned the tables on the metaphysicians and theologians. The charge of nihilism is leveled against all those who, by Nietzsche's reckoning, are too weak to celebrate life in all its meaninglessness. Their lack of strength forces them to grasp at illusions. Their efforts constitute a new form of impiety and idolatry. Zarathustra encourages his listeners to "remain true to the earth" and forego the temptation of metaphysics and theology, of "superterrestial hopes." Such hopes are a devaluation of life, a form of blasphemy against life: "Once blasphemy against God was the greatest blasphemy, but God died, and thereupon these blasphemers died too. To blaspheme the earth is now the most dreadful offence" (*Z* 42). Every movement toward gods and transcendent ideals is a movement away from the here and now, a dissipation of the hope for a higher, this-worldly life: "The concept of 'God' invented as a counterconcept of life. . . . The concept of the 'beyond,' the 'true world' invented in order to devaluate the only world there is—in order to retain no goal, no reason, no task for our earthly reality!" (*EH* 334). No doubt the theologians and metaphysicians, the propagators of a belief in gods, a beyond, or transcendent ideals, would refuse to accept Nietzsche's charge, thrusting the accusation of nihilism back at him who attempts to destroy the only things that could give life meaning. But that is the expectation. The need to invent imaginary worlds in order to redeem this one, the desire for such redemption itself, is the sign of degenerate instincts, of a soul out of order. No amount of argument can turn a decadent into a follower of Dionysus.

With baptism in the Dionysian religion of life, the problem of evil is washed away. All life, including so-called evil, must be affirmed. Nothing may be deprecated, for its existence alone constitutes its justification. Morality, to the extent that it decries the presence of evil, is a defamatory effort to "pass sentence on existence" (*WP* 10). The Dionysian is beyond good and evil in his celebration of life. Even a Cesare Borgia, according to Nietzsche's taste, is more palatable than Christ. For the latter's other-worldly preaching served to depreciate this world (*NB* 20.10.88; cf. *EH* 261). Nietzsche's "transvaluation of all values" is both the heir of nihilism and its overcoming. Characterized by the death of God and the negation of all hitherto reigning values, nihilism is the necessary forerunner to Nietzsche's philosophy. The *re*valuation of this world is possible only once the *de*valuation of the "other world" is complete.

The presence of evil is the precondition for greatness, pressing "the mightiest natural powers—the affects—into service" (*WP* 208). To eliminate evil would be to destroy the possibility of all great passion, and consequently of all greatness. In today's "tepid atmosphere," virtue is merely a euphemism for the dread of individuality. "I greatly fear," wrote Nietzsche, "that modern man is simply too indolent for certain vices: so that they are actually dying out" (*TI* 77). There is reason to be grateful for vice; its presence signifies that the potential for great virtue survives.[6] The revolutionary, individualistic thinkers and actors— those deemed evil by their contemporaries—are to be thanked. They awakened passions that were going to sleep. For the stronger the hold of habit, custom, and mo-

---

[6] This was Socrates' claim in the *Crito* (44d): "Would that the many *could* produce the greatest evils, Crito, so that they could also produce the greatest goods! That would indeed be noble. But as it is, they can do neither."

rality, the severer the atrophy of passion and the attendant eradication of greatness.

Good and evil, as hot and cold, are not so much exclusive categories as they are abstract end points on a continuum. Following Heraclitus, Nietzsche posits the absence of "absolute opposites." What exists are only degrees of scale, quantitative rather than qualitative distinctions: "Between good and evil actions there is no difference in kind, but at most one of degree. Good actions are sublimated evil ones; evil actions are coarsened, brutalized good ones" (HH 58). In the middle ground, between the extremes of good and evil, stands mediocrity—the realm of habit and custom, indolence and impotence. Not unlike Christ's dictum that one must be either hot or cold, or one shall be vomited from the mouth, Nietzsche's philosophy maintained the virtue of extremes. The passions and instincts are such that to be capable of great good one must also be capable of great evil. The energy levels required, as it were, are the same. Recalling that the chief threats to individuality are timidity and laziness, we see how the capacity for extremes allows the great man to escape the mediocrity of herd life. He knows only the poles of the virtue-vice continuum, and these develop in a tensioned simultaneity (WP 567). His virtues are sublimated vices. The capacity for self-sacrifice, self-denial, and discipline, for example, is actually a higher form of cruelty (GM 88). His display of courage in the pursuit of excellence is a sublimated form of vanity combined with envy, jealousy, and avarice.[7]

Good and evil develop in a dialectical fashion, as do all

[7] Nietzsche's inspiration for this understanding was the culture of the ancient Greeks, who were held not to have repudiated but to have regulated the natural drives that find expression in "evil" qualities. The competitive spirit and unquenchable ambition of the Greeks allowed the sublimation of greed and envy into the quest for fame and honor. In turn, cowardice and pettiness were counteracted. Higher egoism (e.g., a desire for honor) grew powerful upon the energies of lower egoism (e.g., avarice and envy), resulting in a heroic culture.

so-called opposites. One cannot exist without the (possibility of the) other: "All good is the transformation of evil; every god has a devil as his father" (GW 14:24).[8] Those who would erase evil from the face of the earth are ignorant of its necessity for the continued development of goodness: "Grand economy . . . cannot do without evil" (WP 164). Progress and growth are products of the struggle between opposing forces. Absence of struggle signifies absence of advancement. One must embrace antagonism with a heroic spirit, that is, with the joyful acceptance of the need and benefits of strife.

Nietzsche's effort to demonstrate that the value of evil lay in its potential for sublimation has its counterpart in his high estimation of the value of decadence. Nietzsche, the great critic of decadence, did not desire its extermination. He did not make the mistake of illustrating the ignorance of those who deprecate evil only to substitute decadence as the bane of life. To affirm life as a whole is to affirm even decadence. In society, decadence is the harbinger of progress. This dialectic also displays its effects within the individual. Inner degeneration signals the possibility of growth, an opportunity to increase strength through struggle. In fact, one should not even desire a

[8] The dialectic works in both directions; good is also the parent of evil. Nietzsche claimed to have arrived at this position at thirteen years of age when he began to "philosophize." At that time he concluded that "God the father" created "God the son" in order to think of himself, and subsequently created "God the devil," realizing that he could not think of himself without thinking of his opposite (GW 14:307; cf. GM 16–17).

Nietzsche was a dialectical thinker. Gilles Deleuze, in his *Nietzsche et la philosophie* (Paris: Presses Universitaire de France, 1962), maintained the thesis that Nietzsche's fundamental characteristic is his antidialectic, which mostly meant anti-Socratic and anti-Hegelian, content and method. Not dialectical negation but affirmation is held to be the project. Deleuze ignored the inseparability of destruction and creation for Nietzsche (cf. EH 328: "Negating *and* destroying are conditions of saying Yes"), as he did the creative, affirmative capacities of dialectical thinking. Moreover, Nietzsche's description of dialectics as "an erotic contest," and "a new artistic form of the Greek agon" (TI 81), identified it as a heroic mode of philosophizing.

weakening of one's elements of decadence; for the greater their strength, the greater the victory of mastering them (*WP* 197). Here Nietzsche displayed a Homeric disposition. Homer disparaged neither the Trojans nor the Achaeans as forces of evil: each side needs the other to display its prowess. Glory is always measured by the magnitude of the danger confronted. Heroes are evaluated by the stature of their foes. With regard to self-overcoming, then, vice is as important as virtue. That is to say, the greater the chaos within, the more worthy the inner struggle, the greater the eventual power of an ordered soul. The Nietzschean hero is not he who is fearless, but he who overcomes great fear, not he who is pitiless, but he who overcomes a debilitating pity. Decadence and growth are inseparable, for the latter is the ongoing overcoming of the former.

Nietzsche's understanding of the necessity of evil and decadence aligns with his antiteleological worldview. The purpose of human life is not the establishment of a utopia in which the victorious forces of good have eliminated opposition and strife. Life has no purpose but itself. The battle between good and evil is not a prelude to some future state of passivity. Indeed, to posit a purpose to life is to demean living to a mere means. For life *is* struggle, nothing more nor less. "Behold," life whispered its secret to Zarathustra, "I am that *which must overcome itself again and again*" (Z 138). The effort to go beyond good and evil was effectively the attempt to strip the teleological trappings from the doctrine of life as struggle. Nietzsche avoided the error of moralists who spoke of the battle between good and evil. This sort of Manicheanism always carries connotations of a desired and expected victory, and hence of final purpose. Strength, weakness, and chance, not moral forces, said Nietzsche, are the determinants of growth. The present occupants of the chain of evolution, therefore, should not flatter themselves either as the purpose of their predecessors' existence or as an unqualified improvement upon them. For evolution is as much the product of decadence as of progress. The development of consciousness itself, Nietzsche held, was less a step along the road to the perfection of a species than a necessary recompense to offset increasing physical weakness. Speech allowed communal defense for those animals that had grown too weak to defend themselves singly. Higher intellect is the characteristic of animals that have lost their sharp claws. In short, man's spiritualization is a function of his physical and instinctual deterioration.

From the overall development of a species to its particular characteristics, Nietzsche's evolutionism is devoid of teleological movement. Utility does not explain origin (*WP* 343). He contended, for example, that "vision was *not* the intention behind the creation of the eye, but that vision appeared, rather, after *chance* had put the apparatus together. A single instance of this kind and 'purposes' fall away like scales from the eyes!" (*D* 77).[9] The disappearance of purpose from nature marks the erasure of good and evil from man's moral tabulations. Without a final purpose to life, there can be no ultimate right or wrong. Life is neither good nor evil; it is the realm of necessity, of chance, of instinctual drives, of growth, decadence, strength and weakness, of the unending struggle for dom-

[9] Such assertions exhibit a strikingly lucid understanding of modern descriptions of cumulative adaptation. Adaptation is not a species' (genetically purposive) response to a changed environment. Statements as "this species developed such and such a feature *in order to* . . ." or "this was nature's way of . . ." imply a teleological understanding of adaptation that is generally not accepted within the scientific community. Adaptation is held to be a form of haphazard mutation in which the mutant's chance acquisition of certain traits or qualities prove useful given altered living conditions. The *failure* of an organism's DNA molecules to duplicate themselves correctly fortuitously produce an offspring whose mutation, while in practice an improvement on its parents' capacities for survival, actually constitutes a *malfunction* of their systems of reproduction. Evolution is the result of the rule of chance and decadence on a molecular level. Nietzsche held that progress in a species is always the product of "degenerate natures": "The strongest natures *preserve* the type, the weaker help it to *evolve*" (*HH* 107).

ination in its crude and sublimated forms on a subindividual, individual, and social level.

If the disappearance of evil is a great liberation from the guilt with which morality would burden man, it also marks the absence of good and the unreasonableness of ascribing moral worth. Man rediscovers his innocence through the loss of his responsibility. It becomes irrational to blame *or* praise. Virtue loses its approbation and vice its opprobrium. Ironically, the "unaccountability" of man that Nietzsche challenged his readers to accept constitutes the greatest threat to his project of stimulating the emergence of heroic types whose life task is defined as the pursuit of excellence. The irony was not lost on Nietzsche.

> The complete unaccountability of man for his actions and his motives is the bitterest draught the man of knowledge has to swallow if he has been accustomed to seeing in accountability and duty the patent of his humanity. All his evaluations, all his feelings of respect and antipathy have thereby become disvalued and false: his profoundest sentiment, which he accorded to the sufferer, the hero, rested upon an error; he may no longer praise, no longer censure, for it is absurd to praise and censure nature and necessity. As he loves a fine work of art but does not praise it since it can do nothing for itself, as he stands before the plants, so must he stand before the actions of men and before his own. He can admire their strength, beauty, fullness, but he may not find any merit in them. (*HH* 57–58)

Nietzsche's object in asserting the unaccountability of man is not to deny all values, but to create new ones. Not all purposes in life but any ultimate purpose of life is denied. Transformation, not annihilation, of values is proposed. The death of God signals the development of an earthly piety. The end of teleology and its moral accountability brings about the need for an earthly responsibility. In brief, nihilism is not so much the end of spirituality and morality as the precondition for their sublimation.

The individual must rescue himself from the abyss of nihilism. In a world without purpose, accountability, merit, or transcendent values, all weaker beings perish in the grip of meaninglessness. Only the strong, those capable of creating their own values, survive. Hence the imperative of a heroic life, a life characterized by nonutilitarian, self-fulfilling action. Only deeds done for their own sake, constituting their own reward and justification, are tolerable in a world without meaning. Struggle must become an intrinsic good, not merely an instrumental one. Ends must be found within means: thus is the terror of purposelessness transformed into the joy of innocence.

With the death of God and the absence of transcendent values the creation of new values assumes a hitherto unmatched urgency. If nihilism is not to destroy life, an earthly judge must be capable of setting goals, allotting praise and blame, and determining values. In such a world "the first problem is the *order of rank of different kinds of life*" (*WP* 324). Formerly, all men could be considered equal in the eyes of God, for God himself provided the model of perfection. Without deities, nihilistic man lacks any ideal for which he may strive. The need for rank emerges to supply man with a substitute for his rejected idols. Under such circumstances, equality would simply mean mediocrity without development, a plebeian world whose heroes have been banished, whose gods have died, whose future is without hope, and whose present is without the stimulus of challenge. In a godless world, the belief in equality is tantamount to the extirpation of the "virtuous" drive to self-perfection as well as the useful "vices" of envy and ambition that have allowed the development of civilization. To the extent that the belief in equality ends the struggle for growth, it denies all hope: "That every will must consider every other will its equal—would be a principle *hostile to life*, an agent of the dissolution and destruction of man, an attempt to assassinate the future of man, a sign of weariness, a secret path to nothingness" (GM 76). To enforce equality is to cut off the heads of those who rise above the crowd and to deny individuals any exemplars to contend with or emulate. The modern world, thought Nietzsche, was desperately in need of new values to fill the vacuum left by the disappearance of God. Not the nihilistic abdication of judgment, but a this-worldly means of evaluating and ranking man was needed. Above all, "Dionysus is a *judge!*" (WP 541).

Nietzsche called himself a psychologist and a physician of the soul. He sought to determine rank, the nobility of a soul, and proposed diagnoses of its disorders. Yet the soul of man is opaque: its analysis is not straightforward, and the symptoms of its diseases are neither obvious nor unambiguous. "What is noble?" Nietzsche asked. Who is the "noble human being"? "It is not his actions which reveal him—actions are always ambiguous, always unfathomable —; neither is it his 'works'. . . . it is the *faith* which is decisive here, which determines the order of rank here. . . . *The noble soul has reverence for itself*' (BGE 196).[10] The higher man, then, is the bearer of a higher egoism, a love of his own individuality. His actions and works are not infallible indices of this self-love or of the strength it requires to be maintained, but they do reflect it. Everything that is said and done as well as that which is left unsaid and undone is a symptom of decadence or a sign of ascending power. How the actor, and in particular the thinker, deals with the inscrutable and terrible question of existence, how much uncertainty he can tolerate, what props he requires to support himself and his beliefs—these are the indicators of his strength of soul.

The phenomenon of man, for Nietzsche, was always a semiological puzzle. There exist no ultimate truths, judgments, or values. Therefore, Nietzsche asked in each case

---

[10] "Self-trust is the essence of heroism," Emerson wrote.

why such and such truths, judgments, and values were adopted, what purpose they served, what sort of man, in short, *needed* to have them. Nietzsche prided himself on his ability to infer the order of a soul using the "most difficult and captious form of *backward inference* . . . from the work to the maker, from the deed to the doer, from the ideal to those who *need* it, from every way of thinking and valuing to the commanding need behind it" (*GS* 329). He saw himself as equipped with "psychological antennae" that allowed a sensitivity to the rank of the objects of his study: "The innermost parts, the 'entrails' of every soul are physiologically perceived by me—*smelled*" (*EH* 233).

What is smelled is the level of decadence or ascending power within the individual. The question Nietzsche posed to all aesthetic phenomena—"Is it the hatred against life or the excess of life which has here become creative?"—may also serve as the criterion for categorizing philosophical, moral, and religious works (*NCW* 671).[11] This interpretive dualism gives rise to much of the ambiguity and outright contradiction in Nietzsche's writings. Philosophy, art, morality, even pessimism and nihilism all have their higher, ascending, and lower, declining forms. They may at the same time be the object of polemic and eulogy. Nietzsche frequently failed to supply the clarifying adjective. Yet one is necessary. Facts do not speak for themselves. There are no constant values ascribable to specific forms of action or thought. The deed that is laudable in the higher man may be condemnable if performed by the lower, and vice versa. The value of a virtue depends on who is exercising it. The internal state of the doer or thinker must be perceived before any deed or thought may be judged.

---

[11] This formulation was altered in *Nietzsche contra Wagner* from its original appearance in *The Gay Science* (p. 329), wherein "hunger," not "hatred of life," served as the antipode to excess of life. Presumably Nietzsche made the change because hunger, while denoting a lack, also connoted a desire (to consume) that could be mistaken as a desire for life.

Nowhere is the dualistic interpretation of phenomena more pronounced than in Nietzsche's evaluation of nihilism. Does a hatred of life or an excess of joy predominantly characterize the individual? The value of nihilism rests on the answer to this question. Nihilism *tout court*, Nietzsche declared, is ambiguous. *Active* nihilism is a sign of "increased power of the spirit"; *passive* nihilism is a "decline and recession of the power of the spirit" (*WP* 17). Nihilism may be a *"divine way of thinking,"* or an invitation to spiritual anarchy (*WP* 15). It depends on why and how one is a nihilist. There are, at base, two possibilities. One may deny God and other worlds out of a reverence for the self, a love of this life, and a desire to be creative; or one may deny God out of an irreverence for the self, and a desire to escape all evaluation, judgment, and responsibility. The former nihilist approaches the overman. The latter nihilist is the last man, whom Zarathustra accuses: "You could not *endure* him who saw *you*—who saw you unblinking and through and through, you ugliest man! You took revenge upon this witness!" (*Z* 276). The last man is the "murderer of God." Zarathustra, for his part, announced the death, identified the culprit, and suggested how one might celebrate the wake.[12]

The theoretical assumptions of the passive and active nihilist are the same: no ultimate values, no God, radical individualism. Yet the practical and spiritual ramifications of these assumptions are extremely divergent. On the one hand, a denial of the worth of life and spiritual torpor develop; on the other, an affirmation of life and creative will. The "facts" of nihilism can be united just as easily with its noxious potentiality as with its practical celebration (*HH* 27). Nietzsche claimed that his "overall insight" was *"the ambiguous character of our modern world*—the very

---

[12] More correctly, Zarathustra himself is a mix of the last man and the overman; he knows about decadence firsthand. Thus he denies God both out of a need to be creative and owing to an inability to endure an ultimate overseer and judge (*Z* 110–11).

same symptoms could point to *decline* and to *strength*" (*WP* 69). Those who are strong enough will be able to transform into a higher pleasure what for others remains a bane. Most importantly, this applies to the fundamental character of life: "The thousand mysteries around us would only interest us, *not* torture us, if we were healthy and happy enough in our hearts" (*GW* 16:55).[13] One man's meat is another man's poison. What is beneficial and what is dangerous to health depend upon who is doing the eating. It is the consumer who determines the value of life— for *himself.*

From *The Gay Science* we learn that "the poison of which weaker natures perish strengthens the strong—nor do they call it poison" (*GS* 92). That poison is not always called poison presented certain problems for Nietzsche, and more so for his readers. Language never fully communicates the subtleties of spirit. Depending upon the context and his imagined audience, Nietzsche's words bear different valences and meanings: "Each written word is ambiguous, misunderstandable, in need of a commentary through glances and handshakes" (*NB* 5.7.85). Language is always tactically employed. "My words," wrote Nietzsche, "have other colors than the same words in other people" (*NB* 20.5.85). Correctly perceiving these colors goes a long way toward making the apparent contradictions in Nietzsche's writing less troublesome. What has been called a dualism in Nietzsche's work appears contrary to his disavowal of absolute opposites and transcendent categories. It is, in fact, better labeled a pluralism. The hard and fast dichotomies of decadence and growth, strength and weakness, noble and plebeian, good and bad,[14] are heuristic devices that allow one to talk about a

[13] The paradigm for this achievement appears to have been Heraclitus, whose "blessed astonishment" was the transformation of the "terrible, paralyzing thought" of a world in constant flux (*PTG* 54).

[14] Bad, as distinguished from evil, connotes for Nietzsche a decadent,

virtual infinity of ranks, orders, and spiritual regimes (cf. *GW* 1:422, *NB* 3.8.83). Just as there are no actual antipodes of good and evil, but only differences of degree, so too are the categories of decadence and growth but a shorthand to describe a myriad of divergent states of the soul. Any attempt to venture into this plethora of ambiguities is bound to place a premium on nuance. One must approach Nietzsche with one's own "psychological antennae" tuned in. The mark of a higher thinker is his ability to do without Manichean conceptualizations, in a word, to do without opposites (*WP* 70, 490). It follows that "the best thing we gain from life" is the "art of nuance" (*BGE* 44). This judgment would seem especially apposite for Nietzsche's critics.

Once again Nietzsche appears to slip through one's fingers as soon as one grasps for stable categories of his thought. The lack of any firm theoretical ground in Nietzsche's work, however, does not constitute a valid charge against it. Indeed, the accusation is shown to be self-condemnatory. The need for fixed values is a symptom of weakness and decline. Nietzsche used his perspectivism, contradictions and all, to expose the plurality of values, and to cast aspersions at any who might attack his philosophical position as self-refuting. There is, noted Nietzsche,

> no limit to the ways in which the world can be interpreted; every interpretation a symptom of growth or of decline.
>
> Inertia needs unity (monism); plurality of interpretations a sign of strength. Not to desire to deprive the world of its disturbing and enigmatic character! (*WP* 326)

The greater the enigma, the more mystery, the better; or so says the spiritually healthy man. But then why write at

---

sick, atrophied drive. Evil has to do with a great passion, which, from a certain perspective, has gone awry.

all? Why proffer interpretations and attempt to clarify the world's enigmatic character? Would not the completely ordered soul do without such attempts, reveling in the meaningless chaos without trying to establish any philosophical ground upon which to stand?

The answer is yes. But the completely ordered soul does not exist. Man, like all forms of life, is in a constant state of becoming. There is no stability, only ascent or decline. To ascend is to overcome decadence through strength. Lack of growth is just another term for weakness. Nietzsche held all ordered society to be in a state of decline. Similarly, the soul that ceases to grow is already decaying. The "well-ordered soul" is in this sense a misnomer: there are only souls being put into order and souls falling into disorder. "Perfection," said Nietzsche, to the extent it has any meaning for the individual, can only be "the extraordinary expansion of its feeling of power, riches, necessary overflowing of all limits" (*WP* 422). Ascending life, growth, and strength all denote the overcoming of decline, decay, and weakness. For the soul, as for society, the aim is not so much the establishment of order as the act of establishing order. Nietzsche displayed and lauded the overcoming of decadence, not its absence. Health and order of the soul are always an overcoming of illness and disorder. Nietzsche maintained that his own greatest and truest experiences were recoveries (*CW* 155; *EH* 222–23). The "cure" for nihilism, pessimism, or boredom is "to remain sick for a long time and then, slowly, slowly, to become healthy, by which I mean 'healthier' " (*HH* 9). The difference between health and sickness remains a matter of degree. As with perfection, health is seen not as an end point to be reached but rather as an increase in strength and a feeling of growing power.

Decadence, then, is not so much to be avoided as combatted: sickness, Nietzsche averred, is a stimulant to life; but one must be healthy enough for it (*CW* 165). The distinguishing feature of greatness is the ability to transform

91

sickness into health, to grow stronger after a draught of poison. Only by allowing oneself to experience decadence can it truly be understood and subsequently overcome. Nietzsche's critiques of decadence were based on first-hand experience. His personal encounters with infirmity, convalescence, and well-being are the substance of his writing. "Apart from the fact that I am a decadent, I am also the opposite," he claimed, "I turned my will to health, to *life*, into a philosophy" (*EH* 224).

The proper attitude for the higher man is summed up in the assertion "What does not kill me makes me stronger" (*TI* 23). But the poisons of the modern world are lethal to many. Nietzsche had no illusions about the possibilities for the general betterment of mankind. Nihilism is a curse for the majority, a blessing only for the few souls strong enough to transform it. "There is an element of decay in everything that characterizes modern man: but close beside this sickness stand signs of an untested force and powerfulness of the soul. *The same reasons that produce the increasing smallness of man* drive the *stronger and rarer individuals up to greatness*" (*WP* 68). Any genuine advance of mankind, which for Nietzsche meant an advance of its highest exemplars, would be preceded and accompanied by disease, disorder, and deterioration (*WP* 69). Hence Nietzsche at once celebrates and loathes the modern world's spiritlessness: it is a world pregnant with greatness, although its pregnancy will be marked by much suffering and nausea.

Decadence is inherent to the human condition because man is a suffering being, and suffering is a form of illness. Indeed, Nietzsche's philosophy, to the extent that it may be summarily defined, is a philosophy of and about suffering.[15] His critiques are censures of the means with which suffering has hitherto been faced. His admonitions are as

[15] Consequently, in Nietzsche's "utopia" society was organized according to its members' sensitivity to suffering (*HH* 168–69; cf. *WP* 542–43).

autobiographical sketches of how suffering may be over-come. Pain, strife, and contradiction are the essence of life, Nietzsche declared, while pleasure and harmony are only appearances (*GW* 7:145; *GW* 3:333). To exist is to suffer. The more developed the consciousness, the greater the af-fliction; for it is not physical pain per se but its lack of sig-nificance that is the greatest torment. Man suffers most from his inability to provide his suffering with meaning. Philosophy, religion, and morality attempt to alleviate this predicament through various "lies." Religion promises an afterlife which allows redemption and compensation for earthly woes. Morality gives man guilt, because punish-ment is easier to bear than meaningless pain. Philosophy speaks of ideal worlds to anesthetize man against the sting of existing in a nonideal world. All this constitutes a de-preciation of life according to Nietzsche. It is man's re-venge on life for his suffering.

Nihilism marks the onset of a skeptical integrity. The lies involved in the justification of suffering are no longer believed. The void of meaning, however, is left unfilled. "Nihilism appears at that point, not that the displeasure at existence has become greater than before but because one has come to mistrust any 'meaning' in suffering, indeed in existence. One interpretation has collapsed; but because it was considered *the* interpretation it now seems as if there were no meaning at all in existence, as if everything were in vain" (*WP* 35). Nietzsche's alternative to this passive ni-hilism is its active counterpart. The presence of suffering, unredeemed by an other-worldly existence and unjustified as a punishment for sins committed, is not denied. It is to be transformed. The greater the suffering, the greater the potential for joy. "How little you know of human *happi-ness*, you comfortable and benevolent people," Nietzsche observed, "for happiness and unhappiness are sisters and even twins that either grow up together or, as in your case, *remain small* together" (*GS* 270). Those who wish to experience the fullness of life must also suffer deeply, for it is in the recovery from a crippling disease that life is most fully affirmed. "Who *suffers* much makes the devil *envious*, and is thrown out into heaven," Nietzsche wrote, describing his own experience (*GW* 14:44).[16]

One liberates oneself from suffering by means of its transformation. A prescription is offered:

> Truly, I have gone my way through a hundred souls and through a hundred cradles and birth-pangs. . . .
>
> All *feeling* suffers in me and is in prison: but my *willing* always comes to me as my liberator and bringer of joy.
>
> Willing liberates: that is the true doctrine of will and freedom—thus Zarathustra teaches you. (*Z* 111)

Will liberates from the bitterest sorrow facing man—consciousness of his own impotence. Willing is the act of self-overcoming in which a pathos of distance between multiple souls is achieved. One steps beyond oneself, beyond one's limits and pain. Suffering becomes nourishment in a period of gestation, with the accompanying faith that the joy of new life will overly compensate for the pangs of birth. Amidst his pain the higher man spurns the anesthetics needed by weaker souls that he may most relish his will to power. For there is no greater exercise of will than that which transforms the agony of existence into the jubilation of life. Nietzsche's words bear out this resolve to face suffering heroically, and thus to overcome it: "Over all lamentation always anew with a song of joy—isn't that true; so is life! So can it be!" (*NB* 15.7.81). To live *is* to be imprisoned: to will one's liberation is to *feel* one's freedom. To resolve that life resound with celebration rather than lamentation is already to know the liberating effect of will.

[16] The words of the forlorn harp player of Goethe's *Wilhelm Meister*, one of Nietzsche's favorite works by his most-admired writer, are recalled: "Who hasn't tearfully eat his bread, / Who hasn't through the troubled night, / Sat crying woefully on his bed, / He knows you not, you heavenly sights." Goethe, one must remember, was a self-avowed pagan and critic of Christianity.

All growth, all health, all wisdom, and in the end, all higher pleasure and joy are the products of suffering and its transformation through will. Redemption is not of another world, but is experienced at the moment of overcoming. As newfound health peaks, a backward gaze bestows the wisdom of Heraclitus: suffering exists only for the limited human mind whose power is insufficient to see its necessity, its potential and benefit (*PTG* 61–62). This is the wisdom of the ascending soul, the soul in search of order. Strife is the essence of its politics.

PART III

INCARNATIONS AND IDEALS

Most people obviously do not at all regard themselves as individuals; their life shows that. . . . Only in three forms of existence does one stay an individual: as philosopher, as saint and as artist.

—*Gesammelte Werke*

It is the fundamental idea of *culture,* insofar as it sets for each one of us but one task: *to promote the production of the philosopher, the artist and the saint within us and without us and thereby to work at the perfecting of nature.* . . . Only when, in our present or in some future incarnation, we ourselves have been taken into that exalted order of philosophers, artists and saints, shall we also be given a new goal for our love and hate.

—*Untimely Meditations*

To become artist (creator), saint (lover) and philosopher (knower) in *one person:*—*my practical goal!*

—*Gesammelte Werke*

F I V E

THE PHILOSOPHER

If a man wants to become a hero the serpent must first
have become a dragon: otherwise he will lack his proper
enemy.

—*Human, All Too Human*

Philosophy receives Nietzsche's accolade as "the most
spiritual will to power" (*BGE* 21). The philosopher attempts to create the world in his own image. His truths,
his philosophy, his entire world are the reflections of his
person, of his will to power in its multiple and variegated
forms, ascending and declining, affirmative and decadent.
Nietzsche's love-hate relationship with philosophy was a
function of this dynamic. It received his highest praise and
his most untempered wrath. His pantheon of philosophers is problematic. Those who are the victims of his
most scathing diatribes are those whose spiritual powers
have raised them to the greatest heights. Precisely the stature of such titans makes their slip into decadence all the
more damnable.

In Heraclitus Nietzsche discovered a kindred spirit. Already in *Philosophy in the Tragic Age of the Greeks* Heraclitus
figured as Nietzsche's most respected philosopher. In
1888, at the end of his career, Nietzsche still "set apart
with high reverence the name of *Heraclitus*" (*TI* 36), in
whose proximity he felt "altogether warmer and better
than anywhere else," and whose understanding of strife
and eternal becoming were more closely related to

Nietzsche's own philosophy "than anything else thought to date" (*EH* 273). Heraclitus's maxim "War is the father of all" was the summons of a comrade in arms. His understanding of life as artistic creation rather than moral evolution was embraced wholeheartedly by Nietzsche. Heraclitus stands alone in that he, unlike Nietzsche's other "educators," from Socrates, Plato, and Epicurus to Schopenhauer and Wagner, was never subjected to accusations of decadence. The Heraclitean world of constant flux was seen by Nietzsche as the projection of a man strong enough to accept the terrifying questionableness of the world of appearance. In his early essay on the Greek philosophers, Nietzsche had this mentor proclaim a worldview that might be read as his own: "I see nothing other than becoming. Be not deceived. It is the fault of your myopia, not of the nature of things, if you believe you see land somewhere in the ocean of coming-to-be and passing away. You use names for things as though they rigidly, persistently endured; yet even the stream into which you step a second time is not the one you stepped into before" (*PTG* 51–52). Nearly two decades later Nietzsche's judgment had not changed: "Heraclitus will always be right in this, that being is an empty fiction. The 'apparent' world is the only one: the 'real' world has only been *lyingly added*" (*TI* 36).

It is from an understanding of Nietzsche's affinity with Heraclitus that we may best account for his antagonistic relation to Socrates. As if to demonstrate his talent for discovering the streaks of decadence in those most revered, Nietzsche chose Socrates as the victim of his first philosophical publication, *The Birth of Tragedy*. Socrates would be attacked where Nietzsche felt him to be the strongest, that is to say, where his philosophy most closely resembled Nietzsche's own and was thus particularly culpable for the germs of decadence it harbored. Nietzsche felt vulnerable to this infection: he battled with Socrates as a physician battles with a disease that he has himself contracted.[1]

In contrast to the (Sophoclean and Aeschylean) tragic hero, who reveled in the terrifying nature of an unknowable but intoxicating world of becoming and appearance, Nietzsche posed Socrates as "the dialectical hero of the Platonic drama" (*BT* 91). The new hero's task was to steal the laurels from his tragic predecessors. It was, for Nietzsche, an ignoble deed. For Socrates constructed a world of stable forms and ideals in order to deny the ubiquity of becoming. In effect, this denial was an admission that he was too weak to affirm a world of appearance and flux. His weapon was the dialectic, and it was used in an attempt to prove that truth could be secured through rational speech and argument. Socrates, perhaps best known for his paradoxical claim both to wisdom and ignorance— that he was the wisest man, according to the oracle, because he knew that he knew nothing, while others did not even know that—is confronted by Nietzsche with the charge of rationalism. Rationalism is defined as the false equation of wisdom with the spurious knowledge gained through methodical inquiry, and the accompanying "faith in the explicability of nature and in knowledge as a panacea" (*BT* 106). Nietzsche denounced it as a philosophical fraud.[2]

[1] Shortly after publishing *The Birth of Tragedy* Nietzsche would write: "Socrates, just to acknowledge it, stands so close to me that I am almost always fighting with him" (*GW* 6:101).

[2] It would be naive to believe that Nietzsche's tactical foray against Socrates demonstrated a lack of understanding of Socrates's skeptical, nonscientific, and even mystical nature. Already in *Philosophy in the Tragic Age of the Greeks* Nietzsche acknowledged that the Greek philosophers employed dialectic and conceptualization as an inadequate but necessary means to communicate the "world symphony" they heard within. "What verse is for the poet, dialectic thinking is for the philosopher. He grasps for it in order to get hold of his own enchantment, in order to perpetuate it" (*PTG* 44). The charge against Socrates is not that he never knew this enchantment, but that he betrayed it by trying to capture and tame it. He

Only during his last days in prison, according to Nietzsche, did Socrates voice doubts about his project. The closest Socrates came to the Heraclitean wisdom of a tragic world of becoming was a laughable attempt to practice music and write a few poems while awaiting execution. Here, in his prison poetry, "that despotic logician" betrayed "the only sign of any misgivings about the limits of logic." In the end, Nietzsche speculated, Socrates wondered if indeed what was "not intelligible" to him was "not necessarily unintelligent," asking himself, "Perhaps there is a realm of wisdom from which the logician is exiled?" (*BT* 92–93). Such misgivings, however, could not erase the decadence inherent in a life of rationalism. In his final request that Crito discharge his debt to Asclepius, the godhead of medicine and healing whom one repaid for regained health, Socrates took his final revenge on life by slandering it, saying in effect: "To live—that means to be a long time sick" (*TI* 29). More than two millennia after Socrates' death Nietzsche hoped to regain the laurels from this philosophical foe, making possible the rebirth of a tragic-heroic culture.[3]

sought to rationalize it. Carl Jung's charge that religion is a defense against the experience of God may be adapted to describe Nietzsche's opposition to Socrates: rationalistic philosophy is a defense against the experience of wonder.

[3] "For Nietzsche, the quarrel with Socrates is part of a vast historical drama which he recounts and which features Socrates as the first villain and Nietzsche himself as the final hero," Werner Dannhauser wrote in his *Nietzsche's View of Socrates* (Ithaca: Cornell University Press, 1974), p. 272. Dannhauser's remark is accurate enough. However, he mistakenly portrayed Nietzsche's antagonism to Socrates as indicative of a basic misunderstanding and lack of respect. Nietzsche insisted that an enemy worth having is worth honoring. Moreover, if his explorations into the psyche of Socrates are extraordinarily insightful, it is because he had experienced the same threat of a fall to decadence. Nietzsche acknowledged the "long war" waged with himself "against the pessimism of weariness with life" (*HH* 213), and his personal letters contain many references to his life as a long sickness he would be anxious to end. His point is not that Socrates was wrong in his evaluation of life, but that he failed to overcome this truth (cf. *GS* 272). The tragic hero combats the ramifications of the terrible but truthful answer given by the satyr Sil-

Nietzsche was convinced that the subtleties of rationalist argument and the discoveries of scientific research
never really touch upon truth. Indeed, the communicabil-
ity of knowledge is itself the best indicator of its limited
reach. Language is the charm we use to deceive ourselves
into believing that reality is within our grasp: "We set up
a word at the point at which our ignorance begins, at
which we can see no further . . . these are perhaps the
horizon of our knowledge, but not 'truths' " (*WP* 267). The
true philosopher is always a skeptic. Nietzsche maintained, however, that skepticism must result from
strength of soul and be embraced as an affirmation rather
than a denial of life. He recommended it only for thinkers
with a strong will (*GW* 14:22). The "beautiful luxury of
scepticism" is reserved for those who are "secure enough,
firm enough, fixed enough for it" (*TI* 74). But this is to put
the philosophical cart before the horse. For the strong-
willed, ascending individual, skepticism is not an intellectual choice, but an indelible feature of his character. The
great man, Nietzsche asserted, is always a skeptic; the
need for faith or convictions is already a symptom of
weakness (*WP* 505–6). The true philosopher embraces
skepticism instinctively. This *"intellectual conscience"* is
what distinguishes the higher from the lower man (*GS* 76).
"The vigour of a mind, its *freedom* through strength and
superior strength, is *proved* by scepticism. . . . A spirit
which wants to do great things, which also wills the
means for it, is necessarily a sceptic. . . . Grand passion
uses and uses up convictions, it does not submit to them—
it knows itself sovereign" (*A* 172). Convictions or beliefs
are the prisons one builds to escape from thinking. It is,

---

venus to the question, "What is the best and most desirable of all things
for man?": "Oh, wretched ephemeral race, children of chance and misery, why do you compel me to tell you what it would be most expedient
for you not to hear? What is best of all is utterly beyond your reach: not
to be born, not to *be*, to be *nothing*. But the second best for you is—to die
soon" (*BT* 42).

therefore, "indecent" for the philosopher " 'to believe'—
or a sign of *décadence*, of a broken will to live" (A 166). Simply put, truth is the pious law adopted by those too weak
to celebrate the Saturnalia of illusion.

Nietzsche's skepticism is evident in his earliest writings.
At fourteen years of age he wrote in his diary of the futility
of any attempt to comprehend God since one was not
even capable of understanding his creations (*DWN* 69).
Two years later he had already established the epistemological foundation of his mature position: "Everything that
confronts man can be comprehended only from the point
of view of his intellectual[4] endowment. Thus everything
for man actually is only appearance; naturally truth must
be something; the knowledge of it is for us only
probability[5]" (*GW* 1:52). Skepticism is an acknowledgment
of the limitations of human knowledge and perception, a
suspicion that nothing can be known with certainty. The
skeptic suspects man of an unscrupulous hunger for truth
and its accompanying infections of self-delusion. As a pro-
phylaxis, Nietzsche offered his writings, a "schooling in
suspicion" (*HH* 5). But skepticism is more than a disposition to intellectual reservation. Nietzsche was a skeptic in
the original sense of the word: he was an inquirer (*skepti-
kos*). And inquiry, for the philosopher, becomes a way of
life; skepticism becomes a "passion" (*GW* 11:30).

The skeptic is an ascetic who prefers to preserve his
strength and integrity by doing without the opiate of belief. Better to hunger, Nietzsche admonished, than to eat
what is impure. The skeptic proves to be the only "hon-
orable type" among philosophers (*EH* 243). Those who
could not match the severity of such intellectual self-denial
were labeled "contemptible libertines hiding in the cloak

---

[4] The German word *geistig* means "intellectual," "mental," and "spiritual." It refers not merely to the capacity for rational calculation or memory but to all faculties of the mind in the broad sense of the word.

[5] "Probability" is the translation of *Wahrscheinlichkeit*, literally, that with
the "appearance of the true."

of the woman 'truth' " (*WP* 257). But the skeptic's passion is engaged not only in the task of preserving his intellectual purity. He ardently seeks to undress beliefs that masquerade as truth.

Consequently, the skeptic must employ knowledge—but only as a means to contradict "absolute knowledge" (*GW* 11:129). For knowledge is always only the "measuring of earlier and later errors by one another" (*WP* 281). Truth or absolute knowledge can never be refuted in good faith. The skeptic merely instills doubt. Belief becomes contaminated with the germs of uncertainty and meets its demise for lack of resistance. Authority that is questioned ceases to function as legitimate authority. A truth that is under suspicion ceases to operate as truth. "I do not refute ideals," Nietzsche wrote in *Ecce Homo*, "I merely put on gloves before them" (*EH* 218). Such an act of irreverence was enough to cause ideals to die of shame. Nietzsche claimed to philosophize with a hammer. But his hammer is not primarily a weapon that breaks apart truths in direct combat. Rather, the *"eternal* idols . . . are here touched with the hammer as with a tuning fork" (*TI* 22). The hollow sound emitted—if it finds the right ears—reverberates until the idols collapse. With Nietzsche, the manner in which truth is approached and handled proves to be its undoing.

Beliefs and convictions are an escape from thinking; and thinking in itself always promotes skepticism. The belief in God, Nietzsche said, was the greatest prohibition to thought. It follows that skepticism finds a natural enemy in religion.[6] But the death of God was taken to be a cultural fact, and Nietzsche was not particularly interested in burying the corpse. His efforts were not so much aimed at fostering doubt among the remaining faithful as at attack-

[6] Nietzsche's "atheism" was a product of his skepticism. He was "too inquisitive, too *questionable*, too exuberant to stand for any gross answer. God is a gross answer, an indelicacy against thinkers—at bottom merely a gross prohibition for us: you shall not think" (*EH* 236–37).

ing the religious remnants that took the form of metaphysics and ethics. Concern lay with the "truths" of ontology, teleology, causality, and morality. These truths were now proffered as independent of theistic doctrine, but, Nietzsche charged, they nonetheless stood upon its half-buried foundations. The first occurrence of the infamous proclamation "God is dead" demonstrates that Nietzsche's concern was not so much with the death of God as with the "shadows of God" that persisted after his death (*GS* 167). The goal is to vanquish these shadows, to rout the metaphysical and moral beliefs that give a transcendent status to the categories of being, causation, truth, purpose, good, and evil. Nietzsche's project was the "de-deification of nature," the attempt to rid the world of the shadows of God that "darken our minds" and cast upon the world of appearance the gloom of lost innocence.

The radical nature of Nietzsche's skepticism allows a relatively straightforward exposition of his attacks on metaphysical notions. His attack on ontology stems from two sources: Heraclitus and Kant, philosophers who severely questioned the limits of human reason and knowledge. Nietzsche followed Heraclitus's program to the end: all is in flux, all is appearance, so-called being is simply the product of man's insensitivity to the ever-changing nature of becoming. Kant was followed halfway down his philosophical path. At the point where Kant's critique of reason becomes the vehicle for ushering in a renewed faith (in God and metaphysics), Nietzsche parted ways. That metaphysical or religious categories are necessary assumptions if we are to think consistently and act morally, as Kant maintained, does not speak to their status as truth. The skeptic has no truck with faith by default. "We have arranged for ourselves a world in which we can live—by positing bodies, lines, planes, causes and effects, motion and rest, form and content; without these articles of faith nobody now could endure life. But that does not prove them. Life is no argument. The conditions of life might include error" (*GS* 177). In a world of constant flux there are no footholds to be found, even though they prove necessary for survival.

It is not clear whether Nietzsche held ontology responsible for teleology or teleology for ontology. Certainly they stand together and subsequently must fall together. If all is appearance and endless becoming, then the search for a final purpose is pointless. Being may indeed have such a purpose, as dictated by its enduring nature, however it unfolds. Becoming, on the other hand, is an unending process without a final state or *telos*. To reject ontology is to take away the ground from which teleology may spring. Teleology speaks of the development of being, its endurance amidst transformation. The world of which Nietzsche spoke evidences only transformation, a world of fleeting appearances rather than abiding natures. If, however, logic would have the causal arrows point from ontology to teleology, Nietzsche assumed that where psychology is concerned the causal arrows flew in the opposite direction. Our myopic vision, which prevents us from discerning the flux of existence, is, as it were, a psychosomatic defect. The need to impose meaning and purpose on our world prompts us to imagine being in place of becoming. Only abiding entities can have ends or purposes. Man's desire to find life purposeful seduces him into believing in being. As early as 1868 Nietzsche posited that ontological categories were the creation of teleological needs: the idea of enduring being and unities carries the idea of purpose within it (*GW* 1:414). Being is the vehicle man constructs to allow the arrival of purpose at its destination.

Ontology and teleology are mutually supporting structures. Both collapse whenever one is sufficiently undermined. In turn, the belief in causality must be abandoned once its teleological, or ontological, foundations have been wrecked. Causality in nature is the anthropomorphism of teleology. The materialist (or deist) rejects providence but retains a belief in causality. Yet both providence and causality are inherently teleological concepts. The theist proposes a universe created and kept in motion by a god who also supplies its purpose. The materialist proposes a universe that, whatever its origin or lack thereof, is run according to the laws of nature. These same laws supply the ends to which nature's inhabitants proceed. The materialist's inability to conceive of events without causes is, however, no better apology for his belief in the laws of nature than the theist's inability to conceive of a universe without a creator and maintainer is a justification of his belief in God and divine intervention. Again, the radical skeptic does not permit the limits of human reason to become a legitimation of faith. "In short: the psychological necessity for a belief in causality lies in the inconceivability of an event divorced from intent; by which naturally nothing is said concerning truth or untruth (the justification of such a belief)! The belief in *causae* falls with the belief in télē" (*WP* 335). Causality is the deification of nature, a projection of man's need for purpose and meaning given in terms of intent and lawfulness. By rights it should disappear once God, as the ultimate giver of purpose, disappears. Its persistence as a ghostly shadow is evidence of man's unwillingness to suspend belief.

The skeptic's rejection of the principle of causality does not put him at risk of an early demise owing to his stubborn reluctance to act with due respect for the so-called laws of nature. He holds these laws to be acceptable conventions, useful for the purposes of sustaining life and human community. Man's inability to survive or prosper without such beliefs, however, does not justify their enshrinement. What is available to man is not truth but interpretation, not explanation but the creative introduction of meaning (*WP* 327). "One ought to employ 'cause' and 'effect' only as pure *concepts*, that is to say as conventional fictions for the purpose of designation, mutual understanding, *not* explanation. . . . It is *we* alone who have fabricated causes . . . motive, purpose; and when we falsely introduce this world of symbols into things and mingle it with them as though this symbol-world were an 'in-itself', we once more behave as we have always behaved, namely *mythologically*" (*BGE* 33). Mythology, the creation of symbol systems with teleological underpinnings, is the mainstay of culture. But as a skeptic Nietzsche wished to distinguish what was necessary for the development of culture, indeed of human life in general, and what was philosophically acceptable. This applies to the most basic symbol system man has created: language. Without grammar, language is impossible. Without language, culture is impossible. And without culture, higher man is impossible. Yet it is this higher man, the radical skeptic, who is suspicious of language in general, and grammar in particular. At base a systematic set of causal relationships between subjects and predicates, grammar is a secret carrier of the belief in causality and, by extension, of the belief in ultimate purposes. "I fear we are not getting rid of God," Nietzsche quipped, "because we still believe in grammar" (*TI* 38). The unconsciously accepted and employed rules of grammar serve as the preparatory exercise for man's belief in a lawlike universe subject to divine, metaphysical, or natural principles. Nietzsche's remark, "Every word is a prejudice" punctuated his discovery of the *"linguistic danger to spiritual freedom"* (*HH* 323). Grammar, "the metaphysics of the people," is to be assaulted as a shadow of God (*GS* 300).

Viewed within the entirety of his writings, Nietzsche's skirmishes with metaphysics serve primarily to introduce his major battle with morality. Nonetheless, his metaphysical engagements set the tone for the larger campaign. Stripped of stability, purpose, and predictability, life becomes a terrifying, essentially tragic experience. But it also regains lost innocence. Guilt is impossible without duties to shirk or (natural) callings to neglect. The Heraclitean world, fearful as it may be, is a world of the greatest liberty. Man is free to create himself, for he bears no transcendent nature, nor is he subject to preestablished goals. Nietzsche espoused "the absolute necessity of a total liberation from ends: otherwise we should not be permitted to try to sacrifice ourselves and let ourselves go. Only the innocence of becoming gives us the *greatest courage* and the *greatest freedom*" (*WP* 416). With no obligations to fulfill, life becomes an exercise in creative freedom, "an experiment . . . and *not* a 'contract' " (Z 229).

The role of philosophy, as Nietzsche saw it, is twofold. First, it sows the seeds of suspicion, destroying the fraudulent regimes of religion, metaphysics, and morality. Second, it engages in creative experimentation with life in an effort to fill the void left by its own handiwork. The result is the transvaluation of values, their destruction and subsequent *experimental* replacement. All systematization signals a lack of integrity (*TI* 25); it constitutes an obfuscation of one's dearth of knowledge by means of conceptual entanglements. The true philosopher does not construct theories that he may escape his own doubts. He searches for practical ways better to live a skeptical life. Thus Nietzsche prescribed: "not a philosophy as *dogma*, but as a provisional regulator of *research*" (*GW* 14:312–13). Skepticism and experimentalism prove to be complementary dispositions (*GS* 115).

Even Nietzsche's ostensibly most dogmatic writings were conducted within a skeptical, experimental framework. His imperatives and purportedly scientific statements on the breeding of higher men, for example, were considered speculative (*WP* 480). The work Nietzsche proposed to publish under the title *The Will to Power* (which may well have borne little resemblance to the posthumously collected notes that came to be so named) was submitted as an "experiment" (*GW* 14:372). If published by Nietzsche it might have been introduced with the qualification he had written for it: "A book for *thinking*, nothing else: it belongs to those for whom thinking is a *delight*, nothing else" (*WP* xxii). Nietzsche's skepticism relegated

all thought and conceptualization to the status of "a fiction" (*WP* 291). His writing was a game of semiotics, an
exercise in the manipulation of metaphors that made no
claim to touch upon anything called truth. His so-called
doctrine of the will to power was set forth as an interpretive framework or heuristics under which the experiment
of a certain way of living could be carried out: "Instead of
belief which is no longer possible for us we place a strong
will over us, which holds fast to a provisional abundance
of fundamental evaluations, as a heuristic principle: in order to see *how far* man gets with it. Like a ship in unknown
seas" (*GW* 14:280). The destination and fate of this philosophical vessel remain untold. In the end, whether his
transvaluation of values could escape the specter of nihilism haunting the modern world remained for Nietzsche a
"*question mark*" (*GS* 285–87).

The first person to venture into these unknown seas is
the philosopher himself. He is his own guinea pig (*GS*
253). His motto might read: Hitherto philosophers have
only interpreted life in various ways; the point is to exhaust its possibilities. The radical skeptic must live with
his lack of beliefs. His life becomes an experiment in just
how much terror and anxiety can be tolerated and transformed.[7] He tests the extent to which the truth that there

---

[7] The extent to which Nietzsche was his own guinea pig cannot be
overemphasized. His philosophy was both incorporated into and the
product of his life. In turn, life's experimental nature proved to be its
own redemption. Nietzsche's letters often reveal how the agonies of his
poor physical health, his social alienation, and his existential anxiety
were transformed into joy by way of probes in the laboratory of the soul:
"My existence is a horrible burden: I would have thrown it away long
ago if I did not make the most instructive tests and experiments in the
spiritual-moral field precisely in this condition of suffering and almost
absolute renunciation—this knowledge-thirsty joy brings me on high,
where I conquer all torment and hopelessness" (*NB* 1.80). In a letter to
his friend Franz Overbeck, Nietzsche made a similar point: "I experience
contempt, suspicion and, in regard to that of which I am able and which
I want, an ironic indifference. Through some bad accidents I have experienced all this in the cruelest form—objectively considered: it was most
interesting" (*NB* 20.12.82). One is to look upon life as actor and spectator:

are no truths can "endure incorporation." "That is the question," wrote Nietzsche, "that is the experiment" (*GS* 171).

Prudence, then, is not a philosophical virtue. It has no place for those who seek adventure in uncharted waters: "The genuine philosopher—as he seems to *us*, my friends?—lives 'unphilosophically' and 'unwisely', above all *imprudently* . . . he risks *himself* constantly, he plays *the* dangerous game" (*BGE* 113). *The* dangerous game is the philosophical life itself. It is a life Nietzsche claimed to have lived, and to have limned in words. To understand his condition and his works, Nietzsche wrote, one must be "the victim of the same passions" (*GW* 21:83). To be the victim of an insatiable skeptical passion is to understand how its incorporation is literally dangerous to life. For the range of experimentation is unbounded. Excess is endemic. What makes the Nietzschean philosopher "unphilosophical" is his heroism: he tempts fate, he commits sacrilege, he suffers, and he celebrates tremendously. In the nihilistic age, where everything is permitted, "experimentation would be in order that would allow every kind of heroism to find satisfaction" (*GS* 82). By these rules the philosopher might even take his life to satisfy his curiosity: "If suicide is also only an experiment! Why not!" (*GW* 3:207).

The skeptic's refusal to take his own life would likely be grounded on his suspicion that the act would not be conducted as an experiment. Most probably, suicide would be the recourse of a sufferer whose resentment at the unknowability and purposelessness of life led him to take revenge upon it. Such revenge would be unjustified. To end one's life in anything but a spirit of pure experimentation is to judge life as a whole. Nietzsche maintained that we are not entitled to such evaluations: "One would have to

the sufferings of the former are redeemed by their experimental value for the latter.

be situated *outside* life . . . to be permitted to touch on the problem of the *value* of life at all" (*TI* 45). "Judgements, value judgments concerning life, for or against, can in the last resort never be true: they possess value only as symptoms. . . . One must reach out and try to grasp this astonishing *finesse, that the value of life cannot be estimated.* Not by a living man, because he is a party to the dispute, indeed its object, and not the judge of it; not by a dead one, for another reason" (*TI* 30). The same spirit of experimentalism that places the skeptic's life in jeopardy also safeguards it from the often fatal grip of despondency. Intellectual integrity precludes the sufferer of life from becoming its ultimate censor.

The philosopher carries heroism into the search for knowledge by offering himself as a grand experiment. His quest for knowledge necessarily leads to self-investigation; for all knowledge ultimately is self-knowledge. At base, he must ask himself *why* he is willing to consider any particular observation or perception to be a party to knowledge, *why* any particular appearance or probability should be dealt with, even heuristically, as truth.

The answers to these questions prompt the philosopher to be skeptical of himself, including his tragic-heroic tendencies. He becomes suspicious of his willingness to sacrifice himself for knowledge. The will to knowledge, in other words, is seen to have its own form of decadence. It often smells of morality, of duty: " 'Knowledge for its own sake'—this is the last snare set by morality: one therewith gets completely entangled with it once more" (*BGE* 72). The unrestrained thirst for knowledge, Nietzsche realized early on, barbarizes man (*PTG* 30–31). Is knowledge to dominate life, or life to dominate knowledge? Nietzsche responded in favor of life. To this end one needs a *"hygiene of life,"* a means of supervising science and the quest for knowledge (*UM* 121). The superintendent is philosophy, which elevates "man over the blind unrestrained greed of his drive for knowledge" by "legislating greatness," that is, by determining what is worth knowing (*PTG* 43). The philosopher discriminates that knowledge which is beneficial to life and that which is harmful. His ironic wisdom begets a willingness to restrain his passion for knowledge so that life itself is not jeopardized.

"The tree of knowledge is not that of life," Nietzsche wrote, quoting Byron: "Man may bleed to death from knowledge of truth" (*HH* 60–61). The truths from which man needs to be shielded are, however, precisely those the philosopher keeps digging up. The point is that even the strongest of spirit must occasionally turn their backs upon the "ugly truths" they battle. Nietzsche warned his fellow inquirers: "Look outward! do not look back! One gets crushed if one is always digging at foundations" (*GW* 20:235).[8] Why, then, play this most dangerous game wherein the limits of one's endurance are forever being tested? Why the endless war with the self? Why reveal ugly truths only to have to shrink from their presence? Why knowledge at all? Nietzsche admitted that he had no ready response to these questions (*BGE* 143). The answer can be found only by living the philosophical life itself: it must prove to be its own justification.

> No, life has not disappointed me. On the contrary, I find it truer, more desirable and mysterious every year—ever since the day when the great liberator came to me: the idea that life could be an experiment of the seeker for knowledge—and not a duty, not a calamity, not trickery.—And knowledge itself: let it be something else for others; for example, a bed to rest on, or the way to such a bed, or a diversion, or a form of leisure—for me it is a world of dangers and victories in which heroic feelings, too, find places to dance and play. "*Life as a means to knowledge*"—with this principle in one's heart one can live not only boldly

[8] "Sieh hinaus! sieh nicht zurück! Man geht zu grunde wenn man immer zu den gründen geht."

but even gaily, and laugh gaily, too. And who knows how to laugh anyway and live well if he does not first know a good deal about war and victory. (*GS* 255)

The great liberation of experimentalism is the transformation of the burden of a duty-bound life into a vast puzzle for the curious. That this curiosity may prove fatal is part of the adventure, though wisdom periodically might moderate the pursuit in order to perpetuate it.

The skeptic's integrity not only releases him from the constraints of morality, it also allows him an escape from his own suspicions: "When the moral skeptic arrives at mistrust of morality there remains one more step for him to take—skepticism of his mistrust. *To deny* and *to trust*—go hand in hand" (*GW* 14:30). Compared to former skeptics who believed they had attained the truth that truth was impossible, Nietzsche held himself to be even more suspicious. No truth is known at all (*GW* 11:3). In other words, one must be skeptical vis-à-vis one's own skeptical passion. One is to doubt that doubting itself constitutes an undischargeable obligation.

In this way Nietzsche prevents skepticism from becoming a burdensome, self-imposed duty. Radical skepticism serves as its own brake, allowing itself an occasional rest from its zealous pursuit: "A philosopher recuperates differently and with different means: he recuperates, e.g., with nihilism. Belief that there is no truth at all, the nihilistic belief, is a great relaxation for one who, as a warrior of knowledge, is ceaselessly fighting ugly truths" (*WP* 325). The imperative not to have beliefs may be applied to the belief that such an imperative exists. The relentlessness of the will to knowledge is checked by the skeptic's mistrust of his own drives: "Scepticism is simply in regard to all authority, that we do not want to be duped, not even by our own *drives*! But what, then, actually does not *want* this. A drive of course!" (*GW* 10:366). In short, the skeptic is a man driven to mistrust his own drives. That life itself not be jeopardized, respite from the infinite regress of self-suspicion is necessary. Such clemency, however, dispenses only reprieves, a fact the philosopher finds both a blessing and a curse.

A purely cognitive being, Nietzsche realized, would be indifferent to knowledge. The philosopher, therefore, is a passionate animal. His passion exhausts itself not in the accumulation of data, however, but in questioning. The fierceness of his inquiry determines his order of rank.[9] A passion for unanswerable questions, and an inability to remain indifferent and distanced from them, is the mark of a true thinker (GW 11:12). Nietzsche testified to the pleasures of this philosophical life: "Abstract thinking is for many a hardship, for me, on good days, a festival and intoxication" (GW 16:106). Abstract thought—that is, thought free from any utilitarian function, *aporetic*, without a destination—is the trademark of philosophy. Its capacity to carry one into an inspired state of wonder, what Nietzsche described as "symbol-intoxication," was the highest pleasure of the most spiritual men (WP 540).[10]

The philosopher's life as a whole is sublimated to the symbolic; the creative force of metaphor is celebrated as the greatest truth. Indeed, in a state of philosophical inspiration the distinction between reality and symbol, truth and metaphor, disappears: "One no longer has any notion

[9] Nietzsche acknowledged rather grudgingly that he suspected this capacity for philosophical passion to be universal: "But to stand in the midst of this *rerum concordia discors* and of this whole marvelous uncertainty and rich ambiguity of existence *without questioning*, without trembling with the craving and the rapture of such questioning . . . that is what I feel to be *contemptible*, and this is the feeling for which I look first in everybody. Some folly keeps persuading me that every human being has this feeling, simply because he is human. This is my type of injustice" (GS 76–77). As shall be shown further on, the quality and duration of this feeling, not its mere presence or absence, was Nietzsche's measure of greatness (cf. GW 6:26).

[10] Goethe's remark to Eckermann is recalled: "The highest to which man may aspire is wonder." Goethe also maintained that "one truly thinks only when that of which one thinks cannot be thought out."

of what is an image or a metaphor: everything offers itself as the nearest, most obvious, simplest expression . . . as if the things themselves approached and offered themselves as metaphors. . . . On every metaphor you ride to every truth. . . . Here the words and word-shrines of all being open up before you; here all being wishes to become word, all becoming wishes to learn from you how to speak" (*EH* 301). The self-conscious power to give meaning to the world through the pleasures of thinking, to justify it through its sublimation in symbol and metaphor, carries the philosopher into a rapturous state of life-affirmation. For Nietzsche, such a state, such feelings, were the essence of philosophy: "Philosophy as love of wisdom . . . not love of men, or of gods, or of truth, but *love of a condition, a spiritual and sensual feeling of perfection*: an affirmation and approval out of an overflowing feeling of the power to accept" (*GW* 16:70). Philosophy, the most spiritual will to power, is the love of wisdom. And wisdom, far from being an accumulation of knowledge, is rather the vision of a world justified and made perfect; this by means of its potential for symbolic sublimation. Philosophy is the love of this vision. But philosophers as far back as Socrates have pointed out that the lover desires but does not possess his beloved. The lover of wisdom is never really wise. He glimpses wisdom, and is momentarily caught up in a wonder that inspires and justifies. Yet each glimpse also serves to mark his want, further inflaming his desire.

The philosopher is he whose "ecstasies of learning" (*EH* 263) lead him to celebrate rather than condemn a life in which learning will have no end. For life is intrinsically paradoxical, questionable, ambiguous. "We despise everything that lets itself be explained," expresses the philosophical sentiment (*GW* 14:7). The philosopher knows no greater joy or blessing than the terrible questionableness of existence, the wonder at being. *This* is life's justification. But this is also the source of his suffering. For the questions he passionately asks have no answers. He is a "wanderer on the earth—though not as a traveller *to* a final destination: for this destination does not exist" (*HH* 203). Too consistent in his skepticism to die for any particular "truth," he is willing enough to sacrifice himself for the right to struggle in its pursuit (*HH* 391). As all "great heroic figures," he is a "seeker" who defines himself by his seeking. Only the philistine mistakes him for a "finder" (*UM* 9). His quest for knowledge does not produce knowledge, but only greater, more profound, more dangerous doubt. The philosopher feeds the serpent of knowledge with his own skeptical passion until the serpent becomes a dragon.

S I X

THE ARTIST

For a philosopher to say, "the good and the beautiful are one," is infamy; if he goes on to add, "also the true," one ought to thrash him. Truth is ugly.
We possess *art* lest we *perish of the truth*.
—*The Will to Power*

The philosophical life is necessarily an artistic one. Throughout Nietzsche's works lies the recurring theme of the philosopher as artist. In 1875 he had already set himself a general task: "to show how life, philosophy and art can have a deeper, more congenial relationship to one another" (GW 6:105). During his final years of work the concept of the "philosopher-artist" continued to occupy his thoughts (WP 419). In its broadest terms, the reason for the coupling of philosophy and art is straightforward. Philosophy is the most spiritual will to power, not because will finds its highest realization in philosophical thought or writing, but because it finds its highest incarnation in the philosopher himself. The philosopher is his own experiment in living, in the enhancement and sublimation of the will to power. He is, in effect, his own artistic creation: "The product of the philosopher is his life (first of all, *before* his *works*). That is his work of art" (GW 7:19).

If, however, the philosopher needs to become an artist in order to create himself, so too does the artist need to become a philosopher in order to fulfill his calling. Only a philosophically skeptical life allows that degree of freedom

119

required for great artistic work. He who is a slave to his convictions cannot be expected to breathe a creative freedom into his works. This is not to deny, for example, the inspiring history of religious art. But the philosopher who treats his life as the sculptor treats his stone demands a greater liberty to carve as he sees fit, unconstrained by extrinsic models and rules. Nietzsche wrote: " 'I no longer believe in anything'—that is the correct way of thinking for a *creative person*" (GW 14:15).[1]

Nietzsche maintained that the highest will to power was found in creation, not contemplation. More often than not, the so-called philosopher is without the strength or courage to test the limits of the incorporation of his thought into life. His arsenal of ready convictions is the register of an inability to will. The ominous shadow of the Creator intimidates the philosopher from assuming the burden of creation himself. His moral, metaphysical, and religious beliefs are a direct reflection of his impotence: "It is a measure of the degree of strength of will to what extent one can do without meaning in things, to what extent one can endure to live in a meaningless world *because one organizes a small portion of it oneself*" (WP 318). Philosophical skepticism allows the artist the freedom to create; artistic creation—minimally the organization of that small portion of the world which is the self—allows the philosopher the strength to bear his own skepticism.

The skeptic's necessary recuperation from his own suspiciousness is found in creation. Art is always the self-conscious affirmation of appearance and life (the two are synonymous for Nietzsche) over knowledge. Nietzsche, who

---

[1] Nietzsche's atheism was party to his aestheticism. His atheism did not constitute a denial of (the possibility of) the existence of God but a rejection of the belief in a "moral god" (GW 10:70), that is, a god who would dictate how man is to live, thus stymieing man's creativity. The worthiest representation of the gods, Nietzsche maintained, was found in the Epicurean maxim: "If there are gods, then they do not concern themselves with us." This was considered "the single true proposition of all philosophy of religion" (GW 11:275).

considered himself the most suspicious man to have lived and the archetypical victim of the passion for knowledge, found in his own works a necessary "self-forgetting," a seeking of "shelter" from himself through the creation of a "suitable fiction" (*HH* 5). The spiritual sufferings inflicted by knowledge, and in particular the knowledge that there are no answers to the most pressing questions of life, is alleviated by art. According to Nietzsche, "the greatness and indispensability of art lie precisely in its being able to produce the *appearance* of a simpler world, a shorter solution of the riddle of life. No one who suffers from life can do without this appearance, just as no one can do without sleep. . . . Art exists *so that the bow shall not break*" (*UM* 213). The appearance produced by art is not only that of a simpler world, but of a better one. The contemplation of art allows one to escape the fatigue and melancholy of life "in the hiding places and *abysses* of perfection" (*GS* 325): "In art, man takes delight in himself as perfection" (*TI* 72). That is to say, art is the means by which man successfully lies to himself. Placed in less moralistic terms, art helps man to forget. He forgets his mortality, his condemnation to individuality, the limitations of his power. Zarathustra speaks of man's need for the seduction of art: "Every soul is a world of its own. . . . There is no outside! But we forget that, when we hear music; how sweet it is, that we forget!" (*Z* 234). Those who listen to Zarathustra's song of the overman are also blessed with a selective amnesia.

The ability to forget as an act of will is considered a sign of strength; this because the self-imposed forgetfulness of art is less deceitful, less delusory, and, most importantly, less defamatory of life than the erection of religious or metaphysical ideals. Moreover, it does not rob existence of all its questionableness and mystery. These claims predominantly occupy Nietzsche's earliest writings. Art is pitted against knowledge, religious or metaphysical, in the cultural and existential arenas. With the young Nietzsche, art invariably emerges victorious. His attacks on Socrates must be seen in relation to these confrontations. Socrates' denial of art, of its merit and necessity, was interpreted by Nietzsche as an attempt to flee the terrible truths of existence. Anyone who was brave enough to confront these truths knew the need of art for recuperation. He who denied the worth of art was denying himself the therapy required by all true "warriors of knowledge." Unable to avail himself of art's healing powers, Socrates could not chance being wounded. Rationalism became his retreat.

Nietzsche's skepticism, which found many of its conceptual foundations in Kant's "anthropomorphism" of knowledge, found in artistic creation its necessary counterweight. Art complements skepticism by counteracting its poisons: "We must get beyond this skepticism, we must *forget* it! How much must we forget in this world! . . . Not in *knowledge*, in *creating* lies our salvation" (*GW* 6:35). The advance of science rent the veil of illusion that had protected man from the grotesqueness of his existential drama. In such times art has an indispensable role to play in making life bearable. A section of *The Gay Science* entitled "Our Ultimate Gratitude to Art" reads: "If we had not welcomed the arts and invented this kind of cult of the untrue, then the realization of general untruth and mendaciousness that now comes to us through science . . . would be utterly unbearable. *Honesty* would lead to nausea and suicide. But now there is a counterforce against our honesty that helps us to avoid such consequences: art as the *good* will to appearance" (*GS* 163). The widespread growth of nihilism is a modern phenomenon; the healing powers of art, therefore, are of especial importance in the modern world. But the relationship between art and nihilism, as Nietzsche demonstrated in *The Birth of Tragedy*, is primordial and recurring, a theme to be found in ancient Greek tragedy, Shakespearean drama, and modern life.

In this sense the Dionysian man resembles Hamlet: both have once looked truly into the essence of things, they have *gained knowledge*, and nausea inhibits action; for their action could not change anything in the eternal nature of things; they feel it to be ridiculous or humiliating that they should be asked to set right a world that is out of joint. Knowledge kills action; action requires the veils of illusion . . . true knowledge, an insight into the horrible truth, outweighs any motive for action, both in Hamlet and in the Dionysian man. . . . Here when the danger to his will is greatest, *art* approaches as a saving sorceress, expert at healing. She alone knows how to turn these nauseous thoughts about the horror or absurdity of existence into notions with which one can live.[2] (*BT* 60)

The value of tragedy is in the overcoming of nihilism by way of its artistic portrayal. Through the transformation of life's horrible truths into works of art, into beauty, tragedy achieves that philosophical-artistic union that is expressive of the highest form of existence. Tragedy, in brief, is "a victory of beauty over knowledge" (*GW* 3:212). The value of any victory, according to Nietzsche, is determined by the strength of one's combatant. The defeat of nihilism,

[2] The sorcery of art is most cogently illustrated in Dostoevsky's *Notes from Underground*. The "hyper-consciousness" of its scribe precludes his acting meaningfully, relegating the opportunity for heroism to his fanciful dreams. His perpetual nausea and frustration, however, is redeemed in some measure by the writing of autobiographical notes, that is, by the transformation of his debased life into a piece of literature. (Dostoevsky, Nietzsche said, was the only psychologist from whom he learned anything.)

Victor Brombert's study of heroism in modern literature is of interest in this regard. Brombert noted the intellectualization of the hero owing to the shrinking of the arena of meaningful action: "Deprived of his heroic being, the modern 'hero,' torn between the desire to act and the conviction that action is absurd, intuits that it is his tragic fate to live up to this dilemma. Action and thought once again clash. But the stress is no longer on the exploit, the deed; it is on the 'heroism of consciousness' " (*The Hero in Literature*, ed. Victor Brombert [Greenwich, Conn.: Fawcett Publications, 1969], p. 21). (Cf. Brombert's *The Intellectual Hero: Studies in the French Novel, 1880–1955* [London: Faber and Faber, 1961].)

the most egregious threat to life, is therefore the highest expression of philosophical-artistic power. Ancient Greek civilization had reached its apogee with the development of a tragic culture, represented by the Dionysian music-drama and the pre-Euripidean tragedy. Herein man witnessed and participated in the transformation of existential terror into ecstasy. The tragic hero celebrated illusion over reality, the appearance of truth, the symbolic, over truth (GW 3:220). He was able to endure life because he had willed his own life to become a work of art. Existence became "justified as an aesthetic phenomenon" (BT 52, 141).

The birth of tragedy, as the original title to Nietzsche's book indicated, was out of the spirit of music. Music is the symbolic conscious of itself. It is capable of arousing and unifying the feelings of pleasure and pain that capture man's existential plight. Music symbolizes the "pure essence of will" (GW 3:228), which "strikes the heart directly as the true, universal language that is understood everywhere" (GW 3:18). It is "beyond all individuation" (GW 3:345) in its origin, standing "in symbolic relation to the primordial contradiction and primordial pain in the heart of the primal unity" (BT 55). The rhythm of music moves one beyond oneself, producing an illusion of the unity of being. And, like tragedy, it affirms, with a Heraclitean wonder, the destruction of all boundaries: "It is only through the spirit of music that we can understand the joy involved in the annihilation of the individual" (BT 104). As the vehicle for man's transformation of existential pain and nausea into ecstatic celebration of appearance and symbol, music proves superior to words and reason, image and concept (BT 55).[3] "Only music," Nietzsche wrote,

---

[3] Although Nietzsche would later come to criticize his youthful enthusiasm for the transformative power of music, he never rejected its sovereignty in the realm of communication. In 1887 he wrote: "Compared with music all communication by words is shameless; words dilute and bru-

"can give us an idea of what is meant by the justification of the world as an aesthetic phenomenon" (*BT* 141).

The growth and eventual victory of nihilism, the specter Nietzsche saw haunting Europe, was considered unstoppable. Moreover, man was without the cultural achievements needed to make life in such circumstances endurable. He could not, for example, redeem existence through the rejuvenation of myth. He had become too suspicious, too unbelieving; he had lost his innocence. Music was seen by the young Nietzsche as the only means of survival available to modern man. The understanding of life as a symbolic phenomenon was held to be the precondition for a cultural rejuvenation and the necessary accompaniment to a people whose spiritual development had brought them to nihilism. Only music would allow a rejuvenating worldview. Nietzsche looked to music, particularly that of Richard Wagner, to stimulate a cultural golden age in Europe. The "fire magic" of his dissonant compositions would allow the rebirth of a purifying, Dionysian wisdom. Wagner could "philosophize in sound," producing an image of a Heraclitean world (*UM* 232, 242). The emergence of a higher culture would follow from the actions of those individuals transformed through this music, those who became bearers of a tragic wisdom. At the height of his enthusiasm, Nietzsche believed that a reproduction of his own inspiration on a relatively limited scale would be enough to usher in a cultural renaissance. In December 1871, after spending a week with Wagner at Triebschen, Nietzsche wrote his friend Erwin Rohde: "What are other artistic memories and experiences measured against these last ones! . . . If I but think that only a hundred people from the next generation have from music what I have, I would expect a completely new culture: Everything that remains and does not want to apply itself to music rela-

---

talize; words depersonalize; words make the uncommon common" (*WP* 428).

tions produces in me, admittedly now and then, down-right disgust and loathing" (NB 21.12.71). Such exaggerated hopes and estimations of Wagner's work would soon prove disappointing. Nietzsche, who had given Wagner his highest praise, would also subject him to his most scathing diatribes.

The break with Wagner, first evident in *Human, All Too Human* and reasserted throughout his later writings, also marked the beginning of what is often called Nietzsche's positivistic period. In fact, Nietzsche's "positivism" was mostly negation. It was a reaction against his earlier romanticism, and in particular his naiveté with respect to the potential of art as a cultural rehabilitator. Even at the high point of this reaction, however, Nietzsche did not deny the necessity of art. He simply accentuated his suspicions of it.[4] Art became problematic. Nietzsche confronted himself with the sort of accusation Rousseau had made of Hobbes: that he had fallaciously inserted the features of civilized, cultured man into his imagined primeval forerunner. Music lost its innocence, becoming a product as much as a producer of culture. Music no longer was considered to be the *immediate* language of feeling, nor did it speak directly to and of the will. Its capacity to furnish life with symbolic meaning was supposed a historic acquisition, a result of its interaction with intellect (*HH* 99). Moreover, music, like art in general, often would prove to be a narcotic rather than a stimulant.

Nietzsche came to realize that art's veil of illusion frequently was used to hide and perpetuate decadence. The fictions of artistic creation were suspected of being a poor substitute for (scientific) explanation, the products of a muddled head incapable of a more rigorous performance. Art, Nietzsche discovered, can beget the delusion of

---

[4] Likewise, even at his most romantic, antipositivistic moments, in *The Birth of Tragedy*, for example, Nietzsche did not deny the need for science; he simply asserted that art must be its "correlative" and "supplement" (*BT* 93).

strength when all that exists is a lavishly decorated impotence: "The poet conducts his thoughts along festively, in the carriage of rhythm: usually because they are incapable of walking on foot" (*HH* 93). Art was impugned to be a crutch masquerading as a sword. It no longer solely served as the weapon of the tragic hero who intrepidly tempted fate and dared embrace the tragedy of life; art also supported the cripple who could not bear the weight of existence unaided.

The intensity of Nietzsche's polemics against artists in general and Wagner in particular resulted from the failure of his most desired projections to materialize. His idealization of Wagner, Nietzsche admitted, had invested the composer with his own qualities. He assumed that the passion Wagner displayed in his music was akin to his own philosophical passion: insatiable for struggle and challenge, incapable of rest, forever overcoming itself in growth. Rather than engaging in the heroic battle against the shadows of God, however, Wagner fell back exhausted onto the couch of religious belief and romantic ideals.

That Wagner was a great man and a great artist was never denied. Indeed, his decadence was all the more condemnable because he proved incapable of matching his artistic genius with a sufficient amount of skeptical integrity. This is the danger confronted by all great artists: the veil of illusion they create becomes so alluring that they invest it with magic. What was supposed to allow temporary respite from the battle with the gods becomes itself the gods' imagined medium. "When the free spirit has divested himself of everything metaphysical the highest effects of art can easily set the metaphysical strings, which have long been silent or indeed snapped apart, vibrating in sympathy . . . he feels a profound stab in the heart and sighs for the man who will lead him back to his lost love, whether she be called religion or metaphysics. It is in such moments that his intellectual probity is put to the test" (*HH* 82). Here Nietzsche spoke from experience, as one who knew the longing for certainty but was capable of using this passion to bolster his suspicions. He explained: "I am, no less than Wagner, a child of this time; that is, a decadent: but I comprehended this, I resisted it. The philosopher in me resisted" (*CW* 155). One must, like Odysseus, secure oneself to the mast of skepticism lest the enchanting voices of the Sirens herald the end of one's quest. And many would be better off with their ears stopped with wax than seduced by the false promise of music. Wagner, Nietzsche's artistic alter ego, failed the test of intellectual probity. Nietzsche's disappointment at this failure led him to reexamine art and the artist with the greatest severity.

The product of this reexamination was the mature formulation of Nietzsche's dualistic understanding of life. His early attacks on rationalism rested on his evaluation of science as the antipode of art, as a slanderer of life owing to its inability to accept life's essential ambiguity and unknowability. Science would rather blind itself than see the terrible questionableness of existence. The modern counterpart to the rationalistic Socrates and his dialectical methods is the scholar buried beneath an ever-growing pile of books, his "fly-swatters against boredom" (*UM* 172); or the scientist whose "resolve to be so scientific about everything [is] perhaps a kind of fear of, escape from, pessimism? A subtle last resort against—*truth*? And, morally speaking, a sort of cowardice and falseness? Amorally speaking, a ruse?" (*BT* 18). Nietzsche's reevaluation of art produced the understanding that art had this same potential for decadence.[5]

---

[5] Nietzsche often stood closer to Socrates than he would openly admit. In the *Republic* (401d) Socrates acknowledged music to be the "most sovereign" form of education because only music could reach the "inmost part of the soul," thus allowing for the soul's beautification *and* its corruption. Nietzsche, like Plato's Socrates, played the role of artistic censor. And while the criteria of censorship differed markedly, both invoked the philosopher to resist the artist. "Fearing for the regime in himself," the man who has fallen in love with poetry owing to his rearing in the arts is

Everything, then, must be judged as to whether it is life-affirming or life-denying, ascending or declining. There are no sacred cows. Knowledge and art, passion and intellect, fact and fiction, must be evaluated according to their stimulation of growth or their perpetuation of decadence. Nietzsche's dualism is characterized by remarkably stringent standards. To escape the charge of decadence one must be a radical skeptic with an unrelenting passion for knowledge and disciplined inquiry. This skeptical probity prevents one from avoiding the terrible truths of existence, and coming to affirm, in effect, not life, but one's romanticized image of it.[6] In order to bear this skeptical passion, however, one also must be an artist, a creator of fictions. One must be able temporarily to rest from skepticism in illusions, all the while realizing their fictive status so as not to become their permanent victim. To escape its decadent form, art must not completely succeed in its own task.

The purpose of art, according to Nietzsche, is the self-conscious self-deception of one whose knowledge would otherwise be unbearable. Nonetheless, the healthy artist does not hide the questionableness of life behind his creations. He sublimates it, which is to say, he affirms life's tragic nature as the precondition for his activity. His creations are a forgetting of truths that cannot be withstood. At the same time, the artist realizes that his existential plight is at base the source of his inspiration, his passion and drive. He thrives on his philosophical terror, just as the philosopher recuperates in his artistic sanctuary. The split personality of the artist-philosopher is evidenced in Nietzsche's frequent admonitions to forget. One is to forget the ugly truths of life in order to live, and live fully.

---

counseled by Socrates to "chant" a philosophical argument, effectively stopping his ears with this "countercharm" (608a).

[6] Such is Nietzsche's objection to Emerson, who was acknowledged as a "brother-soul" (NB 24.12.83), but who unfortunately lacked intellectual discipline and skeptical probity, thus becoming "too much infatuated with life" (NB 26.5.76; cf. Kaufmann's discussion of Nietzsche's relation to Emerson in GS 7–13).

The irony, of course, is that it is through Nietzsche's explanation of the need to forget that one is reminded of what it is one is supposed to forget. The artist-philosopher performs this service for himself.

Works of art, like philosophical writings, are ciphers to be decoded. They represent an amalgam of life-affirming and life-denying drives. The work of art always signifies a struggle with decadence, a subtle mix of decadence vanquished and victorious. The value of works of art is not that they are beautiful in themselves—beauty as such does not exist for Nietzsche—but that they portray the state of their maker's soul. Art per se has no value; one must always ask what kind of art, what kind of artist. Similarly, the love of art has its ascending and declining forms. Is art sought as an elixir the better to affirm life, or as an anesthetic? The purpose of modern art, we are told, is clear: "stupefaction or delirium! To put to sleep or to intoxicate! . . . To help the modern soul to forget its feeling of guilt, not to help it return to innocence!" (*UM* 220). Nietzsche believed that his contemporaries, particularly the romantics, sought in art merely something to "scare away their discontent, boredom and uneasy conscience for moments or hours at a time." For the ancient Greeks, on the other hand, "art was an outflowing and overflowing of their own healthiness and wellbeing. . . . [They] loved to view their perfection *repeated* outside themselves:—self-enjoyment was what led them to art, whereas what leads our contemporaries to it is—self-disgust" (*HH* 251).[7] Most art,

---

[7] That art, and in particular music, must serve the higher goal of spiritual development, and not be mere amusement, was a recurring theme of Nietzsche's writings. At thirteen years of age, though his youthful religiousness defined his understanding of the spirit, Nietzsche had already arrived at this understanding: "[Music's] chief mission is that it leads our thoughts upward, that it elevates, even shocks us. . . . However, if music is used only for merriment, or in order to make an exhibit of itself, it is thus sinful and harmful" (*GW* 21:30). Once Nietzsche had renounced his religious beliefs, a veneration of earthly life replaced other-worldly piety: artists' creativity was to manifest a "gratitude for their existence" (*WP* 451). The self-enjoyment of the spirit and the cele-

presumably, lies somewhere between these two poles. For its interpretation psychological antennae and a good nose are necessities.

The writings Nietzsche left behind are a testament to his understanding of art. They are, like all works of art, of secondary importance, being the relics of a spiritual struggle. The life that produced them remains the justification of their appearance; the works themselves are merely the excrement of digested experience.[8] Experience is not to be equated with a purely intellectual activity; it is the incorporation of one's thought into life. "I have always written my writings with my whole body and life," Nietzsche averred, "I do not know what purely intellectual problems are" (GW 21:81). In the same vein, Zarathustra declared that "he who writes in blood and aphorisms does not want to be read, he wants to be learned by heart" (Z 67). The philosopher whose chief artistic creation is himself cannot separate his writing from his experiences, nor can his readers understand him unless they have shared these experiences.

Nietzsche remained doubtful that his bloody truths could be learned by heart. He feared that his readers would not appreciate what they could not understand owing to their lack of spiritual insight. They necessarily would remain unimpressed by descriptions of experiences foreign to their souls. Of his own writing Nietzsche commented: "I know these things as thoughts, but your thoughts are not your experiences, but echoes from those of others: as when your room shakes when a wagon drives by. I however sit in the wagon, and often I am the wagon itself" (GW 21:81). Nietzsche's doubts as to the spiritual

bration of life through art (most notably in the Greeks) becomes a pious act. It is distinguished from the use of art that Nietzsche consistently condemned: its vulgar function, to employ the French term, as a *distraction*.

[8] "I write only what has been experienced by me, and understand it to be expressed," Nietzsche explained to his publisher (NB 9.82). The verb *Ausdrucken* as translated here by "express," in the sense of expressing a feeling, also means to press out or excrete.

caliber of his readers was based partly on his low estimation of contemporary writers. Few, if any, demonstrated their willingness or ability to write with blood. Their style, or rather lack of style, betrayed their incapacity.

According to Nietzsche, style is the index of the soul. With regard to writing, every sentence, its content, form, and cadence, what is said and what is left unsaid, serve to describe the author. "The wealth of life betrays itself through the wealth of gestures. Everything—the length and shortness of sentences, the punctuation, the choice of words, the pauses, the succession of the argument—must be learned to be felt as gestures" (*NB* 24.8.82). One cannot, however, learn style as a technique. Rather, the gestures of good style follow naturally once the proper feelings and thoughts are cultivated. "To improve one's style," Nietzsche reminded his readers, "means to improve one's thoughts and nothing else!—If you do not straightaway agree with this it will be impossible to convince you of it" (*HH* 342). The impossibility of convincing readers of this point stems from the assumed dearth of shared experiences. Style is that art of life which begets greatness. Those who do not live as an attempt to make of their life a work of art cannot understand why learned technique may not replace passion and spiritual strength. To achieve style one must first have the power to order one's multiple soul, to give it leadership. The closest that technique can come to replacing style is to decorate life and its products. But this is quite the opposite of the truly stylized life, which has no need of decoration because it is itself a work of art. The modern infatuation with technique parallels the modern celebration of works of art without reference to the status of artistic drive that produced them. Both are symptomatic of the modern belief that method should triumph over inspiration. Both are exemplified in the writings of the kind of author Nietzsche vowed never to read: "an author of whom it is apparent that he wanted to produce a book," rather than one "whose thoughts unintentionally became a book" (*HH* 339). Writing, like art in general, should be an imitation of lived experience, its echo become form.[9]

The worth of art rests with its experiential origin. Great art must be the product of the right kind of experience. It should demonstrate the artist's health and strength, that is, his victories over sickness and weakness.[10] Nietzsche offered this advice to writers: "One should speak only when one may not stay silent; and then only of that which one has *overcome*—everything else is chatter, 'literature', lack of breeding. My writings speak *only* of my overcomings" (*HH* 209).[11] He maintained: "Writing ought always to advertise a victory—an overcoming of *oneself* which has to be communicated for the benefit of others" (*HH* 248).

[9] Alexander Nehamas's praiseworthy book *Nietzsche: Life as Literature* (Cambridge, Mass.: Harvard University Press, 1985) offers an original, sympathetic reading of Nietzsche's commitment to life as a philosopher and artist. His treatment of Nietzsche as someone engaged in the creation of himself as a literary figure corresponds well with the understanding of Nietzsche as a self-styled figure of heroic status. However, Nehamas failed to account for the primacy of the lived over the written experience. His claim that Nietzsche "showed that writing is perhaps the most important part of thinking" misses the mark. The error is aggravated by attributing to Nietzsche the further view "that writing is also the most important part of living" (p. 41). The crucial, if indeed not fatal, weakness of Nehamas's thesis is that for Nietzsche literature was not life but life's relic.

[10] Nietzsche was wont to describe the precondition of his writing as illness (e.g., *NB* 13.2.88). Indeed, for most of his life actual writing was accomplished sporadically, during the relatively few pauses in a tortured existence of debilitating headaches, eye and stomach pain, and nausea. His works well bear out Maria Ebner-Eschenbach's aphorism: "No one writes like a god who has not suffered like a dog."

[11] This holds well enough with regard to Nietzsche's public works (including *Thus Spoke Zarathustra*, wherein Zarathustra's failures are the necessary preludes to his victories). Nietzsche's personal letters, however, form a running commentary on his various ills and sufferings. Nonetheless, even here he had the intent of stylizing his writing: "I must develop myself otherwise in my solitude. Namely, however, I must unlearn to write letters in which I show myself suffering. The sufferer is the easy prey for everybody; in relation to a sufferer everyone is wise" (*NB* 12.2.84). This new way of writing letters was never realized. Indeed, Nietzsche ends this very letter with a list of complaints.

Even so, in any great work a "subtler eye" will perceive "that here a sufferer and self-denier speaks as though he were *not* a sufferer and self-denier" (*HH* 212). Modern eyes, however, have little upon which they might exercise their powers. Apart from his own works, Nietzsche lamented, there was "an extraordinary dearth of books in our time that breathe a heroic strength" (*GW* 6:10).

Nietzsche saw himself as a doer of great deeds and a speaker of great words. His deeds, however, were witnessed by no audience, being the silent flights of his spirit. His words, written rather than spoken, served as trophies to mark the victories of inner battles. One suspects that for Nietzsche, as for the ancient Greek warriors, the erection of a trophy was as much an expression of the love of glory as the solemn commemoration of a valiant deed. Regardless, the heroic purveyor of words offers an eclectic self-display. In short, a great writer always wears a mask, and the multiplicity of voices which speak in Nietzsche's books gives evidence of his repertoire of heroic types. For it is the function of art to enable us to see ourselves heroically (*GS* 132–33). Although the hero suffers more from life than the common man, he also rises higher. Good taste and style decree that his words must reflect this elevation without belaboring the depths to which he has descended. Writing must not exhibit, to use Nietzsche's word, the "dyspepsia" of its author. It must not bewail his plight, but account for his prowess.

An accounting of one's victory over decadence is not the victory itself. Indeed, the fact that one must *re*present an experience signifies that it is no longer present. "One does not get over a passion by representing it: rather, it is over *when* one is able to represent it," Nietzsche observed (*WP* 431). The great author looks upon his books as any great artist would look upon his creations—as the mummified forms of his lived experiences, that is, sadly.

Alas, and yet what *are* you, my written and painted thoughts! It is not long ago that you were still so

many-coloured, young and malicious, so full of
thorns and hidden spices you made me sneeze and
laugh—and now? You have already taken off your
novelty and some of you, I fear, are on the point of
becoming truths: they already look so immortal, so
pathetically righteous, so boring! And has it ever been
otherwise? For what things do we write and paint, we
mandarins with Chinese brushes, we immortalizers of
things which *let* themselves be written, what alone are
we capable of painting? Alas, only that which is about
to wither and is beginning to lose its fragrance! (*BGE*
201)

Why then write? In part, one desires to share the fruits of
thought, even if it be in this dried and shriveled state; in
part, to make way for new growth. All thought loses its
fragrance with time. Writing is a purge. The thinker writes
because he can discover no other way of getting rid of his
thoughts (*GS* 146). He sets them in print in order to leave
them behind. For the experience of thinking and its incorporation in life is the true creation; the work of art found
between covers is and should remain excretory.

Any investigation of Nietzsche's aesthetics that does not
come to terms with the theme of life as art remains fundamentally flawed. Art is defined as that which allows us
to make of existence an aesthetic phenomenon. The essence of art is in the perceptions and actions, thoughts and
feelings of the artist, not in his concrete products. The Dionysian artist is he who makes life beautiful because he
perceives it that way. To revitalize an old cliché, beauty is
in the eye of the beholder. If one does not see beauty in
nature and man, the problem is not with life, Nietzsche
insisted, but with one's eyes (*GW* 9:415). Art is the development of the senses such that one sees and hears the
pleasing, of the spirit such that one transforms or hides
the repulsive, of the soul such that its order begets the
graceful.

After this great, indeed immense task of art, what is usually termed art, *that of the work of art*, is merely an *appendage*. A man who feels within himself an excess of such beautifying, concealing and reinterpreting powers will in the end seek to discharge this excess in works of art as well; so, under the right circumstance, will an entire people.—Now, however, we usually start with art where we should end with it, cling hold of it by its tail and believe that the art of the work of art is true art out of which life is to be improved and transformed—fools that we are! (*HH* 255)

Not only the hands, but the mind, eyes, ears, nose, mouth, and skin are the artistic instruments; their object is not merely a page or canvas or stone, but the moments of each day. The goal, Nietzsche declared, is to become the poet of one's own life—including the "smallest, most everyday matters" (*GS* 240). "The most beautiful still appears only in the dark, and sinks, scarcely born, into eternal night—I mean the spectacle of that strength which employs genius *not for works* but for *itself as a work*; that is, for its own constraint, for the purification of its imagination, for the imposition of order and choice upon the influx of tasks and impressions" (*D* 220).[12] Constraint, purification, order, in short, the stylized life: this is what art meant for Nietzsche. Works of art should be monuments to such a life. They are and ought to be beautiful to behold, as relics.

To stylize one's life, to make of one's life a work of art, is not to sculpt oneself into some preconceived form. It is

[12] Nietzsche was still an infant when Henry David Thoreau's *Walden* gave words to the aesthetic life. In the section "What I Live For" one reads: "It is something to be able to paint a particular picture, or to carve a statue, and so to make a few objects beautiful; but it is far more glorious to carve and paint the very atmosphere and medium through which we look, which morally we can do. To affect the quality of the day, that is the highest of arts. Every man is tasked to make his life, even in its details, worthy of the contemplation of his most elevated and critical hour."

not a process of methodically molding oneself to match a foreordained ideal. Such activity would remain entangled in teleology. The ends depreciate the means; having a goal for life makes actual living of secondary, purely utilitarian value. One lives aesthetically not to arrive at an end called the self-as-art, but because only life lived aesthetically yields its fullest realization at every moment. There is no purpose to life as a whole, and Nietzsche did not suggest that we install an artificial one. Kant's description of the activity of art as "purposiveness without purpose"[13] is apposite. Living life artfully is just this purposeless purposiveness. To use one of Nietzsche's favorite metaphors, life as art is like dancing. The disciplined, purposeful movements, stylistically unified, create a work of art. The end, however, is not a completed performance, but the activity itself, the dance in its performance.

Were man a beautiful plaything in the hands of God, Nietzsche wrote, he would find art unnecessary (GW 5:475–76). In the absence of God, the redemption of life rests with man; he must behold himself as a work of art, as his own creation. He must become both the playwright and spectator of the ongoing drama of his will in the world. "As an aesthetic phenomenon existence is still *bearable* for us, and art furnishes us with eyes and hands and above all the good conscience to be *able* to turn ourselves into such a phenomenon. At times we need a rest from ourselves by looking upon, by looking *down* upon, ourselves and, from an artistic distance, laughing *over* ourselves or weeping *over* ourselves" (GS 163–64). Is such a fate a curse or a blessing? Are we really to wish that art were unnecessary? Nietzsche's answer is that only art is capable of transforming the curse of life into a blessing. In art is found the true philosopher's stone that transforms the leaden heaviness of existence into the brilliance and richness of gold.

[13] "Zweckmässigkeit ohne Zweck."

The refuges of perfection Nietzsche sought in art are not to be found in florid settings, but in the terrifying beauty of tragedy and in its bloody victories over fear and suffering. Truth *is* ugly; the good and the beautiful are *not* one. *Hence* the need for art. For art is that which casts truth, goodness, and beauty as a unity. The value of art lies in its transformative power. Art not only veils truth so we may endure life, it stimulates us to live more fully. "Life is worth knowing, says science." But that is not enough. Only art, "the most beautiful seductress," proclaims: "Life is worth living" (*GW* 2:6). The skeptical philosopher has denied that one may assess the value of life—such evaluations possess worth only as symptoms. In affirming life, he declares: I am strong enough, healthy enough to feel life as worth living, to see that truth and good and beauty are one; and this despite my knowing that I speak only of my created fictions.

Nietzsche's works portray the tensioned coexistence of the philosopher-artist. Within his writings art is presented as "the *redemption of the man of knowledge*—of those who see the terrifying and questionable character of existence, who want to see it, the men of tragic knowledge" (*WP* 452). The passion for knowledge leads one to confront Medusa-like truths. Only through aesthetically transfigured reflections can these truths be approached without fatal paralysis. Art, therefore, is what is most needed and most desired by the imprudent philosopher, by him whose life is a dangerous quest for knowledge and an experiment in the making of a masterpiece: "Art as the *redemption of the man of action*—of those who not only see the terrifying and questionable character of existence but live it, want to live it, the tragic-warlike man, the hero" (*WP* 452). In the end, Nietzsche could envision no more heroic a life than one transformed into a work of tragic art.

S E V E N

THE SAINT

Here are hopes; but what will you hear and see of them if
you have not experienced splendor, ardor, and dawns in
your own souls? I can only remind you; more I cannot do.
—*The Gay Science*

"I am convinced that art represents the highest task and
truly metaphysical activity of this life," Nietzsche wrote in
The Birth of Tragedy. A career of skeptical inquiry would
replace this metaphysics with a much more suspicious formulation. Nonetheless, the value of art for life remained
intact. Near the end of his vocation as a thinker Nietzsche
would still proclaim: "Art and nothing but art! It is the
great means of making life possible, the great seduction to
life, the great stimulant of life" (*WP* 452). Nietzsche's esteem for art never served to turn philosophy into its hand-
maid. His understanding of art called for a particular form
of philosophy, just as his understanding of philosophy demanded a particular form of art. This complementarity
also applies to the relationship of the saint to the artist and
the philosopher. A trinity exists within the soul in which
important differences do not dissolve a common identity.

The saint is he who loves, and transforms his world
through love. To love is above all to take pleasure in, affirm, and celebrate the existence of the object of love. It is
the "spiritualization of sensuality" (*TI* 43). The saint's capacity is such that he may transform all that is sensed into
something to be affirmed. Love is the saintly equivalent of

139

philosophical wonder and artistic creativity, allowing a third facet to the philosophical-artistic self. The activity of the saint is best demarcated from that of the artist by distinguishing two kinds of creative drives: the ecstatic passion of the Dionysian man, and the measured force of his Apollonian counterpart. Apollo is the impetus of the aspiration to make of oneself a work of art, the "divine image of the *principium individuationis*" (*BT* 36). He is the god of dreams and illusions, and is capable of turning the curse of existence as an individual into the celebration of beauty. Disciplined form, established boundaries, moderation, and taste are the deity's trademarks. The Apollonian man is the stylist of life par excellence. Dionysus, on the other hand, is the god of intoxication and ecstasy. He is a transgressor of boundaries. His truth is excess. In the Dionysian feast man loses his sense of identity, entering into the mystical frenzy wherein the distinction between creator and created, pain and ecstasy, man and man, disappears: "By the mystical triumphant cry of Dionysus the spell of individuation is broken, and the way lies open to the Mothers of Being, to the innermost heart of things" (*BT* 99–100).[1]

The orgiastic rapture of the Dionysian man is fleeting. In these frenzied moments the perfection of existence is experienced. But as the intoxication wanes, despondency grows. Apollo is therefore called upon to nourish the seeds of yearning planted by Dionysus. Because of the latter's excess and destruction of boundaries, the former's moderation, creativity, and capacity for illusion are

[1] In Greek mythology Dionysus, unlike Apollo, was a god of the people, virtually ignored by Homer, who favored the aristocratic Olympian pantheon. It is ironic but appropriate that Nietzsche's favorite deity is of the commoners, for thus he more closely is identifiable with the saint, described as one whose powers of love allow "a profound feeling of oneness and identity with all living things" (*UM* 161). The Dionysus of Nietzsche's later writings is actually an amalgam of the early figures of Dionysus and Apollo, representing the aristocratic style of the Olympian and the boundary-breaking, mystical frenzy of the *demotikos*.

needed "to keep the animated world of individuation alive" (*BT* 143). Indeed, the Dionysian and Apollonian must coexist in "strict proportion": "Of this foundation of all existence—the Dionysian basic ground of the world— not one whit more may enter the consciousness of the human individual than can be overcome again by this Apollinian power of transfiguration" (*BT* 143).

Tragic drama best illustrates this relation. All tragic heroes, Nietzsche stated, are mere masks of Dionysus: "The hero is the suffering Dionysus of the Mysteries, the god experiencing in himself the agonies of individuation" (*BT* 73). In the tragic drama the Dionysian insight into the terrifying nature of existence is transformed into beauty and form through the potency of Apollonian art. Tragedy is the "symbolization of Dionysian wisdom through Apollinian artifices" (*BT* 131). Its figures are representatives of these contradictory and dynamic forces. The hero is an epigone of Dionysus whose task is to transform his hubristic life into a work of art. To this end he must invoke his patron god of Olympus.

Dionysian ecstasy is the feeling of union with the transcendent, a godhead. An overabundance of power vividly colors perception. One comes to "infuse a transfiguration and fullness into things and poetize about them until they reflect back [one's] fullness and joy in life" (*WP* 421). The Dionysian actor sets the stage for his ensuing Apollonian role, producing the drama of the artist-saint. His moments of Dionysian rapture are a falling in love with existence; his Apollonian creativity is a disciplined attempt aesthetically to rediscover this infatuation.[2] The saint's love is as the food upon which the artist nourishes his creativity: "For it is only in love, only when shaded by the illusion produced by love, that is to say in the unconditional faith in right and perfection, that man is creative" (*UM* 95).

[2] Whitman's words come to mind: "The known universe has one complete lover and that is the greatest poet."

The Apollonian actor reflects a certain piety, a devotion to the task of living a life that is worthy of the glimpses of perfection experienced during the Dionysian moment. This piety is what Nietzsche called a *"sense for the tragic,"* the retention of which was considered the "one hope and one guarantee for the future of humanity." The tragic man bears his existence nobly, stylizing his life by heroic standards; for he has glimpsed the Dionysian redemption and is sustained by his struggle to rediscover it. "The individual must be consecrated to something higher than himself—that is the meaning of tragedy; he must be free of the terrible anxiety which death and time evoke in the individual: for at any moment, in the briefest atom of his life's course, he may encounter something holy that endlessly outweighs all his struggle and all his distress" (*UM* 213). The Dionysian moment is an experience of mystical union that induces "an ecstatic affirmation of the total character of life" (*WP* 539). Being is experienced as *"holy enough* to justify even a monstrous amount of suffering" (*WP* 543). Indeed, the tragic hero throws himself into greater perils and suffering because he has discovered that the fullest affirmation of life occurs as an overcoming of the greatest trials. This transformation of suffering and strife into affirmation, into an experience of the holy, is the foundation of Nietzsche's piety and his self-projection as saint.

Concern for the sacred is not usually attributed to Nietzsche. Yet the higher man is said to have religious roots. The belief in God and immortality must be lost like one's first teeth, Nietzsche wrote, for only then does one become capable of a good bite (*GW* 9:405). The first teeth are necessary if one is to gain sufficient nourishment for early growth. They are designed to be temporary, but provide an indispensable benefit for the child. Religion, to the extent that it may stimulate the sense of the holy, was considered a necessary evil of youth.[3] Nietzsche viewed his

[3] Cf. *TI* 25, wherein Nietzsche questions whether the godless modern

142

own religiousness as he viewed his youthful infatuation with music. Both were necessary stages of his development, allowing the strengthening of soul needed for his eventual free spiritedness. "One must have loved religion and art like mother and nurse—otherwise one cannot grow wise," Nietzsche stipulated: "But one must be able to see beyond them, outgrow them; if one remains under their spell, one does not understand them" (HH 135). Breaking the bonds of religious belief need not and should not entail the extirpation of the drives from which it emerges. Rather, these drives are to be exploited and redirected.

Skepticism is the nemesis of religion. At the same time, the religious instinct stimulates the skeptic's passion. His unwillingness to deceive himself leads to his amorality and atheism. His intellectual integrity is nourished by his sense of higher morality and religiosity. In short, Nietzsche sought to secularize piety, not exterminate it. A section of *The Gay Science* entitled "How We, Too, Are Still Pious" contains Nietzsche's admission: "We godless anti-metaphysicians still take our fire, too, from the flame lit by a faith that is thousands of years old, that Christian faith which was also the faith of Plato, that God is truth, that truth is divine" (GS 283). Religious belief, Nietzsche noted, is never adopted on rational grounds; its rejection, one must concede, is equally nonrational (HH 330). Atheism, as a product of skeptical integrity, is effectively a moral, spiritual, indeed even religious position. The philosopher is submitted as the "further development of the

---

age can breed spirits strong enough to be *active* nihilists, nihilists with teeth: "How much the conscience formerly had to bite on! what good teeth it had!—And today? what's the trouble?—A dentist's question." The religious period of mankind, often thought of as its infancy, had the benefit of spiritual strength and thus created the possibility of spiritual independence. Nietzsche seemed to question whether it might not be better to establish religious training for children, as he himself received, with the design of subsequent apostasy. The alternative would be to pull baby teeth and end up with spiritually malnourished youth.

143

priestly type" (*WP* 89). And Zarathustra acknowledges that his blood is related to that of the priests (*Z* 115).[4] Nietzsche did not escape religiosity, he transformed it. He well deserves the oxymoronic epithet of the most religious of atheists.

The transvaluation of values has its origin in the transformation of religious belief. Nietzsche's "religious, that is to say god-forming, instinct" led him to look with hope to the creation of "new gods" (*WP* 534). The sense of the tragic was promoted in order to raise and purify the flag-

---

[4] In the introduction to his translation of *Thus Spoke Zarathustra* R. J. Hollingdale presented the "Christian parallels to the conceptions which . . . found full expression in *Zarathustra.*" *Amor fati* is likened to divine will; the eternal recurrence to eternal life; the will to power to divine grace; living dangerously to the Christian depreciation of an easy life; the Great Noon-tide to the Second Coming; and finally, the overman to God and the Son of Man as God (*Z* 28–29). Hollingdale's parallels are worthy of reflection, although he misses some obvious ones, for example, the "down-going" of Zarathustra and his subsequent resurrections to the Christian imperative of dying in order to be born again; and golden laughter to divine forgiveness. However, none of these concepts is uniquely Christian. Indeed, they form the basis of religion and mythology in general. There exists a deeper relation between the heroic archetypes that infuse both Nietzsche's work and most, if not all, religious scripture and creed. To argue whether Nietzsche's understanding of Zarathustra's down-going was prompted more by his early belief in the death and resurrection of Christ or by his enamorment with the myth of Dionysus's dismemberment and subsequent revivification is to miss the more important point: the archetypes for these essentially mythological events would appear to be part of what Carl Jung has called man's "collective unconscious." The motifs of the hero, the wise old man, the cave, the shadow, the child, and the trickster or fool, for example, all repetitively employed by Nietzsche, are collective patterns found in almost all religious traditions and mythologies. Nietzsche exploited these archetypes within a philosophical corpus. (Cf. Carl Jung, *Collected Works*, trans. R.F.C. Hull [Princeton: Princeton University Press, 1968] esp. vol. 5, 7, 9, 17, and 18; and his *Nietzsche's Zarathustra*, 2 vols. [Princeton: Princeton University Press, 1988]. See also four other worthwhile books on this theme: Joseph Campbell, *The Hero with a Thousand Faces* [Princeton: Princeton University Press, 1968]; Lord Raglan, *The Hero: A Study in Tradition, Myth, and Drama* [New York: Oxford University Press, 1937]; Otto Rank, *The Myth of the Birth of the Hero: A Psychological Interpretation of Mythology*, trans. F. Robbins and Smith Ely Jelliffe [New York: Journal of Nervous and Mental Disease Publishing Company, 1914]; and Jan de Vries, *Heroic Song and Heroic Legend* [New York: Arno Press, 1978].)

ging religious passions of modern man. The mystical glimpse of the perfected world which originates in religious life is not to be dispensed with: it is to yield a new faith. "But such a faith is the highest of all possible faiths," Nietzsche proclaimed, "I have baptized it with the name *Dionysus*" (*TI* 103). Nietzsche saw himself as the modern founder and propagator of this worthiest creed. Unlike its predecessors, most notably its Christian one, the Dionysian faith was to be exclusive. It was not for humanity as a whole, but only for its greatest exemplars, those heroic spirits who were strong enough to affirm life in its entirety, despite the absence of gods and transcendent meaning.[5]

The Dionysian faith is born out of the ashes of its forebears. Atheism is the culmination of religious ideals, particularly the ideal of truth. "Unconditional honest atheism (and *its* is the only air we breathe, we more spiritual men of this age!) is therefore not the antithesis of that ideal, as it appears to be; it is rather only one of the latest phases of its evolution, one of its terminal forms and inner consequences—it is the awe-inspiring *catastrophe* of two thousand years of training in truthfulness that finally forbids itself the *lie involved in belief in God*" (*GM* 160). Unlike the old religious faith, atheism supplies its will to truth with the imperative of artistic creation. Man must forge himself along with his truths. Such an imperative was impossible for the religious man who honored his celestial creator. For the "guilty indebtedness" man feels toward his divine origin is also the cause of his impotence. Liberation from theism and teleology brings a *"second innocence"* and the freedom to create one's own ends (*GM* 91).

The death of God proclaimed as a fact in *The Gay Science*

[5] Lou Andreas-Salomé's evaluation of Nietzsche's attempts to win her and Paul Rée over as his initial converts is apposite: "We experience it still, that he appeared as the proclaimer of a new religion, and that it would be such that recruits heroes as its disciples" (Gilman, *Begegnungen mit Nietzsche*, p. 423).

was voiced as a hope a decade earlier: "Either we will die from this religion, or religion from us. I believe in the original German expression: all gods must die" (GW 3:259). And a decade before that, at age seventeen, Nietzsche had already expressed his antipathy for the other-worldly ideals that kept man from reaching his this-worldly potential. "That God became man only indicates that man should not search for his blissfulness in infinity, but establish his heaven on earth; the delusion of an extraterrestrial world had brought man's spirituality to a false position regarding the earthly world: it was the product of the childhood of peoples. . . . Under severe doubts and struggles will mankind become manly: it will recognize in itself 'the beginning, the middle, and the end of religion' " (NB 27.4.62). The elevation of man is just this project of establishing heaven on earth. Nietzsche's cultural struggle against decadent religion, therefore, had its parallel in his religious struggle against decadent culture. The creation of higher terrestrial men could take place only within a culture freed from the disabling belief in other worlds. In turn, only a culture rich in spiritual strength could produce such worldly giants. The nonreligious culture that has consequently become nonspiritual has thrown out the baby with the bath water. Modern culture is decadent because it has proved incapable of sublimating religious passions. Consequently, these passions have atrophied.[6] The forecast that "perhaps man will rise ever higher as soon as he ceases to *flow out* into a god" (GS 230) is voiced only as a possibility. Its realization depends on whether (and how) man rechannels his religiosity.

The utilization of religious passions in the service of the Dionysian faith is the force behind Nietzsche's own ascetic tendencies. The ascetic knows the powers of the passions

[6] This is the theme of the *First Untimely Meditation* and the essence of Nietzsche's polemic against David Strauss, a man characterized as having "a narrow, dried-up soul" (UM 45). "Cultural philistinism," Nietzsche's epithet for the Straussian vision of a progressive, atheistic culture, captures well the spiritlessness of the modern alternative to religious life.

and instincts. Indeed, he makes their investigation, development, and sublimation his life's work. His task is the accumulation, conservation, and channeled release of this energy. Nietzsche acknowledged this project as his own, calling himself one of the "last of the Stoics," who was "entwined in an austere shirt of duty" (*BGE* 137). Even after announcing his preference for a *gay* science, Nietzsche nonetheless maintained that all of his achievements had fallen under the rubric of asceticism. It constituted an "indispensable means of education and ennobling" and the only adequate means to develop the will (*NB* 31.12.82; *BGE* 68; *WP* 484). The artist and the philosopher are typically portrayed as anchorites whose sensual self-denial allows greater creativity and spiritualization. Ascetic ideals are acknowledged to have been intrinsic to "all the great, fruitful, inventive spirits," constituting "the most appropriate and natural conditions of their *best* existence, their *fairest* fruitfulness" (*GM* 108).

Nietzsche wrote of the saint in heroic terms. The disciplined will, self-denial, and strong passions of the hero are those ascetic qualities needed to achieve greatness and retain the sense of the holy in life. Sensual dissipation is the morbid alternative.

> Alas, I have known noble men who lost their highest hope. And henceforth they slandered all high hopes.
>
> Henceforth they lived imprudently in brief pleasures, and they had hardly an aim beyond the day.
>
> "Spirit is also a sensual pleasure"—thus they spoke. Then the wings of their spirit broke: now it creeps around and it makes dirty what it feeds on.
>
> Once they thought of becoming heroes: now they are sensualists. The hero is to them an affliction and a terror.
>
> But, by my love and hope I entreat you: do not reject the hero in your soul! Keep holy your highest hope! (Z 71)

The saint sublimates his sensuality to the point where willing itself becomes the highest pleasure. Of course, the dynamic also works in reverse. Those seduced by "brief pleasures" and the distractions of everyday life lose the capacity to derive pleasure from willing, finding its discipline distasteful. Nietzsche was aware of the subtle "gymnastic" needed to keep the will strong enough to take joy in its own exercise. "A lack of self-mastery in small things brings about a crumbling of the capacity for it in great ones. Every day is ill employed, and a danger for the next day, in which one has not denied oneself some small thing at least once: this gymnastic is indispensable if one wants to preserve in oneself the joy of being one's own master" (*HH* 386–87). Ascetic self-denial begets a spiritualized hedonism. However, its discipline is not practiced as a purely utilitarian means to an end, namely, some form of higher pleasure. It is a means and end combined. The experience of self-overcoming, of will exercising itself, is a self-fulfilling activity.

Like anything else, asceticism has its decadent form. Religious asceticism, and in particular its Christian variant, was the misdirected reaction to suffering. Instead of being accepted in all its meaninglessness, suffering was bestowed with the meaning of punishment for sins committed. The Christian ascetic was guilt-ridden: he believed that he deserved to suffer. Indeed, he deserved more suffering than the unaided world could arrange. The more suffering, the more meaning, and the greater his sense of power. Hence the religious ascetic's masochistic activity.

This assumption of guilt was tantamount to a denial of the innocence of life. There was need of an other-worldly realm in which the ledger of guilt atoned for would be kept. The object was to escape the world of suffering by denying it anything but a utilitarian function: life was merely a time for the expiation of sins, a painful prelude to the joys of the afterlife. Ironically, this yearning to escape the human condition brought about the greatest de-

velopment of man's urge to live. The desire to be beyond
this life could be sated only by an increasingly powerful
will over life and self. In turn, the development of a strong
will yielded its own pleasures. The ascetic appears as a
decadent whose denial of life becomes a life-affirming
drive in spite of itself.

> The ascetic priest is the incarnate desire to be differ-
> ent, to be in a different place, and indeed this desire
> at its greatest extreme, its distinctive fervor and pas-
> sion; but precisely this power of his desire is the chain
> that holds him captive so that he becomes a tool for
> the creation of more favorable conditions for being
> here and being man. . . . this ascetic priest, this ap-
> parent enemy of life, this *denier*—precisely he is
> among the greatest *conserving* and yes-creating forces
> of life . . . even when he *wounds* himself, this master
> of destruction, of self-destruction—the very wound it-
> self afterward compels him *to live*. (GM 120–21)

Nietzsche's own brand of asceticism is, as it were, the purified form of this priestly variety. All other-worldly aspirations and attendant feelings of guilt have been purged.
What remains is an austere discipline that has as its aim
the greatest affirmation of life. This is the Nietzschean
project. The friction between Dionysus and the Crucified,
Nietzsche asserted, exposed the core of his thought (*EH*
335).

Nietzsche's writings on love must be understood within
the context of the ascetic sublimation of the senses. The
purpose of self-denial should be the increased capacity for
affirmation. The ascetic does not feed on the brief pleasures of the senses because he wants them to grow more
powerful. Similarly, the true lover does not indulge the beloved but strives to promote his growth. For Nietzsche,
the greatest love is always that which has as its object the
ideal that exists within the beloved. "To love men *for the
sake of God*—that has been the noblest and most remote

feeling attained to among men up till now," he wrote (*BGE* 67). With the death of God other imperatives and possibilities arise. Human love can be raised to a new level of nobility: loving man for the sake of that which is most noble in man. Friendship, the relation between two people in which the craving for mutual possession gives way to "a *shared* higher thirst for an ideal above them" (*GS* 89), was therefore considered the highest form of love.

Because love is effectively a yearning and struggling for perfection, it is inseparable from contempt, that is, the distaste for the exhibition and leadership of the lower self. This contempt, Zarathustra explains, is not like its priestly kind: the "gnawing of a worm" as guilt eats away at self-esteem. It is, rather, "the great, the loving contempt which loves most where it despises most" (*Z* 239). The more the object of love approaches its ideal, the greater the enmity for that which inhibits its complete realization. For each kilo of love, Nietzsche recommended, one ought to add a grain of contempt (*GW* 20:132). This applies to self-love as well as love of others. "He who can *wholly, purely love* himself," Nietzsche maintained, "would be he who at the same time despised himself" (*GW* 7:393). Self-love must elevate. The drive for perfection employs contempt of baser elements as a means to this end, much as an ascetic employs disdain and denial of his base instincts so as to develop his higher instincts.[7]

Self-contempt, however, is not tantamount to a desire to eradicate decadent tendencies. One wishes only to overcome them, realizing that the dynamics of ascending and declining drives define life. The self must be affirmed as a whole. Self-love must counteract the gnawing guilt known to the religious man. He who is godless must be his own pardoner. Self-forgiveness becomes the joyful acceptance of one's decadence as an opportunity for growth. It is part

[7] Zarathustra asserts that the most contemptible man is he who can no longer despise himself (*Z* 46). In the same vein, George Santayana remarked that perhaps man's only dignity is that he may despise himself.

of a wise politics of the soul: "Love yourselves as an act of clemency—then you will no longer have any need of your god, and the whole drama of Fall and Redemption will be played out to the end in you yourselves!" (D 48). One must love oneself, the plurality one is, enough to want to see the drama of life played out. Nietzsche attempted to beat the priestly ascetic at his own game by accusing him of taking the easy road. The "supreme heroic feat of morality" is not the straightforward extirpation of the passions and the consequent reduction of the multiple soul to a tyranny. The ongoing battle of a soul rich in contradictions demands "a lot more spirit and reflection" (HH 75). True self-love "presupposes an unblendable duality (or multiplicity) in one person" (HH 230). It is within the multiple soul that the interplay of self-love and self-contempt occurs. Its political dynamic, life as struggle, must always be affirmed.

Love of others follows the same formula as love of self. Plurality is to be cultivated and embraced: "What is love but an understanding and rejoicing at the fact that another lives, feels and acts in a way different from and opposite to ours? If love is to bridge these antitheses through joy it may not deny or seek to abolish them" (HH 229–30). The ideals the lover stimulates his beloved to realize are not the lover's but the beloved's. Indeed, they are unique to the beloved. Love, in short, is a force that elicits another's individuality.[8]

To love is to idealize, to desire the birth of that which rests in a state of pregnancy. It marks an active, participatory relationship. Love become decadent is pity. The sharing of ideals is replaced by the sharing of suffering. The

---

[8] One has, of course, no guarantee that the ideals we perceive in others actually exist. Again, skepticism makes the situation problematic. The individual remains a world unto itself. One never really loves others but only one's idealized image of them: "When we love we create men in the image of *our* God" (GW 14:38). The question Nietzsche posed to himself, *"What do you love in others?"* was answered: "My hopes" (GS 220).

capacity of love for the raising of man is replaced by a passive state of commiseration. "All great love is above pity," Zarathustra says, "for it wants—to create what is loved!" (Z 114). Creators, as Zarathustra also reminds us, must be hard. Nietzsche's conception of love is far from romantic. The lover must be severe, for the realization of ideals is not without ordeal. Love is above pity because it delights in the overcoming of suffering and therefore promotes the engagement in struggle rather than its avoidance. If anything, love is cruel.

Nietzsche's infamous admonitions to cruelty are not justifications of the feelingless affliction of pain for its own sake. Cruelty is one of the forms love takes in the struggle to realize ideals. It is actually a form of compassion that *uses* suffering as a means to the elevation of man: "The cruelty of the feelingless is the contrary of pity; the cruelty of those full with feeling is the higher potency of pity" (GW 14:54). The kind of compassion Nietzsche advocated was that which hid under a hard shell. In other words, it is a love that is strong enough to suffer with someone and yet not succumb to the temptation to alleviate the suffering. For agony is known to serve growth. Nietzsche did not desire the extirpation of fellow-feeling, but the vanquishing of its decadent form. To be without pity or compassion "means to be sick in spirit and love. But one ought to have much spirit to be *permitted* to be compassionate" (GW 14:54). Love must be strong enough to carry out its harsh task in the transformation of suffering, for only then will its compassion not be an aid and abetment to cowardice and stagnation.

Were pity unsuppressed, it would disable the saint (and the philosopher) from propagating his thought. His path is one of transformed suffering. The prophet always requires hardness and a sort of cruelty to deliver his message. His teachings are known to be the catalyst of strife. When Nietzsche spoke approvingly of cruelty, he was reflecting on the only cruelty he himself had demonstrated:

that involved in disturbing the souls of his readers and friends: "Every profound thinker is more afraid of being understood than of being misunderstood. The latter may perhaps wound his vanity; but the former will wound his heart, his sympathy, which says always: 'alas, why do *you* want to have as hard a time of it as I had?' " (*BGE* 197).[9] Pity is held to be the greatest danger. The threat of falling prey to its debilitating forces remains ever present. Zarathustra first quits his solitude for the love of mankind. His love, however, becomes a near-fatal pity for the lower man, who does not, and cannot, share Zarathustra's aspirations and flights of spirit. After much struggle and learning, a wiser Zarathustra overcomes this pity. But another form of it awaits him as his final test, his "ultimate sin." After overcoming his pity for those who could not know the "pleasures of the spirit," he must confront his pity for those who do, those higher men whose spiritual pleasures are necessarily the product of a long and deep suffering.[10]

Nietzsche condemned pity as the most seductive allurement to the depreciation of life. Life *is* suffering. To the

---

[9] In 1884 Nietzsche speculated in a letter: "It is possible that I will be a destiny, the destiny for all men to come—and consequently it is very possible that one day I will become dumb, out of love of man" (*NB* 3.84). Within five years of writing this, Nietzsche slipped into insanity, marking the beginning of more than a decade of muteness before he died.

[10] The final victory over pity of the protagonist of *Thus Spoke Zarathustra*, Nietzsche's allegorical autobiography, would appear not to have been granted to its author. His one-time acolyte, Paul Lanzky, described Nietzsche's own suffering from pity: "Become hard! says his Zarathustra, the ideal after which he strived, before which he kneeled, as he said to me; but he himself could not be hard, or only appeared so in his writings. . . . And he, the strong spirit who thought little of pity, which for him only meant weakness, suffered too much from this weakness" (Gilman, *Begegnungen mit Nietzsche*, p. 509).Of this weakness Nietzsche admitted: "I only need to expose myself to the sight of some genuine distress and I am lost" (*GS* 270). As is well known, his lapse into insanity in the winter of 1888–1889 was marked by a breakdown in the streets of Turin, where upon seeing a mare being severely beaten he embraced it and cried. This is not to suggest that pity (for an animal) proved to be Nietzsche's ultimate undoing, but the symbolism is too striking to be discounted.

extent that pity reflects a desire that things were otherwise, that suffering were not necessary, it serves to de-
value life: "Life is denied, made *more worthy of denial* by
pity—pity is *practical* nihilism" (*TI* 118). The only means to
affirm life as a whole is to affirm the suffering it entails,
which is to say, to transform it into growth. Nietzsche's
cruel man is not without feeling; if he were, pity would
not present a danger, let alone the greatest danger. Not a
lack of compassion but an awareness of its hazards prevents him from commiserating with his neighbors. The
likely result of vicariously bearing suffering is a greater
propensity to resentment, which benefits neither oneself
nor one's fellow man.

> If we let ourselves be made gloomy by the lamenta-
> tion and suffering of other mortals and cover our own
> sky with clouds, who is it who will have to bear the
> consequences of this gloom? These other mortals, of
> course, and in addition to the burdens they bear al-
> ready. We can offer them neither *aid* nor *comfort* if we
> want to be the echo of their lamentation, or even if we
> are merely always giving ear to it—unless, that is, we
> had acquired the art of the Olympians and henceforth
> *edified* ourselves by the misfortunes of mankind in-
> stead of being made unhappy by them.[11] (*D* 91)

This edification is chiefly a learning of how one may overcome suffering without slandering life in the process.

Nietzsche held love to be the greatest of life's affirmative
forces. But it is always accompanied by the greatest dangers, its decadent forms. On one side is pity, the perver-
sion of love into self-indulgent commiseration. On the
other side is infatuation, the self-delusory projection of

---

[11] The Olympic gods did not create man, nor feel much responsibility
for his sufferings. In Homeric times they were by and large an amoral lot.
The theater of mankind, especially its wars, served the purpose of their
entertainment, and, if one may use the word quite freely, of their edification.

ideals as realized, rather than in need of realization. Pity debilitates to the point where one is without the will to transform life. Infatuation deludes to the point where one sees no need of transformation. Love is the passion for perfection. For it to escape decadence it must remain skeptical, even contemptuous, of its necessarily imperfect object: "There is a slavish love that submits and gives itself, that idealizes, and deceives itself—there is a divine love that despises and loves, and reshapes and elevates the beloved" (WP 506). The grain of contempt added to every kilo of love is an inoculation against infatuation and its delusions. True love does not idealize, but strives to promote the birth of ideals. The lover is a midwife. Love that degenerates into infatuation misinterprets the state of pregnancy, bringing about not the actualization of a potential but its miscarriage. Love that degenerates into pity sees only the sufferings of pregnancy while remaining blind to its hidden wonders.

The saint is the greatest of aestheticians.[12] Through love he creates a world worthy of affirmation. As with the artist, his feat is half transformation, half illusion. It is, as it were, a partnership of actuality and aspiration: the *power* to transform being is produced by the *feeling of power* one receives through the illusion of a perfected world. Better said, the struggle for perfection produces power, and the illusory glimpse of perfection allowed us in art and love is the necessary stimulant to struggle: "Love is the state in which man sees things most of all as they are *not*. The illusion-creating force is there at its height, likewise the sweetening and *transforming* force" (A 133). Nietzsche further observed: "One lies well when one loves, about oneself and to oneself: one seems to oneself transfigured, stronger, richer, more perfect, one *is* more perfect" (WP 426). The illusion of growing power is necessary for one

---

[12] Even in his decadent form, the saint, as "homines religiosi," is considered to constitute the "*highest* rank" of artists (BGE 67).

who wishes to grow more powerful. In the realm of love, the line between illusion and reality is not thin: it simply does not exist. One must transgress the borders of reality during the subtle and intricate gymnastics of realizing ideals and transforming potential into actuality.

The culmination of love's transforming glance is manifest in the mystic vision. Herein not a single person or a particular state of affairs is the object of love—existence as a whole is embraced. The musical raptures of the young Nietzsche were as the premonition of his subsequent ecstasies of wonder. His letter to Heinrich Koselitz (alias Peter Gast) from his retreat in Sils Maria speaks of his flight of spirit: "The intensity of my feelings make me shudder and laugh—already a few times I could not leave the room for the laughable reason that my eyes were inflamed—what from? I had cried too much the day before each time on my walks, and indeed not sentimental tears, but tears of jubilation; wherein I sang and talked nonsense, filled from a new glimpse that I have in advance of all men" (*NB* 14.8.81). In *Ecce Homo* Nietzsche wrote of this sort of mystical experience as "inspiration": "If one had the slightest residue of superstition left in one's system, one could hardly reject altogether the idea that one is merely incarnation, merely mouthpiece, merely a medium of overpowering forces. The concept of revelation—in the sense that suddenly, with indescribable certainty and subtlety, something becomes *visible*, audible, something that shakes one to the last depths and throws one down—that merely describes the facts" (*EH* 300). The experience of the ecstatic became a crucial component of Nietzsche's thought. Its importance is primarily twofold. Mystical experience was considered a mark of higher man and an intrinsic feature of his development. It was also, nonetheless, the object of Nietzsche's most virulent attacks. This sort of ambivalence is endemic to his thought. The intensity of the rapturous state and its capacity to elevate the spirit necessitated the most severe suspicion lest one fall victim to a religious residue. The saint whose mysticism is not matched with skepticism remains a holy fool, duped by his own spiritual infatuation. Such lack of skeptical probity is particularly regrettable because the capacity for ecstatic experience bears witness to the pedigree of the soul.

The criticism of ecstatic experience, and more specifically of its mystical-religious interpretation, first appeared in *Human, All Too Human* and continued, in a somewhat abated form, throughout Nietzsche's later works.[13] The position, once again, is essentially skeptical. The intensity of one's feelings and thoughts is no proof of their validity. Indeed, the more ecstatic one is, the more likely one is fashioning an imaginary world from which truth is absent. Mystic visions and rapture, however strongly they suggest the existence of some deity of whom one has become the mouthpiece, remain a testimony only to the individual's spiritual excitement. Nietzsche remarked: "Mystical explanations are considered deep. The truth is that they are not even superficial" (*GS* 182). This is because they are not explanations at all. The mystic believes his elevated state to be the effect of divine inspiration. In fact, his belief in deities is the effect of his elevated state. This is the most vivid demonstration of the "psychology of error" manifested in all religious activity: "In every single case cause is mistaken for effect; or the effect of what is *believed* true is mistaken for the truth; or a state of consciousness is mistaken for the causation of this state" (*TI* 53). In all likelihood, the cause of the ecstatic state is physiological, best described as a derangement: "All the visions, terrors, states of exhaustion and rapture experienced by the saint are familiar pathological conditions which, on the basis of rooted religious and psychological errors, he only *interprets* quite differently, that is to say not as illnesses" (*HH* 68). The vi-

---

[13] Nietzsche described *Human, All Too Human* as an attempt to freeze to death the ideal of "the saint" (*EH* 284).

sionary, in brief, is the victim of "a profound mental disturbance" (*D* 39).

The intensity of his experience dissuades the ecstatic from imputing its cause to himself. Unfamiliar with the feeling of power it lends, he is wont to attribute his condition to divine origins (*WP* 86). Thus he demonstrates a lack of critical thinking. The unwillingness to make his inner states "a matter of conscience for knowledge" is common to all mystics, including all founders of religion (*GS* 253). Compared with the philosopher who makes his experiences a subject of study and experiment, the "holy epileptics and seers of visions" are "moral cretins" without "integrity in self-criticism" (*WP* 103). Self-criticism of this genre is in no way debasing. Quite the opposite is true. Rather than denigrating himself to the status of a tool in the hands of a deity, the skeptic-ecstatic comes to view his experiences as the products of his own heightened spiritual powers. In a section of *The Gay Science* entitled "Personal Providence," Nietzsche demonstrated the proper interpretation of an experience not uncommon to the saint.

> There is a certain high point in life: once we have reached that, we are, for all our freedom, once more in the greatest danger of spiritual unfreedom, and no matter how much we have faced up to the beautiful chaos of existence and denied it all providential reason and goodness, we still have to pass our hardest test. For it is only now that the idea of personal providence confronts us with the most penetrating force, and the best advocate, the evidence of our eyes, speaks for it—now we can see how palpably always everything that happens to us turns out for the best. Every day and every hour, life seems to have no other wish than to prove this proposition again and again. Whatever it is, bad weather or good, the loss of a friend, sickness, slander, the failure of some letter to arrive, the spraining of an ankle, a glance into a shop,

THE SAINT

a counter-argument, the opening of a book, a dream, a fraud—either immediately or very soon after it proves to be something that "must not be missing"; it has a profound significance and use precisely for *us*. Is there any more dangerous seduction that might tempt one to renounce one's faith in the gods of Epicurus who have no care and are unknown . . . ? Well I think that in spite of all this we should leave the gods in peace as well as the genii who are ready to serve us, and rest content with the supposition that our own practical and theoretical skill in interpreting and arranging events has now reached its high point.[14] (*GS* 223–24)

The problem with such higher feelings is that they are invariably held to demonstrate the existence of higher worlds rather than the untapped potentials of man in this world: "It is a sad fact, but for the moment the man of science has to be suspicious of *all higher feelings*, so greatly are they nourished by delusion and nonsense. It is not that they are thus in themselves, or must always remain thus: but of all the gradual *purifications* awaiting mankind, the purification of the higher feelings will certainly be one of the most gradual" (*D* 25). Experience of a mystical ecstasy is intrinsic to the higher soul. The question is, how

[14] By late 1888 Nietzsche proved increasingly incapable of maintaining a skeptical distance from his own feelings of aggrandizement and personal providence. Not his powers of interpretation but reality itself was seen to develop to the point where the world revolved around this relatively obscure, very ill, and impoverished former university professor. A few excerpts from his frenzied letters of December 1888 reveal his threatening solipsism: "Now I have the absolute conviction that everything has turned out for the best, from the beginning on,—Everything is one, and wants one" (*NB* 22.12.88); "There are, moreover, no more accidents: when I think of someone a letter from him courteously comes to the door" (*NB* Christmas 88); "With each glance I am treated like a prince,—there is an extreme distinction in the way a door is opened for me, a meal set in front of me. Every face transforms when I step into a large store" (*NB* 29.12.88). Within weeks of writing these letters Nietzsche became hopelessly insane.

should these experiences be treated? Nietzsche answered that one must "transcend intoxication," not deny its place and use (*GS* 121). With proper skeptical inoculation, such "sublime agitation" becomes a means to growth. Alternatively, it leads to delusory beliefs in providential deities, to other-worldly hopes, and to the concomitant denigration of earthly life. As with any drug, Nietzsche wrote, the mystical experience may be used as a means of heightening awareness of man's spiritual possibilities, or debilitating his mental faculties: "Their misuse has precisely the consequences as the misuse of any other opiate—neurasthenia" (*WP* 249).[15]

For all its dangers and abuses, the ecstatic experience has an indispensable function. It allows that glimpse of perfection that provides the impetus for the saint's mission of love. Moreover, it saves the philosopher from perishing when the Apollonian artifice proves insufficient. The profundity of the wound from his battle with truth necessitates an equally profound and healing ecstasy. Only the Dionysian moment in its excessive, frenzied jubilation provides the needed counterweight to nihilism. "I have presented such terrible images of knowledge that any 'Epicurean delight' is out of the question," Nietzsche explained: "Only Dionysian joy is sufficient" (*WP* 531). To experience a Dionysian joy, however, is to be burdened with an inextinguishable desire to reexperience it, to explore its manifold possibilities. He whose thought has even once overstepped the bridge of mysticism, Nietzsche

---

[15] Nietzsche realized how tempting the narcotic pleasures of mystical experience could be, as well as how the integrity of the skeptic brings its share of suffering. Still burdened with pity, Zarathustra prefers to leave the forest hermit as the holy fool he is, singing, weeping, laughing, and muttering his praises to God. Unwilling to deny him his delusory pleasures, Zarathustra takes his leave, only later questioning how the saint could remain ignorant of the death of God. The juvenile laughter at their parting reflects the mystic's immaturity—he is not strong enough to examine critically his own experiences or bear the suffering that would ensue.

observed, remains forever stigmatized by his experience (*GW* 14:22). The vigor and severity of Nietzsche's quest testified to his crossing of this bridge.

There is no substitute for the mystical experience itself. Only it can provide the stimulus for a passionate devotion to spiritual development in a world without meaning. One may indeed intellectually theorize about the requirements for a full affirmation of life, but this is no closer to the ecstatic experience of life-affirmation than reflecting on fear or courage is actual fear or courage. Contemplation is not enough; nor can communication of someone else's experience replace the real thing. Indeed, such communication is impossible: "To understand one another it is not sufficient to employ the same words; we have also to employ the same words to designate the same species of inner experiences, we must ultimately have our experience *in common*" (*BGE* 186).

In this light, Nietzsche appropriately might be labeled a worldly mystic; for he acknowledged spiritual insight, not the faculty of reason, as the sole conveyor of the highest truths. Like his mentor, Heraclitus, Nietzsche held that truth is grasped in "rapture" through "intuitions" rather than via "the rope ladder of logic" (*PTG* 69). "We no longer have a sufficiently high estimate of ourselves when we communicate. Our true experiences are not garrulous," he insisted (*TI* 82). Nietzsche's mysticism proves to be the highest potency of his individualism. For truth remains fundamentally personal and essentially incommunicable. In short, "whatever is perfect suffers no witnesses" (*NCW* 665).

Only during the celebrated dawns in the soul is existence indubitably known to be redeemed and justified. Nietzsche saw his writings as the necessarily inadequate attempt to communicate the joy and danger, meanings and misinterpretations of this experience. The inadequacy of the attempt was due in large part to the depravity of his age. Nietzsche was doubtful that any of his contemporaries had shared his spiritual flights. He speculated wildly that one would have to go back thousands of years to find the level of inspiration known to himself (*EH* 301). Consequently he expected little justice from his spiritually crippled readership. To understand "six sentences" of *Zarathustra*, Nietzsche averred, "that is, to have really experienced them—would raise one to a higher level of existence than 'modern' men could attain" (*EH* 259). He identified himself as a voice in the wilderness. His teaching was predictably not heeded, for it was not understood. There simply were no ears to hear, no "fish" to be caught by his "fish hooks" (*EH* 310).

The fish Nietzsche hoped to catch were the great spirits of the age (or as he speculated, of the ages to come, he being a "posthumously born" writer). How, then, was the status of these spirits to be established? Just as a society or culture is evaluated according to its greatest exemplars, its mountain peaks rather than its valleys, so life itself is evaluated according to its experiential heights. "Life consists of rare individual moments of the highest significance and countless intervals in which at best the phantoms of those moments hover about us . . . many people never experience these moments at all but are themselves intervals and pauses in the symphony of real life" (*HH* 189). The great man is he who knows the raptures of the soul, the highest flights of spirit.[16] More precisely, rank is determined not so much by the altitude such a spiritual flier may attain as by the frequency and duration of his flights: "It is not the strength but the duration of exalted sensations which makes exalted men" (*BGE* 73). After his disappointment with Wagner, Nietzsche was especially chary of the intoxicating and delusory capacities of art and religion. That one could soar in rapture testified to the pedigree of the

[16] By extension, this is also the basis of the rank of nations: "To have many great inner experiences and to look down on and beyond them with the eye of the spirit—this is what constitutes the men of culture who determine the *rank* of their nation" (*D* 118).

soul, but it said nothing of the probity of the intellect. The religious saint knows spiritual rapture. His lack of skeptical integrity, however, leads him to depreciate the value of these glorious moments in the symphony of life to the status of mere preludes to an other-worldly composition. The point is to be a pious skeptic, not a holy fool. Nietzsche's aim was theoretically and practically to incorporate the philosopher, artist, and saint into one person. Their existence was to be symbiotic and simultaneous: saintly moments of ecstasy must be integrated with philosophical skepticism and artistic creativity. The goal is a tensioned inner plurality rather than a manic-depressive roller-coaster ride of the soul. The proof of such integration would be an *enduring* and *repeated* state of spiritual elevation.

It seems to me most people simply do not believe in elevated moods, unless they last for moments only or at most a quarter of an hour—except for those few who know at firsthand the longer duration of elevated feelings. But to be a human being with one elevated feeling—to be a single great mood incarnate—that has hitherto been a mere dream and a delightful possibility; as yet history does not offer us any certain examples. Nevertheless history might one day give birth to such people, too—once a great many favorable preconditions have been created and determined that even the dice throws of the luckiest chance could not bring together today. What has so far entered our souls only now and then as an exception that made us shudder, might perhaps be the usual state for these future souls: a perpetual movement between high and low, the feeling of high and low, a continual ascent as on stairs and at the same time a sense of resting on clouds. (*GS* 231)

The saintly rapture of the Dionysian moment, the skeptical integrity of philosophical insight, the Apollonian attempt to turn the curse of individuation into a blessed work of art—all this, Nietzsche proclaimed, would combine in the joyful politics of the heroic soul.

The great men Nietzsche longed to see were the future adherents of the Dionysian faith, a heroic breed whose perpetual inner struggle would be their greatest source of power. As "the last disciple and initiate of the god Dionysus" Nietzsche wished to give "a little taste of this philosophy" to his contemporaries (*BGE* 200). But their spiritual sleep made them deaf to the prophet's call. Nietzsche felt the anguish of this isolation, crying his message louder and ever more desperately holding on to the hope that his scripture would someday aid in the birth and nurture of a new generation of this-worldly saints.

EIGHT

THE EDUCATOR AND THE
SOLITARY

Great Star! What would your happiness be, if you had not
those for whom you shine!
—*Thus Spoke Zarathustra*

The philosopher, artist, and saint may be thought of as the
incarnations of the Nietzschean hero. The solitary and the
educator supply his personae. The knower, the creator,
and the lover are defined by the quite specific objects of
their activity. The philosopher is not merely in search of
knowledge, but of wisdom. Wisdom is arrived at through
the understanding of the limitations of knowledge and the
active, self-critical living of this understanding. The
philosopher's skeptical exercises prepare him for the experience of wonder. The artist is no mere fabricator of art.
His task is the creation of life-affirmative art, his works being tributes paid to life. As his greatest tribute he transforms his life into an aesthetic phenomenon. The saint is
not infatuated with his fellow man; nor does he pity him.
His love is a rapture at the pregnancy of being and an active force in the realization of ideals. The solitary and the
educator, on the other hand, are not so much defined by
what they seek or create. They are rather the means, contrary yet interactive, by which the philosopher, artist, and
saint carry out their tasks. The solitary and the educator
are the two ways of being in the world for one who simultaneously incarnates the philosopher, artist, and saint.

These two modes of life are personified in Zarathustra. His philosophical disposition, poetic impulse, and Dionysian fervor find their expression in his words and actions as an educator and his thoughts and passions as a solitary. He is the self-proclaimed "teacher of the overman," whose instruction begins after ten years of hermitage. His cup of wisdom is filled to overflowing in his isolation. Then, like the solitary sun among the planets, Zarathustra rises to seek out students with whom he may share himself. But if his solitude leaves him weary of his wisdom, so too does his "down-going" leave him weary of man. His activities as an educator are repeatedly interrupted by his rehabilitative retreats into his cave and himself. Thus do Zarathustra's cyclical activities of education and solitude parallel Nietzsche's own life of writing and isolation. The teachings are born in solitude and reflect this parentage. In turn, the substance of the teachings, and their effects, makes solitude both necessary and desirable.

"To rear great men," Nietzsche declared, "is the highest task of mankind" (*GW* 7:381). Only education could provide for the growth of genius. Hence Nietzsche promulgated education as the highest duty.[1] He himself assumed the task of educating the educators. His duty was to teach how to teach so that greatness is made possible and capable of reproducing itself: "Educator educate! But the first ones must educate themselves! And for these do I write" (*GW* 7:215). Before one can sow the seeds of greatness, one must be great oneself. The education of the educator must be a self-education. He must recognize and remove the streaks of decadence within him. Of this task Nietzsche wrote:

> I know for me as well no higher aim than somehow once to become an "educator" in a big way. Mean-

[1] In this regard Nietzsche is at one with Plato and Aristotle. The philosopher is always an educator. And the legislator's highest duty, for Plato and Aristotle, is education. The foremost concern of education, according to Plato's *Republic* (377e), is correct speech about the gods and heroes.

while I must first extract all the polemical, negating, hating, tormenting from me; and I strongly believe we must all do this, in order to become free: the entire terrible sum of all that which we flee, fear and hate must first be accounted for—but then indeed not a glance back in the negative and unfruitful! Rather only more planting, building and creating! Isn't it so, that's called "educating oneself."[2] (NB 10.5.74)

Nietzsche's vision of the ideal teacher is a fusion of the philosopher, the artist, and the saint. Their distinctive virtues are combined in both the style and the substance of instruction. This vision, which was an object of fascination for Nietzsche already in his early works, was said to lift "a corner of the veil of the future" (HH 257). From under this veil Zarathustra would later emerge to proclaim the overman.

According to Nietzsche all philosophy originated and was carried out in the service of education (GW 16:38). The order of the soul Socrates sought to instill among his youthful interlocutors has its parallel in the proper hierarchy of the instincts Nietzsche attempted to stimulate in his readers. A truly philosophical education always entails the active manipulation of the soul.

That education is the primary philosophical task is perhaps not in need of demonstration. However, Nietzsche also insisted that the artistic project was no different. The artist's work serves educational purposes. Those who merely enjoy works of art, and fail to realize that living the

---

[2] The division between negative and positive tasks would prove artificial and impossible to maintain. Throughout Nietzsche's works the creation and destruction of values are concomitant, although in time the tone and character of his diatribes took on a distinctive gayness. Even this levity, however, was pitted against the "spirit of gravity" found amongst rivals. Indeed, in Ecce Homo, written some fourteen years after the above excerpt, Nietzsche acknowledged that following the yes-saying period of The Gay Science and particularly Thus Spoke Zarathustra, his writings took on the task of saying no, of waging war against values, thus paralleling the period directly following The Birth of Tragedy (EH 310). The Genealogy of Morals, for example, bears the subtitle A Polemic.

artistic life is the true masterpiece, are wont to ignore art's educational role. Nietzsche reminded his readers that the nobler function of art, its capacity to be more than decoration and diversion, must not be overlooked: "Everyone who enjoys believes the tree was concerned about the fruit; but it was, in fact, concerned about the seed.—It is in this that there lies the difference between all who create and all who enjoy" (*HH* 298). The creator always looks beyond his concrete achievements to his instructive task, the work of planting the seeds of order in the souls of men.

In like manner, the saint avoids the dogging menaces of infatuation and pity that he may demonstrate how love and the cruel discipline of the taskmaster are compatible. He is "the Roman Caesar with Christ's soul" (*WP* 513). He is the bearer of a worldly creed that commands the perfection of men. "My religion, if I may still so name anything," wrote Nietzsche, "lies in working for the production of genius; education is everything to hope for" (*GW* 7:214). The devotion Nietzsche felt to education was, for lack of a better word, religious: it was, at base, a work of hope.

The inclusion of the philosopher, artist, and saint under the rubric of the educator, and the evaluation of education as the highest possible duty, was maintained by Nietzsche throughout his life. The drafts of his prefaces to the unpublished "Transvaluation of All Values," written in 1888, demonstrate this continuity. His forerunners' efforts at education were viewed as decadent, having devalued the individual against an other-worldly ideal. They weakened that which needed to be strengthened if the perfection of man was to be approached, namely, self-love or egoism.

> As a matter of fact, this is my theorem: the teachers who were the leaders of mankind were decadents: *therefore* the transvaluation of all values in the nihilistic ("the beyond" . . .) They called themselves moralists, whatever they were otherwise, philosophers perhaps, priests, prophets, seers, saints: they believed morality

one and all, they were unanimous,—to "improve"
mankind. . . . What will *I* set myself as a task in this
book?—Perhaps also to "improve" mankind, only differently, only reversed: namely to save it from morality . . . the restoration of mankind-egoism! (*GW*
18:361)

Just as Nietzsche proposed values that were the negation
of all previous values, so he proposed himself as the educator who was the antithesis of all previous educators.[3]
Nietzsche's notion of proper breeding had its closest
parallel not in any modern age attempts at the creation of
a master race, but in its Platonic predecessor. Platonism
was a repeated target of Nietzsche's polemics. But the Platonic notion of discipleship and a new republic of higher
men with philosophical, artistic, and saintly credentials
was central to Nietzsche's project. The training of disciples
whose mettle is of the highest quality with the purpose of
creating a higher culture of spiritual giants is the hope
smoldering in both Plato and Nietzsche.[4] Public education
was of little concern, as it was deemed capable of fostering
only mediocrity. The rare and noble souls that lie in bud,
waiting for the proper stimulants for growth, must be
sought. Indeed, the focus should be on a single student.
"Great success," Nietzsche contended, "is reserved above
all to him who wants to educate, not everybody or even

[3] Moses Hadas's attempt to demonstrate that all later educators of antiquity were modeled on Plato's Socrates falls nicely in line with
Nietzsche's self-understanding as the usurper of Socrates' esteemed position (Moses Hadas and Morton Smith, *Heroes and Gods: Spiritual Biographies in Antiquity* [New York: Harper and Row, 1965]).

[4] Nietzsche's own lack of such personal pedagogical relationships was
dismaying for him. Good students, in effect, were hard to find; and those
he did wish to take under his wing, namely, Lou Andreas-Salomé and to
a lesser extent Paul Rée, were loath to become his disciples. A letter to
Salomé reveals his hopes: "I very much wish to be permitted to be your
teacher. In the end, to tell the whole truth: I now am looking for people
who could be new heirs; I carry around with me some things which absolutely are not to be read in my books—and am looking to find myself
the most beautiful and fruitful farmland for it" (*NB* 26.6.82).

limited circles, but a single individual, and in so doing looks neither to the right nor the left" (D 114). Devotion to a single student is necessary because his proper development depends upon specific stimulation given his particular mix of metals. His instincts must be discovered, deciphered, and strengthened or weakened depending on their capacity for leadership in the internal political realm.

The educator is always aware of whom he is speaking to and what effect his speech will have. "An educator never says what he himself thinks, but always only what he thinks of a thing in relation to the requirements of those he educates. . . . He must be capable of employing every means of discipline: some he can drive toward the heights only with whips of scorn; others, who are sluggish, irresolute, cowardly, vain, perhaps only with exaggerated praise" (WP 512–13). Like Socrates of the *Republic*, the educator stokes or dampens the passions of his disciples the better to pursue justice in the human soul. Nietzsche's own educational maxim read: "He who is a teacher from the very heart takes all things seriously only with reference to his students—even himself" (BGE 72). The individualistic nature of education, therefore, is a consequence of the educator's need to reveal himself selectively, according to the needs of his students.

Individualism in education, however, is just the opposite of unrestrained development. The uniqueness of the student calls for a personalized form of discipline; it is not an excuse for intellectual or spiritual self-management. In his early unpublished lectures entitled "On the Future of our Educational Institutions," Nietzsche formulated his opposition to a laissez-faire philosophy of education. The all-around license of the so-called free personality was seen as the onset of barbarism. In an educational setting, freedom is a euphemism for anarchy: "All education begins with the opposite of that which one now praises as academic freedom, with obedience, with subordination, with discipline, with servitude" (GW 4:118). This judgment remained with Nietzsche. He always maintained that the good school was the hard school where one learned how to obey and to command (*WP* 482–83).

Education, in effect, is a protracted discipline (*BGE* 92–94). It has little to do with the accumulation of knowledge and much to do with the learning of self-control. The understanding is that eventually the student will internalize the force of education, coming to discipline himself.[5] He will, in effect, learn to be the master, or perhaps better said, the coordinator, of his instincts. The task of the educator, then, is to prune the instincts of his students, cutting some back in order that others might receive more light and nourishment.

> The rationale of education would seem to require that at least one of these instinct-systems should be *paralysed* beneath an iron pressure, so as to permit another to come into force, become strong, become master. Today the only way of making the individual possible would be by *pruning* him: possible, that is to say *complete*. . . . The reverse is what actually happens: the claim to independence, to free development, to *laisser aller*, is advanced most heatedly by precisely those for whom no curb *could be too strong*—this applies *in politicis*, it applies in art. But this is a symptom of *décadence*: our modern concept 'freedom' is one more proof of degeneration of instinct. (*TI* 95–96)

In sum, the educator trains his student in the art of arranging the soul, and training always involves authority and discipline.

Just as trees must be pruned one at a time, so too must students be individually educated. The unique requirements of each student comprise, however, only one of the reasons for Nietzsche's rejection of public education. Not

[5] In the same vein, Nietzsche held that the value of pursuing a rigorous science was not a gain in knowledge, but the development of intellectual discipline and endurance (*HH* 121).

the acquisition of facts or skills or technique, but the transmission of passion and will from teacher to student defined education. What the teacher has to teach simply is not transmissible to a crowd. He is not a purveyor of knowledge, a talking book, but a purveyor of personality, a model of an ordered soul (*GW* 3:256). For education to have its proper effect, the student must be exposed to the educator in the practice of his political art.

The educator is to serve as a model for his students, and authority and discipline are considered to be indispensable. Nonetheless, the educator's role is not that of Procrustes. The student is to discover in his teacher the paradigm of how to become his own master. In the third *Untimely Meditation*, "Schopenhauer as Educator," Nietzsche wrote of the teacher as the "revered object" that prompts the student to discover his own laws and ideals. The educator is effectively a catalyst that allows the student to achieve the hierarchy of instinct that most enhances his power: "Your true nature lies, not concealed deep within you, but immeasurably high above you, or at least above that which you usually take yourself to be. Your true educators and formative teachers reveal to you what the true basic material of your being is, something in itself ineducable and in any case difficult of access, bound and paralysed: your educators can be only your liberators" (*UM* 129). Education is not the determination of *who* the student should be, but of *how* he might become who he and only he is. "*Until now*," Nietzsche observed, "there were . . . models that were suspended before mankind. But the goal is: that *each draft* his prototype and realize it— the individual model." Nietzsche's role as educator follows: "I want to help everyone who searches for a model by showing *how* one searches for a model" (*GW* 10:405, 404).

Zarathustra repeatedly reminds his disciples of his role as educator. His frequent weariness of his acolytes is invariably the result of their inability to become individuals, an inability that marked the failure of their education. "One repays a teacher badly if one remains only a pupil," he tells his followers, lest their belief in him become a hindrance to their own development (Z 103). And he states, "I am a law only for my own, I am not a law for all" (Z 296). Like the old Zen parable of the master pointing to the moon and the disciples gazing at his finger, Zarathustra's teaching is often taken as the truth itself, when in fact it only points to the means for each to find his own truth. Zarathustra demonstrates how *he* came to order his soul; his experience will prove useful to his listeners, but not as a blueprint for patterning their lives. Indeed, his 'truth' is that such blueprints do not and cannot exist. "This—is now *my* way: where is yours?" he challenges his followers: "Thus I answered those who asked me 'the way'. For *the* way—does not exist!" (Z 213). The true educator celebrates success when his students become worthy of demanding their independence. The fruit of education is the achievement of maturity and individuality. The disciplined training that allows the student to end his servitude to custom and morality ultimately results in the end of his servitude to higher men. "Now I bid you lose me and find yourselves," Zarathustra encourages his disciples, "and only when you have all denied me will I return to you" (Z 103). But this time Zarathustra will return as a peer, not a pedagogue.

The radically individualistic nature of education is the source of the ensuing isolation of its beneficiaries. To struggle to be a law unto oneself, to speak of *one's* way but not *the* way, is to experience the force of a Nietzschean solitude. Ironically, the true educator is he who successfully demonstrates this solitude to his students. He serves as the model of how one may escape herd life and bear one's individuality heroically. In this sense, education is the sharing of solitude. He who has transformed his condemnation to individuality into jubilation wishes to celebrate this victory with others. And only he who has mastered his solitude is worthy of being an educator, a catalyst in the formation of other solitaries. Nietzsche proclaimed: "My whole *Zarathustra* is a dithyramb on solitude" (*EH* 234). But if Zarathustra sings a song to Dionysus, he also offers a hymn to his other patron deity. When the educator and the solitary are wed, Phoebus Apollo—Delphic purveyor of wisdom, deity of self-sufficient individuality and god of light—emerges. As Zarathustra's first words indicate, the educator is a lone star that wishes to shine for others; its internally produced light testifies that it is a sun, subject to no laws but its own, revolving around nothing but itself.

The higher man, stated Nietzsche, "has solitude not because he wishes to be alone but because he *is* something that finds no equals" (*WP* 514). Yet he also desires it. Free-thinkers are always "born, sworn, jealous friends of *solitude*" (*BGE* 55). For it is the condition that allows, indeed necessitates, the confrontation of individuality. In his first autobiography, written at thirteen years of age (and, one might say, carried on in other forms until his collapse), Nietzsche had already identified himself by his need for and pleasure in solitude: "From childhood on I sought out solitude and found myself most at ease there where undisturbed I could give myself over to myself. And this was usually in the free temple of nature, and I found thereby the truest joy" (*GW* 21:10). Writing to his sister at age thirty-one, Nietzsche's situation and sentiment had not changed: "The weather is splendid, the woods scented, I walk a great deal, converse in the best and most distinguished manner, namely with myself" (*NB* 10.8.75). His isolation continued unabated; if anything, it came to increase. In 1884 he could announce, "I still have found nobody with whom I could talk as I talk with myself" (*NB* 5.84). Such statements reveal as much joy in the fact of solitude as regret at its imposition. Conversations with himself were Nietzsche's only authentic intercourse in a world without kindred spirits. "I am *solitude* become man," he wrote in a draft of *Ecce Homo*, "That no word

174

ever reached me forced me to reach myself" (*EH* 343). What Nietzsche found necessary to his life as a *philosophus radicalis*, namely, independence and solitude, were felt as deprivations so far as Nietzsche the man was concerned (*NB* 14.11.88). The price of living a radically individualistic philosophy was solitude, often experienced as loneliness.

In his letters Nietzsche often laments his solitary existence. He appears to have suffered all his life with the vain hope of discovering a soul mate. Excepting his relatively brief and in the end antagonistic relationship with Richard Wagner, however, Nietzsche could find no equal. In 1887 he wrote of his alienation to Franz Overbeck, one of his closest friends (whom, however, Nietzsche obviously held to be of a lower rank): "If I exclude R. Wagner, so far no one has approached me with a thousandth the passion and suffering that I might come to an 'understanding' with him; I was in this way already alone as a child, I am still so today, in my 44th year of life" (*NB* 12.11.87). The burden of solitude, and his passionate response to it, was vividly portrayed by Nietzsche years before he began his own life of wanderings after giving up his post at the University of Basel.

> The last philosopher I call myself, for I am the last human being. No one converses with me beside myself and my voice reaches me as the voice of one dying. With thee, beloved voice, with thee, the last remembered breath of all human happiness, let me discourse, even if it is only for another hour. Because of thee, I delude myself as to my solitude and lie my way back to multiplicity and love, for my heart shies away from believing that love is dead. It cannot bear the icy shivers of loneliest solitude. It compels me to speak as though I were Two. (*GW* 6:36; translation from *PTG* 18)

The pathos of this cry reappears throughout Nietzsche's works and letters, until the total isolation of lunacy put an end to his writing.

Solitude was deemed a "virtue" by Nietzsche (*BGE* 195). But it was not an ascetic virtue. Opposed to the "fruitless, perhaps melancholy solitude" of the nun, the true thinker finds in solitude his greatest fruitfulness (*D* 187). Being absorbed in the realm of one's own thoughts signifies a freedom from the surrounding world. This freedom is the thinker's most cherished condition. His self-isolation from the world of affairs speaks of "a certain heroic basic disposition." His own ideals rather than the tide of the *Zeitgeist* pull him along (*UM* 176). He becomes peripheral. But he also becomes autonomous: "He who does not have two-thirds of his day to himself is a slave, let him be what he may otherwise: statesman, businessman, official, scholar" (*HH* 132). The pursuit of political, economic, or academic power is of no interest. For the attempt to reap the fruit of one's worldly involvement produces the loss of all "genuine productivity." The attempt to affiliate oneself with the *Zeitgeist* only demonstrates one's servility to it. The "profound speechlessness of pregnancy" cannot withstand worldly activity or a running commentary on the day's events. The victims of contemporaneity prove the lack of the basic disposition Nietzsche most demanded: "The event of the day drives them before it like chaff, while they think they are driving the event—poor devils!—If one wants to represent a hero on the stage one must not think of making one of the chorus, indeed one must not even know how to make one of the chorus" (*D* 107).

Casting the solitary in the role of the hero on stage is somewhat misleading. For the true solitary does not wish to be on stage at all, nor does he seek applause for his part. He is too suspicious of all that needs to parade itself. Public displays of courage are most likely motivated by the fear of being thought a coward. The solitary's courage is of another sort: he has no care for the opinions of others. His fear is that self-display will entice him to perform, to betray his true calling: "When I am among the many I live as the many do, and I do not think as I really think; after a time it always seems as though they want to banish me from myself and rob me of my soul—and I grow angry with everybody and fear everybody. I then require the desert, so as to grow good again" (*D* 201). The solitary does not fulfill his heroic destiny as a leader among men. For then he would have to compromise his cherished condition and demonstrate his affiliation with his followers. "It is not a matter of going ahead (—for then one is at best a herdsman, i.e. the herd's chief requirement), but of being able *to go it alone*, of being able *to be different*" (*WP* 196).[6] The fear of losing oneself to the many prompts the solitary to spurn public acclaim. In *Ecce Homo* Nietzsche attempted to portray himself as one who never sought honors (*EH* 255). From his "hermitage" in Sils Maria, he wrote to his mother and sister: "The last thing I would want is 'fame' and 'publicity' and 'pupil-veneration'. . . . I want to feel right in the middle more solitary than already now and perhaps also frightfully grow in the contempt of man" (*NB* 9.85).[7] The virtue of solitude is a jealous one; it will tolerate nothing that might jeopardize its preeminence.

[6] Even in Nietzsche's ostensibly most politically oriented and power-hungry statements actual political power and leadership are not foreseen. For example, he wrote of "philosophical men of power" and "artist-tyrants" as the new "masters of the earth." Politics, one learns, will have a different meaning under this "master race" that will employ Europe "for getting hold of the destinies of the earth." But the Europe being so used is said to be "democratic," and the only legislation mentioned is "the severest self-legislation" of the new aristocracy, which is stipulated to be international (*WP* 504). In other words, the hope is not for philosopher-kings with national or global mandates, but for philosophers who, operating within existing political regimes, are capable of expanding the ranks of their own spiritual elite across the globe. However, even this project is made problematic by Nietzsche. For the higher man is above all a solitary individual. Chances are he will not recognize a kindred spirit (*WP* 516). If he does, he is much more likely to fight with his peer than conspire with him: "It is completely false that the great spirits had judged essentially the same about being and man. . . . geniuses have had *individual* views—and have carried them into the things: which is why they have deeply contradicted each other and have always believed they must destroy all others" (*GW* 11:9). In short, "there exists no *consensus omnium sapientium* whatever in regard to any single thing" (*HH* 62).

[7] At best Nietzsche was half-hearted in these sentiments. He found his lack of recognition most distressing and unjustified. Moreover, as his cor-

The solitary's rejection of fame may appear to be at odds with his characterization as a heroic type. In fact, the hero is always caught in this contradiction. He strives to assert his individuality, to distinguish himself. He therefore excludes himself from the common life. Yet without the security of a group identity he becomes susceptible to the seductions of fame. Morality and custom are the means whereby the worth, dignity, and function of the common man are acknowledged. The hero is without these forms of social recognition. Indeed, he seeks to be honored for his rejection of these standards. He acts and struggles for the sake of action and struggle, placing himself beyond morality and utility. But the demands of this self-supporting mode of life leave him all the more eager to gain the foothold of fame.

What primarily makes solitude a heroic virtue is its *agonal* character. With whom, then, does the solitary struggle? The answer, of course, is himself. The solitary is not only his own best friend and conversationalist, but also his own best critic and fiercest antagonist. "This thinker needs no one to refute him," Nietzsche remarked: "He does that for himself" (*HH* 371). The "nymph Echo" keeps the solitary from becoming too self-assured by resounding the

---

respondence reveals, Nietzsche was very much concerned with his reputation and quite active in its promotion. Less than a year after the above letter was written, for example, he had his publisher send out over forty copies of the newly published *Beyond Good and Evil* for purposes of publicity, and this above all the copies he had sent to friends and academic colleagues (*NB* 2.8.86). It would appear that Nietzsche understood himself to exemplify Tacitus's dictum that "Even for the wise the lust for fame is the desire they give up last." In quoting this line, Nietzsche indicated that the desire is never really given up, that at the very least, he who does without applause must be "assured of his own hand-clapping" (*GS* 260). The torment of his relative anonymity ended with Nietzsche's applauding very wildly for himself, as evidenced throughout the pages of *Ecce Homo* and, more alarmingly, in his last letters. He came to believe in the reality of his own aspirations for fame. Still a relatively obscure retired professor of philology, Nietzsche would proclaim: "Today there is no name that is treated with so much honor and respect as my own (*NB* 21.12.88).

hollowness of his words (GS 203). His "shadow" keeps him from becoming complacent. It dogs him, ensuring that he never forgets his task. The falseness of his every move and gesture is made apparent. One of the most enduring images of Nietzsche's work is the shadow, which follows the wanderer as his alter ego. "The Wanderer and the Shadow," an essay that eventually became the final addition to *Human, All Too Human*, is effectively a sketch of the friend-foe relationship Nietzsche maintained with himself. The wanderer cannot run away from his shadow, and in his shadow he finds both the comfort of a constant companion and the severity of an inseparable critic. "One day the wanderer slammed a door behind himself, stopped in his tracks, and wept. Then he said: 'This penchant and passion for what is true, real, nonapparent, certain—how it aggravates me! Why does this gloomy and restless fellow keep following and driving *me*? I want to rest, but he will not allow it' " (GS 246–47). Echoes and shadows are what the solitary must contend with. Plato had Socrates express envy of his interlocutors because they could return home to rest after a day of discussion, untroubled by the voice of the most unrelenting critic, a critic Socrates always met when he was alone. Likewise, Nietzsche had Zarathustra inform his listeners of the plight of all who practice solitude: "But you yourself will always be the worst enemy you can encounter; you yourself lie in wait for yourself in caves and forests" (Z 90).

The internal battle of the solitary is undeniably a torment, but it also provides him with his profoundest pleasures. Thinking and living his thoughts constitutes a full-time occupation, regardless of how such "idleness" might be perceived by others.[8] His isolation does not speak of a

---

[8] Nietzsche's original title for *Twilight of the Idols* was *The Idleness* [or *Leisure*] *of a Psychologist*. His attitude toward leisure, its meaning and purpose, is very much at odds with modernity's equation of it with relaxation. Aristotle's view of leisure as neither work nor play but a time for contemplation is Nietzsche's own.

lack of creativity, for his life is a poem subject to ongoing interpretation. He is more than willing to spurn the theater of worldly affairs and the enticements of the arts because he finds "enough tragedy and comedy in himself" (*GS* 142). The solitary turns his condition into an aesthetic accomplishment, exercising the Apollonian "urge to perfect self-sufficiency" (*WP* 539).

The first question concerning the order of rank pertains to the degree of one's solitude (*WP* 472). "He shall be the greatest who can be the most solitary," Nietzsche flatly declared (*BGE* 125). How, then, does one become the most solitary? Who bears this loneliest solitude? It is the heroic individual: the man who finds no equals on earth and therefore shuns the diversions of community. He does not need to share in the social nourishment of his fellow man because he consumes himself. But neither does he find company in the heavens; he spurns even a divine audience for his deeds. Thus he distinguishes himself from the "Herakles of duty." This self-proclaimed hero of morality exhibits his lack of independence by inventing a god; for he finds virtue without a witness intolerable (*GM* 69). "In the end," Nietzsche asserted, "all those who somehow have a 'god' in their company still have not at all that which I know as 'solitude' " (*NB* 2.7.85).

Some perish from this solitude, driving "so deep into themselves that when they re-emerge it is always as a volcanic eruption." Others, those "demigods" Nietzsche so admired, survive: their works of genius evidence their victory (*UM* 140). Nietzsche experienced both fates. In this matter the appropriate question is not why Nietzsche became insane, but why he became incapable of bearing his insanity. For the solitary is always courting madness. His self-challenge is to see how much truth can be endured, and his truth is none other than his life sentence of spiritual solitude. The extent to which he can transform this condemnation into a triumphant celebration of the self is the mark of his heroism. He becomes a demigod. When the truth becomes more than he can bear, his work of genius founders. He loses all sense of limits, of style. He can no longer present the chaos he is as a cosmos, an aesthetic whole. The will to power atrophies; the soul loses its leadership, its cohesion. In December 1887 Nietzsche wrote of his attempt to push his solitude to the extreme in an effort to reach a "new and higher form" of life. How "young" he would become in the effort, Nietzsche stated, remained unknown to him (*NB* 14.12.87). Within a year of this announcement he had entered a terminal infancy.

Such is the danger of a radical individualism whose passion is without bounds. History was the witness, Nietzsche claimed, with words that bore a prophetic eeriness: "All superior men who were irresistibly drawn to throw off the yoke of any kind of morality and to frame new laws had, *if they were not actually mad*, no alternative but to make themselves or pretend to be mad" (*D* 14).[9] Madness proves to be the final release from the individual's perpetual struggle. No longer does the affliction of a multiple soul torment. The end of strife arrives: "Who would venture to take a look into the wilderness of bitterest and most superfluous agonies of the soul in which probably the most fruitful men of all times have languished! To listen to the sighs of these solitary and agitated minds: Ah, give me madness, you heavenly powers! Madness, that I may at last believe in myself!" (*D* 14, 15). The tragic hero has had his fate foretold. After a life of enraging the gods, he petitions for a final reprieve.

[9] Nietzsche's insanity is generally attributed to a softening of the brain, a condition his father suffered from. It is also possible that his supposed, but unconfirmed, contraction of syphilis may have caused his madness and eventual semiparalysis. Nonetheless, Nietzsche's speculations on self-induced insanity were substantiated by remarks made by visiting friends. After his meeting with the invalid in 1890, Heinrich Koselitz wrote Carl Fuchs: "It seemed—horrible!—as if Nietzsche was feigning madness, as if he was glad to have ended like this!" Franz Overbeck received a similar impression the previous year. (Quoted in R. J. Hollingdale, *Nietzsche: The Man and His Philosophy* [Baton Rouge: Louisiana State University Press, 1965], p. 291.)

But to whom does he petition? "Where is the lightning to lick you with its tongue? Where is the madness, with which you should be cleansed?" Zarathustra asks, for there is no one outside of the self. He responds: "Behold, I teach you the Overman: he is this lightning, he is this madness" (Z 43). The educator summons greatness, the ultimate solitude. The solitary appeals to the deity within to lift him above and beyond himself. If the request is granted, the heroic Sisyphus will stand purified of his mortal woes, victorious upon the summit. He lives to declare himself no longer man, before being crushed by his burden.

N I N E

APOTHEOSIS AND LAUGHTER:
THE OVERMAN

To live alone "without God and morality" I had to invent a counterpart for myself. Perhaps I know best why man alone laughs: he alone suffers so deeply that he *had* to invent laughter.

—*The Will to Power*

Nietzsche was a pious skeptic. His piety is manifest in his devotion to the task of producing greatness. His skepticism is manifest in his testimony to the limits of human knowledge. The concept of God lies beyond these limits. Moreover, it is a drain on the forces needed to perfect man, for the other-worldly slanders and hobbles the worldly. Nietzsche's denial of God, therefore, is an act of both piety and skepticism. In the absence of God, however, a substitute is needed to represent the state of perfection to which man must strive: the overman is this substitute.

Once you said 'God' when you gazed upon distant seas; but now I have taught you to say 'overman'.

God is a supposition; but I want your supposing to reach no further than your creating will.

Could you *create* a god?—So be silent about all gods! But you could surely create the overman.

Perhaps not you yourselves, my brothers! But you could transform yourselves into forefathers and an-

cestors of the overman: and let this be your finest creating! (Z 109–10)

Greatness is the nearing of perfection; the overman is the
ideal of human being. He fosters the emergence of greatness.

"Who no longer finds greatness in God, finds it not at
all—he must deny it or create it," Nietzsche wrote (*GW*
14:80). To deny greatness predicates nihilism, the condition that characterizes the modern world. There exist no
standards by which human existence may be evaluated
and justified. To create greatness is Nietzsche's higher
form of (active) nihilism, his substitute for religion. Not a
postmortem union with God, but the apotheosis of living
man is proposed. Nietzsche saw himself as the educator of
the forefathers of the overman, the propagator of a new
and saving faith in man.

What is the overman? He is the apotheosis of the hero
as incarnated in the philosopher, artist, and saint. Who is
the overman? This question has no answer, expect perhaps that given by Odysseus to the Cyclops. The overman
remains ever elusive. Mankind, Nietzsche stated, is only
the means of pursuing a goal. This goal is the overman;
but the goal is never reached, only striven for. As an ideal,
the overman is approached, even touched, but not possessed. He is occasionally glimpsed, and lived for a moment in rapturous passion and thought. But the Dionysian
moment is just that—momentary. And the traces it leaves
behind in memory are as the aftertaste of a fruit whose
possession becomes one's obsession.

"Our deficiencies are the eyes with which we behold the
ideal," Nietzsche observed (*HH* 231). Such is the lot of
man. He is a suffering mortal. But he briefly may experience the ecstasy of a laughing god. In his effort to retrieve
and perpetuate these moments he comes to know the
pleasures of the will to power. He has discovered that the
greatest freedom is found only in the continual overcom-

ing of the greatest resistances (*TI* 92–93). Thus he delights in struggle. "It is *not* the satisfaction of the will that causes pleasure . . . but rather the will's forward thrust and again and again becoming master over that which stands in its way. The feeling of pleasure lies precisely in the dissatisfaction of the will, in the fact that the will is never satisfied unless it has opponents and resistance" (*WP* 370). What stands in the way of the overman, however, is precisely one's humanity. One is *not* the overman; therefore one must will him, and this willing is always an overcoming of the self, the creation of a better—that is, more powerful— self. In this willing the suffering mortal partakes of divinity. His willing is his act of creation. It is his redemption from suffering. The joy of willing is what lured Zarathustra away from the gods, "for what would there be to create if gods—existed!" (*Z* 111).

This question must also be asked of the overman. What would there be to create if the overman existed? What self-overcoming, what joyful willing could an overman experience? He knows none. The overman is the perfectly ordered soul and does not partake in the heroic struggle of existence. He is a united self, a self without a shadow. The zenith of mankind is at midday, marked by the rule of Zarathustra. But Nietzsche acknowledged that this is only the "moment of the shortest shadow" (*TI* 41). For a completely shadowless existence is impossible for man. His shadow, however short, remains to remind him of his boundaries and encourage him to jump beyond them. This sort of spiritual gymnastic, Nietzsche observed, produced a strong soul. It remains, nonetheless, a soul divided.

The overman should not be projected as one of Nietzsche's heroic incarnations or personae, for he contains none of the contradictions that prove to be the driving force behind the philosopher, artist, saint, educator, and solitary. He is their deification. His presence is felt at the victorious culmination of a battle, as a temporary release from struggle. He is man at his best, at his most divine, when the struggle to become momentarily achieves the bliss of being. But he is meant to be incorporated into life as a whole, and not merely appear at its distant peaks. As such the overman serves as the antidote to man's guilt and shame for his failures and limitations. His presence signals the liberation from the stultifying sense of duty to be more than one is. He bears the "seal of liberation": "No longer being ashamed in front of oneself" (*GS* 220). He is incorporated to the extent that the passion for excellence is not at the same time a self-flagellation for inevitable shortcomings. The shame of defeat is replaced by the shame of remorse itself. Laughter takes the place of the " 'bite' of conscience" when the struggle becomes too much (*WP* 135).

One must be able to laugh, and in particular laugh at oneself, if the task of self-perfection is not to become a means of taking revenge upon life. The hero must continually demonstrate that struggle is his greatest joy, that his self-despising is only part of a greater self-love, that his destruction and no-saying are the prerequisites for creation and yes-saying—in short, that his desire for change is an affirmation of the state of becoming. He must prove himself not only beyond good and evil, but also above his self-created higher morality.

> We must discover the *hero* no less than the *fool* in our passion for knowledge; we must occasionally find pleasure in our folly, or we cannot continue to find pleasure in our wisdom. Precisely because we are at bottom grave and serious human beings—really, more weights than human beings—nothing does us as much good as a *fool's cap*: we need it in relation to ourselves—we need all exuberant, floating, dancing, mocking, childish, and blissful art lest we lose the *freedom above things* that our ideal demands of us. It would mean a *relapse* for us, with our irritable hon-

esty, to get involved entirely in morality and, for the sake of the over-severe demands that we make on ourselves in these matters, to become virtuous monsters and scarecrows. We should be *able* also to stand *above* morality—and not only to *stand* with the anxious stiffness of a man who is afraid of slipping and falling any moment, but also to *float* above it and *play*. (GS 164)

The aim is somehow to stand *above* ideals even as one reaches for them. The task of affirming life requires that it resonate not only with the heavy steps of the hero but with the prance of the child and the echoes of childlike laughter. In the highest form of affirmation the devotee to struggle discovers "the dance is his ideal, also his art, and finally also his only piety, his 'service to God' " (*GS* 346). Zarathustra proclaims: "And let that day be lost to us on which we did not dance once! And let that wisdom be false to us that brought no laughter with it" (Z 228).[1]

The presence of laughter in wisdom and dancing in struggle is made necessary by the essentially tragic nature of existence. It is a sort of whistling in the dark, except that the thrill of danger and the pleasures of willing, of overcoming one's fears, brings the whistler to the point of truly enjoying his predicament. He feels that it is an adventure to live. One must be one of "the *heroic* spirits who say Yes to themselves in tragic cruelty: they are hard enough to experience suffering as a *pleasure*" (WP 450). Man invented humor in order to bear his suffering. For those active nihilists who have outlawed the possibility of being "comforted metaphysically," Nietzsche recommended laughter: "the art of *this-worldly* comfort" (*BT* 26). To laugh at oneself is to delight at one's own misfortunes. It is the highest

---

[1] This disposition is already foreshadowed in *Human, All Too Human,* wherein Nietzsche praises Socrates for "possessing that *wisdom full of roguishness* that constitutes the finest state of the human soul," and submits the dictum, "Growth in wisdom can be measured precisely by decline in bile" (*HH* 332, 393).

form of cruelty which redeems itself by affirmation: "For in laughter all evil is present, but sanctified and absolved through its own happiness" (Z 247). To experience the full weight of nihilism and still be able fully to celebrate life is the mark of the highest man. Hence Nietzsche proposed to rank philosophers according to the quality of their mirth (*BGE* 199). Zarathustra claims to have "canonized laughter." The final task of the higher man is to learn how to laugh (Z 306).[2]

Before attaining this goal the higher man passes through "three metamorphoses." First, there is the camel or "weight-bearing spirit," which seeks solitude in the desert

---

[2] One of the most striking passages of *Thus Spoke Zarathustra* is "Of the Vision and the Riddle." Zarathustra's vision is of a shepherd who while sleeping has a snake crawl into his mouth and lodge in his throat. In order to remove the snake the shepherd must bite off its head. "Solve for me the riddle that I saw, interpret to me the vision of the most solitary man," Zarathustra challenges his listeners. The solution, it would appear, lies in the transformation of suffering into jubilation that the most solitary man must achieve. Zarathustra urges the shepherd to bite off the snake's head, a thought that contained all of his horror, hate, disgust, and pity. After biting off and spitting out the snake's head, he springs up:

> No longer a shepherd, no longer a man—a transformed being, surrounded with light, *laughing*! Never yet on earth had any man laughed as he laughed!
> O my brothers, I heard a laughter that was no human laughter—and now a thirst consumes me, a longing that is never stilled. (Z 180).

In his moment of self-overcoming the lowly man becomes the overman, a laughing god. It is a consuming vision of the ultimate transformation of the terrible truths of existence into joy.

This vision appears as a variation of a dream Nietzsche had discussed with some of his students at the University of Basel. He dreamt that he was transparent and was irresistibly moved to swallow a live toad. He is reported to have interpreted the dream as follows: "Self-knowledge can only thus be paid for, that I do not shrink back even from the most disgusting of things" (Gilman, *Begegnungen mit Nietzsche*, pp. 102, 163). The image reappears in the rhymes that precede the text of *The Gay Science*, wherein the proffered cure for dyspepsia is the swallowing of a fat toad (*GS* 49). And as a "convalescent" Zarathustra explains that the "great disgust at man," man's impotence, is the croaking, gnawing question that torments him—"knowledge chokes" (Z 235–36).

so that it may dutifully bear its burden. The camel then becomes a lion, a willful creature of strength: the "thou shalt" becomes an "I will." Finally, the lion becomes a child—"innocence and forgetfulness." The child "wills *its own* will"; it is not subservient to the dictates of any morality. Its greatest joy is in the playful creation of its world (Z 54–55). In the section entitled "Of the Sublime Men," Zarathustra clarifies what he meant by the three metamorphoses. The camel and lion represent the heroic archetypes. They are burden-bearing and courageous beasts of war. They are serious and passionately devoted to struggle. And they, too, must be overcome. Struggle must become play. The hero must become childlike.

The final labor of the hero is to overcome his own heroism: "He must unlearn his heroic will. . . . He has tamed monsters, he has solved riddles: but he should also redeem his monsters and riddles, he should transform them into heavenly children" (Z 140). He must, Nietzsche stipulated, reveal not only the neck of an ox but the eye of an angel. The hero identifies himself with his battles and the strength and courage needed to wage them. He inevitably denies who he is with an eye to who he shall become. Consequently he is incapable of fully celebrating himself. The young Nietzsche's agreement with Schopenhauer's pessimistic belief that "a happy life is impossible: the highest that man can attain to is a *heroic one*" (UM 153) no longer holds. The goal is to be both happy and heroic. One must learn to float and dance *above* oneself. One must become an *over*hero.

> Yes, you sublime men, you too shall one day be fair and hold the mirror before your own beauty.
>
> Then your soul will shudder with divine desires; and there will be worship even in your vanity!
>
> This indeed is the secret of the soul: only when the hero has deserted the soul does there approach it in dreams—the overhero (Z 141).

In short, the hero must liberate himself from his own dog-ging shadow. He must discover a unity of soul that puts an end to struggle and suffering, allowing an ultimate cel-ebration of the self: "And only if he turns away from him-self will he jump over his own shadow—and jump, in truth, into *his own* sunlight" (Z 140).

In a section of *Daybreak* entitled "We gods in exile!" Nietzsche declared that "for the present the 'proud suf-ferer' is still the highest type of man" (D 182). Those who suffer most deeply, Nietzsche wrote, can bear their pain only in the thick of battle (NB 28.4.74). Thus the proud sufferer welcomes strife: he is the heroic individual. He is man's highest exemplar, but he remains a man nonethe-less. The overman has not yet appeared; the gods remain in exile. In their absence, the hero should be neither un-dervalued nor overrated. "The kind of people who alone matter," Nietzsche declared, are "those who are *heroic*" (GS 235). The hero remains "the most acceptable form of human being, particularly if one has no other choice" (NB 12.82). What other choice is possible for man? There is none. An apotheosis is required. Man must become *over-man*, the hero an *over*hero. Knowledge, as Zarathustra stipulates, must learn how to smile. The hero must quit the ponderous march of the armored warrior and learn the dance of victory: "*Light* feet are the first attribute of divin-ity," Nietzsche wrote, distinguishing the overhero from his mundane counterpart (TI 48). The musical accompani-ment to dancing is no longer the heavy, Wagnerian scores fit for the romantic hero's labors, but music that, like the overman himself, "does not *sweat*" (CW 157). For "in all moments when we *do* our best, we are not working. Work is only the means to these moments" (GW 14:10).

The image of the highest man as a child at play is taken from Nietzsche's earlier discussion of the Heraclitean world. Sand castles are formed at the beach only to be gleefully trampled down and rebuilt. The world of becom-ing is the game of the gods: "In this world only play, play as artists and children engage in it, exhibits coming-to-be and passing away, structuring and destroying, without any moral additive, in forever equal innocence" (*PTG* 62; cf. *BT* 142). The hero may not enter this world without a transformation. Struggle is his means of passage. Play has no purpose outside itself. It is analogous to struggle engaged in for its own sake, and is reflected in the heroic understanding of life as adventure. The Greeks with their heroic and Olympian mythology, Nietzsche believed, best exemplified the understanding of life as a game, a game in which the stakes were honor and ignominy, life and death (*GW* 5:288). If modern man were to regain such a "mature" attitude he would have to rediscover "the seriousness one had as a child at play" (*BGE* 76).[3]

To the extent that he remains tied to his ideals—however useful they have been in elevating him—the hero lives in a state of self-depreciation: "All ideals are dangerous: because they debase and brand the actual; all are poisons, but indispensable as temporary cures" (*WP* 130). The overhero recognizes this; his struggle ceases, albeit temporarily, that he may enjoy the ideal as it is realized in himself. After the painful labor of pregnancy he has finally given birth, and if he is truly to celebrate he must in some sense break free from his modus operandi of struggle.

To attain an ideal, Nietzsche wrote, is to transcend it (*BGE* 73). To be heroic, ultimately, is to go beyond heroism. The hero must rise above his ideals. In the end, he refuses to reach for transcendent forms, having rid his world of all gods and idols; but he also refuses to renounce the quest for greatness. To deny that one may climb higher is to embrace nihilism. But to climb only that one may draw near supposed gods, Nietzsche maintained, is also

[3] While play is a nonutilitarian activity, this is not to deny its fecundity. Likewise, the dancing Nietzsche applauds is no mere entertainment, but a Shiva-like dance of creation and destruction, of creative and destructive playfulness. "I should believe only in a God," Zarathustra stipulated, "who understood how to dance" (*Z* 68).

nihilism. What is the alternative? One must climb upon and above oneself: "And when all footholds disappear, you must know how to climb upon your own head: how could you climb upward otherwise?" (Z 174). In brief, one must pull oneself up by one's own bootstraps, practicing the "art of apotheosis."

To be both that to be overcome and that to be attained, this is the Nietzschean drama: "Become who you are! First it is necessary to emancipate oneself from one's chains, and finally one must still emancipate oneself from this emancipation" (NB 8.82). The hero, as "the highest manifestation of the will" (BT 104), proves himself above the common man by freeing himself from the chains of custom and morality through the exercise of will. He must then prove himself above humanity itself by rising above willfulness: "Higher than 'thou shalt' is the 'I will' (the heroes); higher than 'I will' stands: 'I am' (the gods of the Greeks)" (WP 495). The 'I am' of the gods is their declaration of perfection. They are self-sufficient entities whose worthiest act could be none other than self-contemplation and self-affirmation. The overhero or overman approaches this godly self-love. To desire to be other is to deprecate life as it is. Yet life *is* growth, the will to growth and greater power. Hence one must fully love the self as it unfolds, as its potential becomes actual. "One loves from the very heart only one's child and one's work; and where there is great love of oneself, then it is a sign of pregnancy," Zarathustra asserted (Z 181). In the overman Nietzsche had created an ideal to be striven for and yet, if only momentarily, also incorporated. Nietzsche was a Daedalus, a master craftsman who fell in love with his own creation. Thus could he love an ideal as himself.

Whatever his aspirations, the higher man is no god. As long as he remains a suffering mortal, as long as his apotheosis remains limited to the elusive and illusionary Dionysian moment, he remains imperfect, a nongod, man. In brief, as long as man remains (self-)conscious, he remains

192

imperfect. For consciousness is always a recognition of limits. Nietzsche denied outright "that anything can be made perfect so long as it is still made conscious" (*TI* 125). Unlike the animals, man knows he is not a god, and he suffers for his knowledge. The glimpse of the overman is as a moment of creative forgetfulness in which this knowledge no longer torments. Already in the second of the *Untimely Meditations*, years before the concept of the overman appeared, Nietzsche had outlined the human need for forgetfulness: "In the case of the smallest or of the greatest happiness, however, it is always the same thing that makes happiness happiness: the ability to forget or, expressed in more scholarly fashion, the capacity to feel *unhistorically* during its duration. He who cannot sink down on the threshold of the moment and forget all the past, who cannot stand balanced like a goddess of victory without growing dizzy and afraid, will never know what happiness is" (*UM* 62). Unhistoric living is characteristic of the heroic existence. Only thus may profound pleasures be embraced without allowing failures and limitations, experienced or expected, to interfere. In Nietzsche's eyes, "only heroes are truly individually alive. In them does the present recognize itself and live on" (*GW* 2:382). The hero is nearly overcome by his task, by his life of incessant struggle. But in the glory of its successes he claims a total victory, a victory over even the memory of his former trials.[4] This jubilation of the here and now, extended indefinitely, is what defines the overhero. He must be able to say with Nietzsche, "Today I love myself as my god" (*GW*

[4] In *Ecce Homo* Nietzsche projected his euphoric state backwards, claiming to have achieved the victory of the overhero without ever having engaged in heroic battles: "I cannot remember that I ever tried hard—no trace of *struggle* can be demonstrated in my life; I am the opposite of a heroic nature. 'Willing' something, 'striving' for something, envisaging a 'purpose,' a 'wish'—I know none of this from experience" (*EH* 255). The falseness of this claim is patent to anyone who has read Nietzsche's previous work. But it is quite consistent with his understanding of the overhero as one who "knows how to *forget*" (*EH* 225).

14:43), all the while forgetting that tomorrow he might despise himself, as likely he did yesterday.[5]

"Let us live above ourselves," Nietzsche advocated, "in order that we may be able to live with ourselves" (NB 11.3.82). To endure the human condition, the Nietzschean hero must struggle to be more than human. His drive to self-perfection knows no limits. In order to bear his imperfections he abolishes the gods through an act of will: "*If* there were gods, how could I endure not to be a god! *Therefore* there are no gods!" (Z 110). In their stead he sets up his own ideal, the overman, as the divinity harbored within himself. Finally, as his power grows in the struggle to realize this ideal he experiences his apotheosis, momentarily becoming the overman, the child and dancing fool. He shudders with a divine laughter. For only the laughter of the gods allows him to forget that, after all, he is but a man.

[5] To love oneself as one's god is the apogee of hubris; yet it is intrinsic to Nietzsche's philosophy in general and his teaching of the overman in particular. Hollingdale's contention that Nietzsche's hubristic claims "must be accepted as the wild over-compensations of an ailing and half-blind man; they must not be confused with his *philosophy*" (*Nietzsche: The Man and His Philosophy* [Baton Rouge: Louisiana State University Press, 1965], p. 216) would discredit far more of Nietzsche's work than expected. His hubris was apparent at an early age; only the prudence to hide it decreased as he grew older. It is impossible to separate the hubristic drive from the philosophy within a corpus of work self-consciously written as a heroic attack on morality and religion. Indeed, philosophers from the days of Socrates, unjustly or not, have been persecuted precisely because philosophy was realized to be a hubristic enterprise.

PART IV

THE CIRCLE OF RETURN

T E N

AMOR FATI AND THE ETERNAL RECURRENCE

No victor believes in chance.
—*The Gay Science*

Nietzsche's writings on *amor fati*, love of fate, and the eternal recurrence cannot be understood in isolation. One must return to Nietzsche's life and philosophy as a whole to find their meaning. These concepts, as with Nietzsche's thought in general, were the product not merely of a sophisticated intellectual exercise, but of a lived experience. They are not to be grasped by readers who have not shared in its revelation. For Nietzsche they represented the crowning achievement of life. The concepts of *amor fati* and eternal recurrence served as ultimate tests of the order of rank. To embrace one's fate, indeed, to desire its repetition eternally, is the greatest affirmation of life and love of self. It is *the* defining characteristic of a higher man.

At thirteen years of age Nietzsche wrote of his God: "But thy holy will be done! I want to accept joyfully everything there is, happiness and unhappiness, poverty and wealth and even look death daringly in the eyes" (*GW* 21:35). Here, for the first time, love of fate is expressed, albeit in theistic terms. To deny or regret the smallest detail of one's life, including one's suffering, is to blaspheme. In effect, one would be slighting the providential wisdom of God. True to his Lutheran upbringing, Nietzsche maintained a strong belief in providence as a child. As a youth, this belief gave way to an ambiguous notion of a "higher force" whose protoprovidential capacities were thought discoverable: "There are no accidents; everything that happens has meaning, and the more science searches and looks, the more obvious becomes the thought that everything that is or happens is a link of a hidden chain. . . . What happens does not happen by chance, a higher being calculatingly and meaningfully presides over all creation" (*DWN* 177). This passage was written in 1862. Within a few years Nietzsche would abandon all providential belief. The universe was no longer conceived as a lawful order of being, a cosmos, but as a chaos, a place of constant flux and strife. The Judeo-Christian God would be replaced by the Heraclitean deities. Accident, not law, became the moving force behind events.[1] All order is illusion and imposed meaning. The universe is not unfolding the way it should. But we can interpret it so.

Nietzsche's atheism did not spell the end of his attachment to the idea of love of fate. With God out of the way, man comes into his own. What cannot be controlled can be interpreted creatively. The sign of a higher morality is a full affirmation of life as it unfolds. Citing Emerson, Nietzsche was wont to say that for the higher man each day is holy, that is, each day is made holy by the full exercise of his creative powers.[2] Already as a philology student at Leipzig Nietzsche had expounded this view in a letter: "Indeed it remains within our power to use each event, small and large accidents for our improvement and fitness, and as it were to exhaust it. . . . It rests upon our

[1] *Accident* is a misleading word. As Nietzsche pointed out, only in a world of purpose and lawful order does it have meaning (*GS* 168). Accidents happen in the temporary absence of law or purpose. A world without purpose or law, then, has no place for accidents.

[2] The incarnations of the higher man for Emerson, as the following passage from his essay "History" indicates, were identical to Nietzsche's: "To the poet, to the philosopher, to the saint, all things are friendly and sacred, all events profitable, all days holy, all men divine."

disposition: the worth we attribute to an event has that value for us. Thoughtless and immoral people do not know of such an intentionality of fate" (*NB* 20.2.67). Fate is no longer a providential distribution of meaning and justice; it is simply what befalls us. However, one must be of the disposition and have the power literally to make the best of it. One must be like those "masters of musical improvisation" who are capable of "breathing a beautiful meaning and a soul into an accident" (*GS* 243). One then ceases to have "wishes," Nietzsche wrote, because one learns to harvest the best fruits of knowledge from whatever land one passes through (*NB* 18.10.75). Indeed, man is the "soil" upon which the "seedcorn" fate is scattered: it is the quality of the soil that determines if anything of beauty or use will grow (*HH* 293).

Amor fati is not fatalism. The fatalist believes himself to be as a leaf in the wind: the forces of nature, of history, of chance, are simply too great to be affected or combatted. Resignation yields rest and comfort. *Amor fati* induces struggle with these forces. Fate is not merely what happens *to* one, but what happens as a result of one's active involvement with life. The love of fate is the love of this involvement and of its outcome. One cherishes the opportunity to do battle with *fortuna*.

The fatalist actually resents fate. He has not learned how he might joyfully partake as the "iron hands of necessity . . . shake the dice box of chance" (*D* 81). The lover of fate, on the other hand, makes everything that comes his way a cause for celebration. Temporary defeats are welcomed as preparations for greater victories. Pain and privation are seen as tools in the workshop of wisdom. One is having constantly to hone these tools against *fortuna*'s stone, the better to achieve tomorrow what has eluded one today. Those practiced in this trade are rewarded for their efforts.[3] They ride the waves of destiny to win their prize:

[3] Nietzsche interpreted his numerous and chronic physical ailments in this light. In 1884 he wrote: "Each step on the way of my task demands

the opportunity to create from their haphazard voyage something of meaning and beauty. Fate becomes a sort of providence for those capable of breathing soul into accident. To love one's fate means fully to affirm one's life, not resentfully to oppose it. The paradox, however, is that it is the most difficult of struggles to love fate. Only constant self-overcoming develops the power necessary to embrace destiny. Only a changing self can accept what is. Once again, it is only through the eyes of deficiency that ideals are seen. The hero negates and affirms himself, endlessly struggling to be at rest, waging inner war that he may truly love himself. Love of fate is won, temporarily, in this ongoing battle for peace. *Amor fati* is the disposition of the overman. For man it is a fleeting mood.

In *The Gay Science* Nietzsche first introduced the term *amor fati* as something yet unachieved: "I want to learn more and more to see as beautiful what is necessary in things; then I shall be one of those who make things beautiful. *Amor fati*: Let that be my love henceforth! . . . some day I wish to be only a Yes-sayer" (*GS* 223). To wish is not to be. Indeed, one must *be* a no-sayer, a destroyer and struggler, if one is to *become* something different, namely, a yes-sayer. The ideal that drives one to grow and change must, if one is to embrace fate, eventually sublimate into the love of what is.

The extent to which one demonstrates this love reveals one's affinity with the overman: "My formula for greatness in a human being is *amor fati*: that one wants nothing to be different, not forward, not backward, not in all eternity. Not merely bear what is necessary, still less conceal it—all idealism is mendaciousness in the face of what is necessary—but *love* it" (*EH* 258). *Amor fati* is the "highest state" attainable to man, constituting a "Dionysian relationship to existence" (*WP* 536). An abundance of strength

---

dreadful payment and now, as I understand my life more, it seems to me that all my bodily misery of the last 12 years falls under the category of such installments" (*NB* 13–14.11.84).

and joy allows one to affirm all—past, present, and future. The affirmation of the present and future may be facilitated through hope. One may joyfully greet one's trials believing that their hardships will yield greater strength, that the toil will prove worth the trouble. But what of the past? To want nothing to be different in the past is the true measure of *amor fati*. Here acceptance is not enough. It cannot be mixed with hope to yield a higher grade of satisfaction. One must indeed *love* one's fate to desire that it be as it was without the slightest modification. Otherwise the will, impotent regarding the past, will be wrathful and full of vengeance. "To redeem the past and to transform every 'It was' into an 'I wanted it thus!'—that alone do I call redemption!" Zarathustra proclaims (Z 161–62). True love of fate demands that one no longer need hope in order to live joyfully.[4]

Fate is loved when one is consumed by living it. Life must not serve as a means to some other end, even if that end is growth. The experiences of life, past and present, are not to be seen as stepping-stones to preferred states in the present or future: "Becoming must be explained without recourse to final intentions; becoming must appear justified at every moment . . . the present must absolutely not be justified by reference to a future, nor the past by reference to the present" (*WP* 377). Living, like loving, must be its own reward.

The eternal recurrence is best understood as the test of one's *amor fati*, and hence of one's greatness. For the most part, Nietzsche did not attempt to prove his proposition that all things repeat themselves endlessly, as the rotation of an infinitely large circle through all eternity.[5] Rather, ac-

---

[4] One is reminded of Goethe, Nietzsche's closest approximation of the overman, who wrote: "Hope is the second soul of unhappiness."

[5] Although Nietzsche considered the eternal recurrence the "most *scientific* of all possible hypotheses" (*WP* 36), this was not to deem it true. What man finds useful or necessary to believe does not bear on the validity of these beliefs. The eternal recurrence is more of a creed for atheists than a cosmological theory: "Who does not believe in a *circular process of*

ceptance of the eternal recurrence was considered the means of separating the wheat from the chaff. It was proposed as a criterion of selection (*WP* 255). Dionysus, one recalls, is a judge. He whose affirmation of life is not strong enough or complete enough for him to desire nothing more than to repeat the same life, endlessly, without the slightest alteration, is considered unfit for the new faith. However, the eternal recurrence is not simply a concept to be grasped and subsequently accepted. It must be lived, experienced in a moment of rapturous affirmation. It must emerge from the torments of nihilism, allowing the ultimate redemption from the greatest affliction. Nietzsche was not anxious to convert: "Are you prepared? You must have lived through every degree of scepticism and with lust bathed in ice-cold streams,—otherwise you have no right to this thought [of the eternal recurrence]; I want to protect myself well from the credulous and enthusiastic" (*GW* 11:188). Preparation, however, is not an intellectual

---

the universe must believe in a *willful* God" (*GW* 11:178). But the belief found necessary by atheists does not prove the eternal recurrence any more than the belief found necessary by theists proves the existence of God. Nietzsche's notes in *The Will to Power* (secs. 55 and 1066) that attempt to refute mechanism were his only efforts at substantiating his hypothesis of the eternal recurrence. Here he demonstrated that if mechanism were strictly true then "the great dice game of existence" must "pass through a calculable number of combinations" in an infinite period of time, and thus reach an end point (*WP* 549). The fact that an end point has not been reached serves as a negative proof of the necessary circularity of the process.

The problem with this proof is evident in Nietzsche's choice of metaphor. It is true that the possible combinations of a limited number of forces, construed as rational numbers like the natural numbers represented on dice, is calculable and finite, and that no matter how large the number of forces, their possible combinations will be exhausted given an infinite amount of time. But we have no a priori reason to construe the universe, or the forces therein, as the sum or product of rational numbers. If, for instance, the forces of the universe are also represented by irrational numbers, that is, numbers that cannot be expressed as a quotient, having no finite decimal value (e.g., 22/7 or π), then their combinations (through addition or multiplication) do not necessarily have a finite value. So conceived, the interaction of forces in the universe need never reach an end point or return to an original position.

exercise. The eternal recurrence is not so much an experiment in thought as an ecstatic experience. One must earn one's position of honor by living one's heaven and hell on earth.

Nietzsche held that all existence was inextricably meshed. To alter the slightest detail affects the whole. The constitution of an individual is not selective: it entails all of its pleasure and pain, knowledge and ignorance, limitations and experience. The constitution of history is no different. Circumstance begets identity. It follows that were *anything* different in history, one would not have come to be as one is. To have arrived at the moment of experiencing the Dionysian rapture, then, is to embrace everything that led to this moment:

> The first question is by no means whether we are content with ourselves, but whether we are content with anything at all. If we affirm one single moment, we thus affirm not only ourselves but all existence. For nothing is self-sufficient, neither in us ourselves nor in things; and if our soul has trembled with happiness and sounded like a harp string just once, all eternity was needed to produce this one event—and in this single moment of affirmation all eternity was called good, redeemed, justified, and affirmed. (*WP* 532–33)

In the *Untimely Meditations* Nietzsche submitted that "if that greatest of all wishes were fulfilled for only a day, how gladly one would exchange for it all the rest of life!" (*UM* 159). In effect, the moment of experiencing the eternal recurrence is the fulfillment of this wish. Nietzsche has gone one better than Plato's endeavor with Gyges' Ring. Nietzsche claimed to have achieved in practice what previous thinkers had only theorized about. He who experiences the eternal recurrence not only is granted the power to do as he pleases, but comes to interpret his past as perfect. He is grateful for all; he has no unfulfilled wish because he wishes things to be exactly as they were, are, and shall be. In short, to experience a moment of perfection is to desire nothing to be different; for the slightest change would have aborted the arrival of such an all-redeeming moment.

"Immortal is the moment when I produced the recurrence," Nietzsche declared: "For the sake of this moment I *endure* the recurrence" (*GW* 14:132). The terror and meaninglessness of an eternally recurring life, without justification or purpose, is borne because of a moment's ecstasy, a moment in which one feels strong enough to justify life *tout court*. The first proclamation of the eternal recurrence occurs in *The Gay Science* under the heading "The Greatest Weight." Would you curse the demon that informed you of the eternal recurrence, asked Nietzsche, "or have you once experienced a tremendous moment when you would have answered him: 'You are a god and never have I heard anything more divine' " (*GS* 273–74). To experience the eternal recurrence is to know that its affirmation can have no substitute. Nietzsche spoke of it as a watershed in history.

Apart from its being a test of spiritual greatness, the eternal recurrence also serves as a moral prod for the higher man. He must seek at all times to act in a way he would wish to repeat eternally. Each action must be justified on its own merits, apart from its purely utilitarian function as payment for a future good. Such an imperative is the positive feature of an active nihilism: one is to live *in* the here and now, *for* the here and now. It is constitutive of the disposition of the overman, of his higher morality, his celebration of life, and his heroism.[6]

[6] In discussing *Thus Spoke Zarathustra*, Carl Jung made a similar point, noting that "the full realization of the here and now is a moral accomplishment which is only short of heroism: it is an almost heroic achievement" (*Nietzsche's Zarathustra* 2:1289). According to Nietzsche, this realization is only fully achieved by the overhero. It is ushered in, however, by a heroic morality, a morality freed of means/ends calculation (*GW* 16:189). The antipode was defined by Nietzsche as the "morality of utility" (*BGE* 178), the "cunning" slave morality, which seeks to maximize

Herein lies the feat: to live life as a series of aesthetically self-fulfilling moments, without expectations or hope. It is a burden enough to crush most men: "The question in each and every thing, 'Do you desire this once more and innumerable times more?' would lie upon your actions as the greatest weight" (GS 274). Nietzsche explained in a passage entitled "The Most Dangerous Point of View" that indeed he did mean each and every thing. All actions, from the apparently trivial to the so-called world historic, are considered to be of equal value (GS 213). For each moment is laden with the burden of being self-justifying, of being worthy of eternal repetition regardless of its consequences. The danger of such a perspective is in its capacity to overwhelm the individual with a daunting responsibility for the worthiness of his every move and whim. Moreover, every thought, word, and deed provides a snapshot of the soul, revealing its development, its present state of order, and its potential. One is and reveals at all times the cumulative product of one's life. Every moment stands as a link in the chain of necessity and yet carries the responsibility of unfolding in a way that redeems itself. There are no exceptions and no escapes from such exhibition: the soul stands in permanent display. Nietzsche argued that one must strive to reveal a masterpiece that justifies scrutiny.

In the idea of the eternal recurrence Nietzsche had combined the most stringent determinism and its accompanying sense of irresponsibility with the highest level of moral idealism.[7] All the interconnected links in the chain of necessity join to produce the self. Yet one feels only the free-

---

goods and benefits and minimize suffering (whether in this world or the next).

[7] Cf. WP 546: "The two most extreme modes of thought—the mechanistic and the Platonic —are reconciled in the *eternal recurrence*: both as ideals." Mechanism or determinism and Platonism, by which Nietzsche meant (moral) idealism, are reconciled in the eternally repeating, inescapable chain of events whose every moment is to be lived as a moral struggle to approach the ideal form of life.

dom to act and the accompanying duty to make one's actions worthy of themselves. Not unlike the classical hero's task of fulfilling his fate by displaying excellence in battle, the task of the Nietzschean hero is joyfully to struggle to achieve what could not be otherwise. He must strive to become who he is.

ELEVEN

BECOMING WHO YOU ARE

For I am *he*, from the heart and from the beginning, drawing, drawing towards me, drawing up to me, raising up, a
drawer, trainer, and taskmaster who once bade himself,
and not in vain: "Become what you are!"
—*Thus Spoke Zarathustra*

"Character is destiny," Heraclitus announced, and once
again Nietzsche concurred with his philosophical mentor.
Without doubt Nietzsche believed the individual to be a
product of nature, not nurture, the bearer of innate drives
and valuations that can be neither created nor destroyed.
At best these drives may be reordered, rearranged, and
coordinated, stimulated or subordinated. "There is no annihilation in the sphere of spirit," Nietzsche stipulated
(*WP* 323). Nor is there creation ex nihilo, only actualization
of what already exists as potentiality. The correct arrange-
ment of the soul is that which best realizes its innate capacities.

The task of ordering souls above all requires self-knowledge—an awareness of one's drives, their respective
strengths, weaknesses, and interactions. Philosophers and
prophets, artists, seers, and saints have attempted to apply their trade to the betterment of mankind. But they mis-
took the effect for the cause. Changing worldviews and
instituting moral regimes are not the means to new and
better human beings. Rather, new and better human beings are the means to changed worldviews and moral re-

gimes. For thought is always only the pale reflection of fundamentally immutable drives.

Nietzsche held that philosophy was simply a conceptualization and intellectualization of one's spiritual constitution. In 1869 he wrote to his friend Paul Deussen: "The right philosophy for each individual is ἀνάμνησις. . . . You want a philosophy that at the same time gives you a practical canon: only ask yourself more precisely about the particular driving forces of your past actions: one cannot with consciousness create oneself any new driving forces" (*NB* 19.12.69). Two years earlier Nietzsche had already voiced the fundamental tenets of his own aristocratic philosophy. The order of rank of men is by and large a product of birth or inheritance. A man may discover noble drives in himself, but he cannot create them. Education and proper environment are merely the means of nurturing the greatness that in rare individuals already lies in seed: "There is an ethical aristocracy, on the other hand, just as there is a spiritual one. The immutable character becomes influenced by its environment and education in its expressions, not in its essence" (*GW* 1:404). Education provides the soil in which youth may strike root and achieve maximum growth; but to produce an oak tree one must start with an acorn, not a mustard seed. Two decades later Nietzsche would make the same point: "Against the doctrine of the influence of the milieu and external causes: the force within is infinitely superior; much that looks like external influence is merely its adaptation from within" (*WP* 47). Environment is not so much a determining force on the individual as a force to be determined and exploited by the individual.[1]

---

[1] The almost universal categorization of Nietzsche as a historicist or cultural relativist, that is, someone who maintains that one's historical or cultural environment determines one's thought, values, and capacities, is quite false. Even those who display a sophisticated understanding of Nietzsche's pathos and project generally fail to recognize or reflect upon his ahistoricist and nonrelativist tendencies. Allan Bloom, for example, mistakenly wrote that Nietzsche held man to have "no other mode of

Greatness, then, is always the product of the disciplined stimulation of strong drives. Nobility is of the blood. It is "incontestable," Nietzsche wrote, that "we are all related and allied to the saint, . . . philosopher and artist" (*UM* 161). But the propinquity of this kinship is far from uniform, and its full development is denied to many. Only those with a heroic disposition will burden themselves with the task of realizing these ideals within themselves. And only the philosopher, artist, and saint, Nietzsche declared, are "no longer animal": "Nature, which never makes a leap, has made its one leap in creating them" (*UM* 159). To escape the constraints of animal nature, one must already be above it in constitution.

Complacency, however, is not the complementary attitude to such an aristocratic philosophy. For the higher man's potential is forever in need of discovery, and his actualization of potentialities remains a struggle, a continuous self-overcoming. Man has a multiple soul. Unlike the lower animals, he is a battleground for warring instincts. Participation in the conflictual politics of the soul is the dictate of higher morality—the mark of heroic individualism. But this imperative of self-development does not contradict Nietzsche's tenet of innate determination. Growth is nothing but the rearrangement of drives, a change of political regime. The players remain the same, but they are reorganized, their powers enhanced or diminished. The "constellation" of an individual's personality is as fixed as

---

support than a particular culture. The actuality of plants and other animals is contained in their potentialities; but this is not true of man. . . . Nietzsche's contribution was to draw with perfect intransigence the consequences of that idea and try to live with them" (*The Closing of the American Mind* [New York: Simon and Schuster, 1987], p. 203). In fact, Nietzsche maintained that great men conversed with each other throughout the ages from their mountain peaks, for they found few if any receptive ears and recognizable voices in their own time. A strong culture is held necessarily to be founded on an ahistorical understanding of greatness. The "exalted spirit-dialogue" within the transcultural "republic of genius" is possible because history allows great individuals of all ages to live "contemporaneously" (*UM* 111; cf. *GW* 4:142).

that of the stars, even if different lights will shine more brightly in the course of its years (*HH* 227): "We do not believe that a man will become another if he is not that other already; i.e., if he is not, as is often the case, a multiplicity of persons, at least the embryos of persons. In this case, one can bring a different role into the foreground and draw 'the former man' back—The aspect is changed, not the essence" (*WP* 211).[2] Which foreground one presents, which mask one wears to create the illusion of a united self, is a question of style. Great style, for Nietzsche, is not something everyone can achieve. Organized mediocrity is still mediocrity. Just as the caliber of society's highest exemplars determines the value of that society, so too the caliber of the inner drives, assuming they are correctly ordered, determines the greatness of the individual.

Zarathustra, the moral iconoclast, issues his own commandment: "You shall *make amends* to your children for being the children of your fathers: *thus* you shall redeem all that is past! This new law-table do I put over you!" (*Z* 221). The inheritance is fixed for each individual. Its best exploitation constitutes the challenge of a higher morality. One must properly invest all of one's inheritance to become more than a parasitic heir. Upon this spiritual capital one's progeny may look forward to even greater wealth. This is the pious task of the active nihilist. This is the task of producing greatness, both in the self and in the world. Man

[2] A remark in *Human, All Too Human* qualifies—although, far from contradicting, actually reinforces—Nietzsche's frequent pronouncements as to the innate determination of man and the practical unalterability of character: "That the character is unalterable is not in the strict sense true; this favourite proposition means rather no more than that, during the brief lifetime of a man, the effective motives are unable to scratch deeply enough to erase the imprinted script of many millennia. If one imagines a man of eighty-thousand years, however, one would have in him a character totally alterable: so that an abundance of different individuals would evolve out of him one after the other" (*HH* 35). Nietzsche's perspectivism effectively concentrated this evolution into a normal life span; indeed, it was a means of living "an abundance of different individuals" simultaneously.

must effectively acquire what he already owns. That is to say, moral duty lies in that higher egoism that induces the individual to fully develop himself. Nietzsche endorsed Goethe's dictum: "What you have inherited from your father, / Earn it that you may possess it" (GW 2:361). The hope was to free man from the stultifying morality of self-lessness. Both 'good' and 'evil' qualities were to be engaged to ensure maximum growth and strength. The most pious man, Nietzsche maintained, was he who served his god with his evil qualities as well as his goodness (GW 14:79). The selfishness of the parts is to be encouraged and exploited for the benefit of the whole. Nietzsche's most beloved dictum was taken from Pindar: "Become who you are." Its exegesis would provide a summary of Nietzsche's entire philosophy.

The frequent repetition of Pindar's words should be understood as advice for a select readership, not a moral recipe for the masses. Those born without noble souls have little to develop into. Everyone is a multiplicity of potential selves, but the pedigree of those selves and their capacity for order varies. For the many the dictum is therefore inapplicable. For the few it is appropriate. And for the very few, those rare individuals of genius whose development needs no encouragement, it is unnecessary, being, as Nietzsche points out, the dictate of conscience (GS 219): " 'Become who you are:' that is a call that is only ever allowed for the few, but for the very few is superfluous" (GW 9:404). While Nietzsche delighted in his mostly silent conversations with "the very few"—that "republic of genius" of which he felt himself to be the newest if not greatest member—it was primarily with "the few" that he was concerned. These are the higher men of a nihilistic age who might be enchanted by his writings, spurred on to develop their heroic potential by Nietzsche's vivid accounts of his own victories.

Zarathustra's announcement that he is the taskmaster who has realized Pindar's dictum is preceded by a passage that indicates how this discriminating disciple of Dionysus usurped the role of his Christian counterpart:

> My happiness itself shall I cast far and wide, between sunrise, noontide, and sunset, to see if many human fishes will not learn to kick and tug at my happiness,
>   until they, biting on my sharp, hidden hooks, have to come up to *my* height, the most multicoloured groundlings of the abyss to the most wicked of all fishers of men. (Z 252)

Zarathustra's wickedness is none other than his cruelty as a taskmaster to himself and those he loves. His concern is to develop his powers and the accompanying joy in life; his gift to others is a sharing of the product of his efforts. Zarathustra's evangelism is but a display of his own happiness surpassing Christ's ministry in its capacity to affirm life within an ironic life-project. The irony lies in the realization that the hooks are all too likely to remain empty. But such results are irrelevant. The activity of the fisher of men, regardless of his catch, must be self-fulfilling.

In other words, for all his evangelical endeavors, the higher man primarily addresses an inner audience. He is caught up with and in himself. His overwhelming project is to unify a multiple soul. This effort to "impose upon becoming the character of being" is the mark of "the supreme will to power" (*WP* 330). The higher man's self-appointed destiny is to make a cosmos of his chaotic inheritance.[3] In turn, his every word and deed bears witness to the struggle. Those unobsessed with this task are also those incapable of stylizing their lives. Their actions are not ciphers of their souls. The anarchy within produces

---

[3] Much of the recent (deconstructionist) writing on Nietzsche is occupied with his diffusion, dispersion, fragmentation, or destruction of the subject or self. In disregarding his eulogies of and proposals for its creative reunification, however, these commentaries fail to account for Nietzsche's primary concern as an educator, a philosopher, and an aesthetic stylist.

reactions as random as their external stimuli. Deeds no longer serve as indicators of constitutional order. Considering how "little personality" most men have, Nietzsche remarked, most actions will be "merely epidermal, merely reflexes that respond to a stimulus" (*WP* 136). The scholar's work, for example, gives little notice of *who* the scholar is. His readings or the events of the day determine what sort of reactions he shall have upon the page: "In the philosopher, on the contrary, there is nothing whatever impersonal; and, above all, his morality bears decided and decisive testimony to *who he is*—that is to say, to the order of rank the innermost drives of his nature stand in relative to one another" (*BGE* 19–20). The philosopher, unlike the scholar, lives a stylized life. And style, Nietzsche wrote, is the proof that one believes in one's words, indeed, that one does not merely think one's thoughts but "feels" them (*NB* 24.8.82). To order the soul, to stylize one's life, and to display oneself in great works are different ways of saying the same thing. They are all characteristic of him whose unending struggle and foremost passion is to become himself: "Everyone *possesses inborn talent*, but few possess the degree of inborn and acquired toughness, endurance and energy actually to become a talent, that is to say to *become* what he *is*: which means to discharge it in works and actions" (*HH* 125).

The discharged phenomena of a stylized life produce a holograph of the soul. However a work or an action is examined, one receives a picture of the entire soul from which it emerged, a three-dimensional image capable of being viewed from various perspectives. Even the smallest fragment of the individual's activity, like a broken piece of holographic plate, can be projected to yield an image of the whole. The opposite of a technical flourish or appended decoration, style is what gives the work its organic character.

Nietzsche's own style necessarily had many forms to match the plurality within his soul. The number of masks he wore and the resulting ambiguities and contradictions of his writing exhibit, however, a more comprehensive unity: the unity of form and content, of the multiplicity of perspectives with, for example, the multiplicity of aphoristic entries or the multiplicity of tempers taken by each of his books. To reveal the power needed to bring something to order, one must display both the chaotic tendencies and the achieved cosmos. For the benefit of the "shortsighted" Nietzsche asked the rhetorical question: "Do you think this work must be fragmentary because I give it to you (and have to give it to you) in fragments?" (*HH* 243). An explicit answer is given a decade later in *Ecce Homo*: the unifying feature of Nietzsche's style is precisely its plurality. "To communicate a state, an inward tension of pathos, by means of signs, including the tempo of these signs— that is the meaning of every style; and considering that the multiplicity of inward states is exceptionally large in my case, I have many stylistic possibilities—the most multifarious art of style that has ever been at the disposal of one man" (*EH* 265). What holds the various "stylistic possibilities" together in Nietzsche is an overpowering *agonal* spirit. It is this "constraint of a single taste" that allowed Nietzsche to form his multiple personae into artistic wholes (*GS* 232). His books, whatever voices they evinced, bore the mark of a heroic disposition.

The hero may be said to lead his life poetically. Poetry grasps at particulars that it may touch the universal, trucking with words that the ineffable might be approached. The hero writes the poem of his life with his deeds. Each of his actions reveals the totality of his character.[4] "My the-

---

[4] In his *Maxims and Reflections* Goethe wrote that poetry "expresses something particular without thinking of the universal or pointing to it. Whoever grasps this particular in a living way will simultaneously receive the universal, too, without even becoming aware of it—or realize it only later" (quoted in Walter Kaufmann, *From Shakespeare to Existentialism* [New York: Anchor Books, 1959], p. 54). Goethe's, above all others', was Nietzsche's model of the aesthetic life, a life that solicits responsibility for

ory: in *every action* of a man the *entire development* of his psychic life is gone through," Nietzsche submitted (*GW* 16:263). It follows that "everything bears witness to what we are, our friendships and enmities, our glance and the clasp of our hand, our memory and that which we do not remember, our books and our handwriting" (*UM* 129). One is at every moment the construct of previous experiences; each action is an index to the entirety of one's history (*GW* 14:31). Here Nietzsche's understanding of the stylized life and the idea of the eternal recurrence merge. For the higher man there are no insignificant thoughts, words, or deeds. He understands himself to be the sum of his effects (*WP* 296). Everything is a testament to his past, a prophecy of his future, and a revelation of who he is in the present. His life, in its smallest details, is laden with the burden of justifying itself, apart from any utility, as a poem justifies its reading.

The paradox contained within the dictum "Become who you are" reveals the nature of living one's life as a work of art. The self is not so much created as unfolded. The uniqueness of the individual makes this revelation appear as creation, for what unfolds is nowhere duplicated. At the same time, retrospect allows recognition of one's "granite stratum of spiritual fate" (*BGE* 143). As the individual "creates" himself over time, facet after facet of the preexisting self is revealed. Yet *the* self is never completely discovered. Its unfolding is as the paring of an infinitely large onion. The sense of penetration is ever present, but the core is never reached: "How can man know himself? He is a thing dark and veiled; and if the hare has seven skins, man can slough off seventy times seven and still not be able to say: 'this is really you, this is no longer outer shell!' " (*UM* 129). Zarathustra himself admitted not knowing the height of his own mountain peaks (*Z* 168).

---

the totality of its experience. In his autobiographical outline of 1810 Goethe wrote: "Principal insight: ultimately everything is ethical."

For the true self, Nietzsche claimed, lies not so much within as above and beyond one. It is glimpsed during flights of spirit and cannot be captured or harnessed. The true self is the seed of aspiration. Its growth describes the entwinement of the real and the ideal.

Three years before the publication of his first book, while still a student, Nietzsche wrote that youth's ideals cast a spell on the man from which he never emerges, even though the "idealizing gaze" has long since died out from his eyes (*DWN* 453). This proved to be a prophetic statement. The ideals that came to life in Nietzsche's earliest works never died. They were continually struggled with, overcome, resuscitated, and transformed. A section of *Human, All Too Human* stands as a prescient autobiographical note:

> An idealist is incorrigible: if he is ejected from his Heaven he makes an ideal out of Hell. Let him be disillusioned and behold!—he will embrace this disillusionment just as fervently as a little while before he embraced his hopes. Insofar as his tendency is among the great incurable tendencies of human nature he is able to give rise to tragic destinies and afterwards become the subject of tragedies: for tragedies have to do with precisely what is incurable, ineluctable, inescapable in the fate and character of man. (*HH* 218–19)

The tragic hero writes his biography with his own blood. His struggle to become an individual ends with the cry "Ecce Homo!" It is a cry that became the title of Nietzsche's final autobiography, written in the last year of his productive life and appropriately subtitled *How One Becomes What One Is*. In that same year, 1888, Nietzsche prefaced his *Vita* with a note acknowledging that his "Schopenhauer as Educator"—the essay that first proclaimed the necessity of ascending the stepladder of the soul that one might achieve the heroic life as incarnated in the philosopher, artist, and saint—contained "the whole plan"

according to which he had hitherto lived (*NB* 10.4.88).
Shortly thereafter Nietzsche wrote *Twilight of the Idols*. This
work ends with a reflection on his own destiny, one he
could not escape and therefore chose to celebrate:

> Affirmation of life even in its strangest and sternest
> problems, the will to life rejoicing in its own inex-
> haustibility through the *sacrifice* of its highest types—
> *that* is what I called Dionysian . . . *to realize in oneself*
> the eternal joy of becoming—that joy which also en-
> compasses *joy in destruction*. . . . And with that I again
> return to the place from which I set out—the *Birth of
> Tragedy* was my first revaluation of all values: with
> that I again plant myself in the soil out of which I
> draw all that I will and *can*—I, the last disciple of the
> philosopher Dionysus—I, the teacher of the eternal
> recurrence. (*TI* 110–11)

The circle of return is completed. The hero exhausts his
potential and resolutely meets his fate. His down-going,
in the end, is always a self-sacrifice. He burns in the fire
of his own teaching.

CONCLUSION

> We criticize a man or a book most sharply when we sketch
> out their ideal.
>
> —*Human, All Too Human*

For all his solitude, Nietzsche undeniably lived in the company of friends and critics, living and dead. His work may
be shown to reflect this intellectual environment. His work
also may be placed within a broader historical and cultural
context. For the most part, I have chosen to do neither.
This it not to gainsay its interest or importance. My reasons are thematic. Nietzsche's effort to live a heroic life
was an attempt to overstep the boundaries of his age. He
sought to become untimely. Described in terms of a politics of the soul, his endeavor provides the thematic core of
this commentary. It is in these terms that his heroic individualism is best approached. For we are thus allowed an
understanding of Nietzsche as a man engaged in the
struggle to become autonomous—to become himself—by
means of a spiritual politics.

One might approach Nietzsche as he did Socrates, identifying the prey as the residue of a historical and cultural
process. Certainly Nietzsche made himself fair game. Yet
such an endeavor would now be too commonplace to redeem itself, as Nietzsche's work redeems itself, by the
originality of its tactics and the daring of its attacks. Indeed, any systematic attempt to capture Nietzsche within
a contextual net might well entail a reversal of roles. The
hunter would become the hunted, his methodology
turned against him by his quarry. Nietzsche foresaw that

his dance would foil and frustrate all those whose spirit of gravity forbade partnership in a gay science.

Independence, freedom, and creativity—so strived for and so cherished by Nietzsche—appear as fictions when viewed retrospectively, within a context that defines the nature and price of every struggle. From a certain perspective the process of becoming who one is seems mechanically, or at best organically, determined. Nietzsche refused to dismiss this paradox. Consequently his name is often held to be synonymous with radical historicism and cultural relativism, and with all the nihilistic forces they engender. In this matter Nietzsche is mistakenly portrayed as the champion of that which he ceaselessly combatted. His intellectual integrity would not allow him to deny the reality of these forces: he challenged his readers to rise above them. Nietzsche's originality and daring is most evident in his tragic effort to escape the trap of nihilism that he himself had uncovered.

Nietzsche announced the shipwreck of humanity. He charted the course that led to its devastation. And he reported the aimless dispersion of the flotsam. The debris was being carried by historical currents whose effects, Nietzsche noted with irony, were being plotted with scientific rigor even as the disintegration accelerated. But he also described an experiment in which he became the surging waves themselves, intoxicated with freedom and power, reaching beyond themselves to attain a greater height. Certainly one could render an account of this experiment in terms of its contextual undercurrents, the submarine formations that structured it, and the celestial bodies exerting their invisible gravitational force. But that would be another project.

My purpose, in short, was to bring Nietzsche's thought to life, not to bury it under the weight of the past. But what of Nietzsche's future, our present? What should Nietzsche mean for us today? There is a certain momentum that propels commentary toward a specific accounting of its contribution to and place within current discourse and practice. What is the value of reading Nietzsche? How, in short, should Nietzsche be *appropriated*?

These questions, too, have been intentionally avoided: in part, because they cannot be answered, at least not in a single voice. Nietzsche taught that human plurality finds its roots in the plurality of the soul. There are many ways of reading Nietzsche into our lives. *The* way does not exist. Indeed, the question of how best to appropriate Nietzsche should not be answered, at least not until he has been wrestled with on his own terms. We are probably incapable of entering Nietzsche's labyrinth untethered to our desires, duties, and projects. Moreover, given the dangers lurking within this maze, and the possibility of becoming hopelessly lost within it, rejecting Ariadne's thread would appear imprudent. Even so, we must recognize that security has its costs. One must be a long time lost, that most imprudent of philosophers wrote, before one is permitted to find oneself. Such is the price to be paid, Nietzsche testified, for certain experiences. And like Theseus, the legendary recipient of Ariadne's gift and father of Athenian democracy, Nietzsche would have achieved nothing great had he not time and again spurned security. However or whenever we choose to leave Nietzsche's labyrinth, it should be entered without the bias that its contents were meant to be placed in the service of our preconceived goals like so many tools standing in reserve. A truly creative effort, Nietzsche indicated, is predicated on the rejection of such an instrumental orientation.

A politics is to be confronted in Nietzsche. Its thrust, however, is not toward the realization of specific goals but rather toward the exploration of the human condition that any such attempted realization must address. That there exists a politics of the soul; that Nietzsche therewith described human being, investigated its plurality, and experimented with its potential; and that we are confronted with the indissoluble question of its meaning: certainly these are political challenges of the first order. Still, if we are to draw a practical lesson from our exposure to the politics of Nietzsche's soul, and articulate it in words that speak to our political life, then it must be such as challenges its own generic appeal. The human condition is not one, but many. Within society, as within the soul, there are no recipes for justice, however much the ingredients may remain the same; there is no substitute for courage and struggle.

"Truth," Nietzsche wrote, "seldom lives where her temples are built and her priests ordained" (NB 6.4.67). This, he lamented, was the indictment of all modern philosophizing: "Limited by governments, churches, academies, customs and the cowardice of men to the appearance of scholarship; it sighs 'if only' or knows 'there once was' and does nothing else" (UM 85). Nietzsche sought to do more. So must his interpreters. We tend to talk so abstractly about poetry, Nietzsche observed, because we are bad poets. The same might be said of philosophy, and in particular Nietzsche's philosophy. For he held that there was only one way truly to assess a philosophy, and that was to attempt to live in accordance with it. He who does not live out a philosophy is not involved with philosophy at all, but is engaged only in a "critique of words by means of other words" (UM 187). Much scholarship on Nietzsche is open to this charge. For the most part, Nietzsche has been interpreted as if his final work bore the miscegenational title Ecce Logos. In contrast, the preceding pages furnish an investigation of Nietzsche's works in the way I believe he meant them to be understood: not abstractly but philosophically, which for Nietzsche meant personally. This is not to place biography above the text, but to understand the text as biographical.

To live one's philosophy, we are told, is to live heroically, to become an individual. Nietzsche knew this life as his reality and his ideal. With all gods and idols banished, the only worthy ideals are found in the creative unfolding

221

of the self. Hence the importance of the politics of the soul. For only the sublimation of struggle, a spiritual agony, enables the real and the ideal to merge. Nietzsche's writings are the inspiring, disturbing, often contradictory, and always passionate biographical notes of a man engaged in the paradoxical struggle to become who he is.

When Zarathustra leaves his cave for the final time, we find him glowing like the morning sun. Unlike the philosopher who leaves Plato's cave, Zarathustra is not blinded by the glare of ideals—for he is his own light. But this does not mean he will be better able to communicate his visions to the deluded dwellers below whose gazes remain fixed on shadows. Nietzsche's spiritually aristocratic character is patent. No less than for Plato is his city populated with souls of different metals. No less than for Plato does the politics of the soul remain his primary concern. No less than Plato would he respond to the question, What is the best form of political regime? with the answer of Solon— "For whom?" But unlike Plato, he has no concern with the noble lies involved in expatiating this answer. That such lies were necessary he had no doubt; but their content and delivery are not of interest. Herein does Nietzsche's truly antipolitical character emerge. For as a philosopher he lives both apolitically and impolitically: apolitically, owing to his narrowly conceived audience—"Our presuppositions: no God: no purpose: finite force. Let us guard against thinking out and prescribing the mode of thought necessary to lesser men!!" (*WP* 324)—and impolitically, owing to what his audience narrowly conceives—"Our supreme insights must—and should!—sound like follies, in certain cases like crimes, when they come impermissibly to the ears of those who are not predisposed and predestined for them" (*BGE* 43). The predisposed and predestined are those higher men capable of turning the nemesis of nihilism into a joyous Nike. Nietzsche wrote for these tragic-heroic types, unconcerned and careless of other ears: "These alone are my readers, my rightful readers, my predestined readers: what do the *rest* matter?—The rest are merely mankind" (*A* 114).

The philosopher is engrossed in his own problems; he has little time for the world of politics around him. If for no other reason, this is because no change in that world could bear upon the eternal questions with which he is obsessed. Political answers to these questions are not even considered superficial: "Every philosophy which believes that the problem of existence is touched on, not to say solved, by a political event is a joke- and pseudo-philosophy. . . . How should a political innovation suffice to turn men once and for all into contented inhabitants of the earth?" (*UM* 147–48). Occupied with ordering his own soul, the philosopher has little time for instituting social order, even if it might prove useful for his comfort or security. Indeed, he is not overly concerned with protecting his sanctuary; for any opposition he encounters may be transformed into a stimulant to growth. Only a philosopher's dis-ease, his displeasure with himself and his life, might tempt him out of his garden to try his hand at the manipulation of the soul writ large. This temptation, Nietzsche charged, is already a mark of decadence. For the challenges and dangers are greater within the politics of the soul. This politics is the truly heroic vocation.

The public life has little to offer the philosopher. But with his tragic disposition demanding that the joys of heroic struggle daily overcome the terror and nausea of existence, he, in turn, has little to offer the public. He may speak of the higher pleasures but must also acknowledge that their price is much suffering, that the love of wisdom is a tormenting passion. On the other hand, the politician is much more popular. He may promise his followers a life of the least displeasure, the least pain. Indeed, he has no right to offer them anything else (*GS* 86). Hence the philosopher is fated to remain apart from social politics as long as he philosophizes. He is a solitary. But he is also an educator. And in the philosophical garden the parallel between the politics of the soul and social politics proves spiritually edifying. The practical application of this correspondence beyond a small discipleship, however, has always proved dangerous and ultimately futile. Nietzsche recognized this, although his writings indicate less concern for the dangers than with the futility.

Antiquity bequeathed a conception of politics as the most excellent of arts. Only politics was capable of ordering the conflictual dynamics of human affairs, assigning everything its place, and thus allowing social life its harmony and humanity its fullest development. Nietzsche's understanding of the multiple soul was founded on such a dynamics of agonism and order. The ancients, however, were inclined to believe not only that public affairs entailed the manipulation of souls but that the manipulation of souls necessarily introduced itself into the text of politics writ large. Nietzsche acknowledged the former belief and rejected the latter. He would echo Plato's declaration in the *Republic* (591c–592b) that the man who has intelligence will mind "the political things" not of his fatherland, but only of "the city within himself." For Nietzsche, a successful politics of the soul excluded political engagement in the social realm. If we are to contend this conviction—if we wish to speak of the synchronic relation of politics within *and* without the soul as that which allows for the fullest realization of human potential—then we must contend Nietzsche. We must accept the challenge to understand him.

In the preceding pages Nietzsche's writings have served as the basis for a scatological inquiry, in the original sense of the word. We are left with the fossilized remains of a man's experiences, and must seek to reconstruct and understand the form of life that produced them. To write about Nietzsche without neutralizing conceptualization is not to say one has written *the truth* about Nietzsche. At best, one has found a more appropriate set of metaphors to interpret what he means. Our truths, Nietzsche reminded us, are always a product of the most popular metaphors. Truths, he suggested, are like coins that lose their face with handling. The value of their metal comes to be accepted when in fact they have no worth except as currency (*GW* 6:81). Nietzsche forged his own metaphors—among others, the soul as a state and society, and the heroic struggle as its politics—to be creatively exploited, by himself and by his readers. We might learn from Nietzsche's tragic example to be wary of the temptation to enshrine the sculptures of our speculation. For in the end, the coins Nietzsche had stamped with his image were manically peddled as truths, as natural metal unformed by human hands.

As if to outline his incarnations, ideals, and attempts at self-apotheosis, Nietzsche wrote: "Around the hero everything becomes a tragedy, around the demi-god a satyr-play; and around God everything becomes—what? Perhaps a 'world'?" (*BGE* 84). Eventually Nietzsche's tragic heroism and satyrlike frolics were no longer embraced with irony. They were transformed into a world around him, a world he had created for himself in thought and experience, but a world in whose transcendence he ultimately came to believe. As either the cause or the effect of his madness, Nietzsche's skeptical probity disintegrated. His works remain as a biography of a soul saddled with this austere virtue, and perhaps broken by it. Until his collapse, Nietzsche's philosophical skepticism proved to be an insatiable passion. That all truth is illusion, all knowledge but metaphor, was for him not an excuse for intellectual or spiritual surrender, but the fuel that fired inquiry and experimentation. To expound Nietzsche is an exercise not in resolving such paradoxes, but in demonstrating their force.

WORKS OF NIETZSCHE CITED

(*Note*: Works appear in chronological order of composition. Dates of original publication of those works published by Nietzsche are given in parentheses; dates of composition of those works left unpublished by Nietzsche are given in brackets.)

Der Werdende Nietzsche: Autobiographische Aufzeichnungen [1859–1869]. Ed. Elisabeth Foerster-Nietzsche. Munich: Musarion Verlag, 1924.

The Birth of Tragedy (1872). Trans. Walter Kaufmann. New York: Vintage, 1967.

Philosophy in the Tragic Age of the Greeks [1873]. Trans. Marianne Cowan. Washington: Regency Gateway, 1962.

Untimely Meditations (1873–1876). Trans. R. J. Hollingdale. Cambridge: Cambridge University Press, 1983.

Human, All Too Human: A Book for Free Spirits (1878; the 1886 edition contains "Assorted Opinions and Maxims" [1879] and "The Wanderer and His Shadow" [1880]). Trans. R. J. Hollingdale. Cambridge: Cambridge University Press, 1986.

Daybreak: Thoughts on the Prejudices of Morality (1881). Trans. R. J. Hollingdale. Cambridge: Cambridge University Press, 1982.

The Gay Science (1882, 2d ed. 1887). Trans. Walter Kaufmann. New York: Vintage, 1974.

Thus Spoke Zarathustra: A Book for Everyone and No One (1883–1885). Trans. R. J. Hollingdale. New York: Penguin, 1969.

Beyond Good and Evil: Prelude to a Philosophy of the Future (1886). Trans. R. J. Hollingdale. New York: Penguin, 1972.

On the Genealogy of Morals: A Polemic (1887). Trans. Walter Kaufmann and R. J. Hollingdale. New York: Vintage, 1967.

The Case of Wagner (1888). Trans. Walter Kaufmann. New York: Vintage, 1967.

Twilight of the Idols: or How to Philosophize with a Hammer [1888]. Trans. R. J. Hollingdale. New York: Penguin, 1968.

The Anti-Christ [1888]. Trans. R. J. Hollingdale. New York: Penguin, 1968.

Ecce Homo [1888]. Trans. Walter Kaufmann. New York: Vintage, 1967.

Nietzsche contra Wagner: Out of the Files of a Psychologist. In *The Portable Nietzsche* [1888], trans. Walter Kaufmann. New York: Viking, 1968.

Dithyrambs of Dionysus [1888]. Trans. R. J. Hollingdale. N.p.: Anvil Press Poetry, 1984.

The Will to Power [1882–1888]. Trans. Walter Kaufmann and R. J. Hollingdale. New York: Vintage, 1968.

Gesammelte Werke, Musarionausgabe. 23 vols. Munich: Musarion Verlag, 1920–1929. (Dates of composition follow by volume number: 1:1857–1868; 2:1869–1874; 3:1869–1871; 4:1872–1876; 5:1872–1876; 6:1872–1876; 7:1872–1876; 8:1876–1878, 1886; 9:1875–1880, 1886; 10:1880–1881; 11:1880–1882; 12:1881–1887; 13:1883–1885; 14:1882–1888; 15:1885–1887; 16:1882–1888; 17:1888; 18:1884–1888; 19:1884–1888; 20:1859–1888 [poetry]; 21:1844–1888 [autobiography]; 22, 23:Indexes.)

Nietzsche Briefwechsel, Kritische Gesamtausgabe. 15 vols. Ed. Giorgio Colli and Mazzino Montinari. Berlin and New York: Walter de Gruyter, 1975–1984.

INDEX

INDEX

drives (*cont.*)
   pher's, 213; the skeptic's, 115–
   16. *See also* instincts
dualism, 74–77, 87–89, 128–29

Ebner-Eschenbach, Maria, 133n
Ecce Homo, 65, 105, 156, 167n, 174,
   177, 178n, 193n, 214
Echo, 178
Eckermann, 116n
education, 170–74
educator, 5, 165–74, 182; and the
   artist, 167–69; and the overman,
   185; and the philosopher, 166n,
   167–69, 223; and the saint, 167–
   69; and the solitary, 172
egoism, 73–76, 80n, 86, 168–69,
   211. *See also* love of self
Einstein, Albert, 20n
Emerson, Ralph Waldo, 20n, 38,
   60n, 61n, 86n, 129n, 198
Epicurus, 100, 159
Eris, 65
eternal recurrence, 5, 144n, 197,
   201–6, 215, 217
Euripides, 14, 64

fame, 177–78
fatalism, 199
Freud, Sigmund, 57n
Fuchs, Carl, 181n

Gay Science, The, 35n, 60, 61, 62,
   87n, 89, 122, 143, 145, 158,
   167n, 188n, 200, 204
Genealogy of Morals, The, 167n
German philosophy, 19
German Reich, 19
Glaucon, 13n
Goethe, 61, 75n, 94n, 116n, 201n,
   211, 214–15n

Hadas, Moses, 169n
Hamlet, 122–23
Hector, 25
Hecuba, 60
Hegel, 43

Heidegger, Martin, 34n
Heracles, 13, 17, 180
Heraclitus, 80, 89n, 95, 99–100,
   106, 161, 207
Hercules. *See* Heracles
hero, 11–27; alienation of, 46, 59;
   overcoming heroism, 189–94;
   and politics, 53n; solitude of,
   174–78; tragic fate of, 11–12, 26,
   48; worship of, 21–22, 43. *See
   also* heroic individualism; heroism; higher man
Herodotus, 22
heroic culture, 14–15, 17, 22, 102,
   125, 146
heroic individualism, 3, 7, 14, 43–
   45, 64, 180–81, 190, 209, 218–19
heroic struggle, 3, 12–13, 23–27,
   32n, 67, 81–82, 164, 178–79,
   186–87, 189–94, 200, 223–25
heroism, 42–48, 123n, 225; and
   art, 134, 138; classical, 13–14,
   18, 21, 23, 42, 47–48, 101–2, 206;
   definition of, 25; the philosopher's, 112–14; tragic, 102n, 124,
   141–42, 181, 216–17. *See also*
   hero
Hesse, Hermann, 60n
higher man: "three metamorphoses," 188–89; becoming, 211–12.
   See also hero; heroism
Hippolochus, 13n
Hobbes, Thomas, 126
Hollingdale, R. J., 12n, 59n, 144n,
   194n
Homer, 13, 22, 25n, 42, 71, 82,
   140n
Hook, Sidney, 20n
Human, All Too Human, 15–16, 18–
   19, 41n, 126, 157, 179, 187n,
   210n, 216
Hume, David, 56
Huxley, Aldous, 53n

individual, as multiplicity, 37, 51–
   52, 63
individualism, 28–48, 161
infatuation, 154–55

INDEX

The Princeton University Press series "Studies in Moral, Political, and Legal Philosophy" is under the general editorship of Marshall Cohen, Professor of Philosophy and Law and Dean of Humanities at the University of Southern California. The series includes the following titles, in chronological order of publication:

Understanding Rawls: A Reconstruction and Critique of A Theory of Justice by R. P. Wolff (1977). Out of print

Immorality by R. D. Milo (1984)

Politics & Remembrance: Republican Themes in Machiavelli, Burke, and Tocqueville by B. J. Smith (1985)

Understanding Marx: A Reconstruction and Critique of Capital by R. P. Wolff (1985)

Hobbesian Moral and Political Theory by G. S. Kavka (1986)

The General Will before Rousseau: The Transformation of the Divine into the Civic by P. Riley (1986)

Respect for Nature: A Theory of Environmental Ethics by P. W. Taylor (1986). Available in paperback

Paternalistic Intervention: The Moral Bounds on Benevolence by D. VanDeVeer (1986)

The Longing for Total Revolution: Philosophic Sources of Social Discontent from Rousseau to Marx and Nietzsche by B. Yack (1986)

Meeting Needs by D. Braybrooke (1987)

Reasons for Welfare: The Political Theory of the Welfare State by R. E. Goodin (1988)

Why Preserve Natural Variety? by B. G. Norton (1988). Available in paperback

Coercion by A. Wertheimer (1988). Available in paperback

Merleau-Ponty and the Foundation of an Existential Politics by K. H. Whiteside (1988)

On War and Morality by R. L. Holmes (1989). Available in paperback

The Rhetoric of Leviathan: Thomas Hobbes and the Politics of Cultural Transformation by D. Johnston (1989). Available in paperback

Desert by G. Sher (1989). Available in paperback

Critical Legal Studies: A Liberal Critique by A. Altman (1989)

Finding the Mean: Theory and Practice in Aristotelian Political Philosophy by S. G. Salkever (1990)

Marxism, Morality, and Social Justice by R. G. Peffer (1990)

Speaking of Equality: An Analysis of the Rhetorical Force of 'Equality' in Moral and Legal Discourse by P. Westen (1990)

Friedrich Nietzsche and the Politics of the Soul: A Study of Heroic Individualism by L. P. Thiele (1990). Available in paperback